Ageing in the Modern Arabic Novel

Ageing in the Modern Arabic Novel

Samira Aghacy

EDINBURGH
University Press

Edinburgh University Press is one of the leading university presses in the UK. We publish academic books and journals in our selected subject areas across the humanities and social sciences, combining cutting-edge scholarship with high editorial and production values to produce academic works of lasting importance. For more information visit our website: edinburghuniversitypress.com

© Samira Aghacy, 2020, 2022

Edinburgh University Press Ltd
The Tun – Holyrood Road
12 (2f) Jackson's Entry
Edinburgh EH8 8PJ

First published in hardback by Edinburgh University Press 2020

Typeset in 11/15 Adobe Garamond by
Servis Filmsetting Ltd, Stockport, Cheshire

A CIP record for this book is available from the British Library

ISBN 978 1 4744 6675 2 (hardback)
ISBN 978 1 4744 6676 9 (paperback)
ISBN 978 1 4744 6678 3 (webready PDF)
ISBN 978 1 4744 6677 6 (epub)

The right of Samira Aghacy to be identified as author of this work has been asserted in accordance with the Copyright, Designs and Patents Act 1988 and the Copyright and Related Rights Regulations 2003 (SI No. 2498).

Contents

Note on Translation and Transliteration — vi
Acknowledgements — vii

Introduction — 1
1. Ageing in Traditional Neighbourhoods: Conformity and Transgression — 20
2. Hoary Monuments, Residual Bodies: Senescence in the City — 48
3. Menopausal Tremors: Refurbishing the Body — 74
4. Senile Masculinity: The Male Body in Crisis — 104
5. Yarns of Later Life: Transgressive Strategies — 133
Conclusion — 167

Bibliography — 172
Index — 183

Note on Translation and Transliteration

I have used English translations for the fictional works in question. In the absence of known English translations, I have used my own translation and indicated that both in the text and the notes. All translations of primary critical texts are mine unless stated otherwise.

I have chosen the most commonly used transliteration in English. I have represented the *'ayn* (') and the *hamza* (') by their conventional symbols.

Acknowledgements

I would like to thank the Lebanese American University for providing the cultural and academic atmosphere, and the facilities, for research and personal development. I wish to extend special thanks to the staff at the University Library, particularly to Aida Hajjar, whose service to the library is simply outstanding.

I am deeply indebted to Dr Maya Aghasi for reading the manuscript and for exceptionally insightful and thought-provoking comments. Special thanks are also due to Dr Laila Khoury for being a wonderful friend and mentor, and for making me believe that a friendship can last a lifetime. I would also like to thank Nazik Yared, a dear friend and colleague, who has left her imprint on this project directly and indirectly.

Finally, I would like to thank Edinburgh University Press for their amazing services, endless support, and swift responses to all queries.

In fond memory of Najla Dabaghi, an exceptional and inspiring woman who lived a full and spirited life until her death at age 99.

Introduction

According to a UNDP report (2011), the number of citizens aged over 65 in the Arab region is expected to rise to 17 per cent by 2050. As a result of 'high fertility rates in earlier periods', 'population ageing' is 'expected to increase more rapidly in the coming decades, with the number of older people more than quadrupling by 2050 (from 22 to 103 million) and the percentage of older persons exceeding 15% in over 13 of the 22 Arab region countries'.[1] Despite such expectations, a general complacency, denial and silence persist, which explains the dearth of works devoted to the old in Arab/Islamic culture, and why, up until recent years, one can readily think of only a few fictional works in which the focus is primarily on older individuals.

The paucity of literature related to ageing in the Arab world can be attributed to the demographic domination of youth and to a general sense that age is a liminal stage between life and death, carrying traces of degeneration and decay. If traditional autobiography is normally linked with older male individuals who centre on activities and achievements in earlier life stages, the immediate personal concerns of the older person are absent, particularly the fact that male individuals are measured solely by achievement in the public sphere. Studies on ageing are lacking in modern Arabic literature, except for a few on disability and on relations between the old and the young. Among such works are Abir Hamdar's *The Female Suffering Body* (2014); Nawar al-Hassan Golley's *Reading Arab Women's Autobiographies* (2003); Dayla Cohen-Mor's *Fathers and Sons in the Arab Middle East* (2013); Valerie Anishchenkova's *Autobiographical Identities in Contemporary Arab Culture* (2014); Robin Ostle, Ed de Moor and Stefan Wilde's *Writing the Self* (1998); and Suad Joseph's *Intimate Selving in Arab Families* (1999).

This study utilises biological and cultural theories of ageing that shed light on the representation of ageing in the contemporary Arabic novel. The essentialist model regards ageing as biologically determined[2] and views older individuals as an undifferentiated, homogeneous group with identical needs and interests. It considers age as a fixed and ahistorical category leading to inevitable decline and reduced to a pathological problem tied to medico-social discourses on ageing, all of which fail to address the idiosyncratic nature of individuals with multiple facets to their personalities and identities.

Since the first visible signs of deterioration are reflected on the surface of the body, the latter is perceived as the prime signifier of age. The meanings attached to an ageing identity combine an awareness of a changing body with a consciousness of the restrictions imposed upon it by the prevailing cultural norms, which consider ageing as a period of discontinuity from earlier life stages, fully separated from the activities of daily life. According to Margaret Morganroth Gullette, human beings are 'aged by culture', or by '*Age ideology*', as she refers to it.[3] The ageing body, assumed to be natural and immutable, is always associated with decline no matter how fit and energetic it might be, since, as Leslie Fiedler puts it, to 'be *properly old*' one is expected 'to withdraw from sexual competition and prepare for death'.[4] According to this model, ageing is seen as a stable category within a static system that regulates all, transcends time, location, class, religion and cultural background, and views ageing individuals as identical and 'distinct from ordinary [younger] human beings'.[5] Elizabeth Grosz refers to this rigidifying category as 'the existence of fixed characteristics, given attributes, and ahistorical functions that limit the possibilities of change and thus of social reorganization'[6] and that turn the old into unproductive individuals facing degeneration and death. Such forced disengagement centres on submission and closure in the 'mutual withdrawal of the individual and society from each other with advancing age',[7] thus confirming the depletion of the ageing individual's role in society, and the irrelevance associated with old age.

This perspective of ageing tends to blur the line between men and women and view them as a static and insulated category where 'rigid role divisions dissolve and men and women become more alike, taking on the characteristics of their gender opposite'.[8] The prevailing view is that, as men and women age, the gendered gap between them narrows, reducing them to an undifferentiated group of de-gendered neuters whereby the dualistic structure of old and young remains prevalent and youth and age are hierarchically arranged to the detriment of the latter.

The constructionist social model extricates itself from biological reductionism, which constrains age within 'a universal wholly biological process'[9] and views the ageing body as interactive, socially determined and 'inscribed and reinscribed with cultural meanings'.[10] Judith Butler's performativity theory centres on the constructed nature of identity and, more importantly, on identity as performance: 'the reiterative practice of regulatory norms that produces and stabilises the embodied identity they name', a repeated set of actions that necessitate the possibility of versatility and change.[11] As a result, identity becomes meaningful only in relation to the norms constructed by society and other institutional processes. In other words, identities reflect what people do rather than what they are supposed to represent. Identity is also a manifestation of underlying power relations and changing social configurations that give way to varied experiences and intersect with age, class, gender, religion, history and location,[12] allowing for 'more diversity than unity, more paradox than consistency, more ambiguity than certainty'.[13] As a result, the elderly individual is 'as much entangled as anyone in the becoming of the world',[14] suggesting that old age is a cultural construct whose boundaries shift with changing times and localities, producing a variety of lifestyles where the elderly individual defies the essentialist model by being active, and functional.

Instead of 'adhering to absolute and objective truth', the focus is on 'fragmentation rather than universalism . . . pushing away from the general and encompassing toward the particular'.[15] According to this social model, the ageing process is one of 'continuity' with the earlier phases of life, a time of 'ongoing personhood'[16] that affirms diversity rather than uniformity where the individual's present actions and behaviour are consistent with 'earlier habits, ideas, and practices'.[17] Accordingly, ageing is not 'a clear coherently defined subject amenable to analysis in precise terms';[18] it is interactive, dynamic, fluid and unpredictable, providing opportunities for change and 'continued human development'[19] so that the lives individuals lead in the present are 'a direct outgrowth of the whole of their lives'.[20]

My approach acknowledges ageing as a process that integrates organic and socially inscribed processes. I adopt what Sally Chivers refers to as a

'Janus-faced old age'[21] which presents deterioration and decline as well as activity and well-being, uncovering an 'emerging interest in the lives of fit and active older people'[22] without disregarding the biological factor.

Instead of viewing the biological and discursive body in dualistic terms, the study concentrates on the inextricable link between them, creating an alternative configuration, an 'undisciplined' old age 'where knowledge relations disassemble and disrupt dominant truth-making practices'[23] and fuse the biological with the social, making the ageing process multiple and plural. Situated at the intersection of biological experience and discourse, the ageing body is not solely static and predictable, leading to physical and mental decline, but is also rooted in everyday practices, shaped by social and cultural meanings, and mediated by underlying relations of power that intersect 'with biological, biographical, socio-historical'[24] and diachronic/synchronic time.

The study also focuses on the disparity between the ageing individual's external physique, which is visible to the world, and the invisible inner self, which is irreconcilable with the external markers of age. Simone de Beauvoir observes: 'Old age is more apparent to others than to the subject himself', and owing to the internalisation of the social norms of ageing, she declares: 'Within me it is the other – that is to say the person I am for the outsider – who is old: and that Other is myself.'[25] In a similar vein, Kathleen Woodward speaks of the 'specular body' which is 'anchored in visuality' and which *mirrors* degeneracy and decline.[26] Featherstone and Hepworth refer to the 'mask of ageing'[27] whereby the older person feels essentially unchanged although the biological body tells another story. Pamela H. Gravagne describes it as 'the looping effect between the idea of old people and old people's idea of themselves',[28] where the outer physique is a rigid alien structure of confinement which can mask the possibilities of expressing the self within, a self that feels young and bouncing.

Keeping in mind the scarcity of works on ageing in the Arab/Islamic world, this study attempts to fill a void and shed light on a forgotten segment of Arab society. The focus of the study on the daily, mundane experiences of ageing characters in a variety of fictional works will, to use the words of Trevor Le Gassick, offer a 'revealing window into the closet workings of a society's values and orientations'.[29] This is one way to break the silence about ageing, since the novels are valuable sources through which to understand the quotidian experience of ageing. In the study, I examine works whose perspectives on ageing include biological and mental decline, fears and uncertainties, as well as gratifications, indulgences, possibilities and successes. For instance, in Randa Khalidy's semi-autobiographical novel titled 'An Unheroic Autobiography', the eighty-year-old female protagonist, who has had a long history of suffering at the hands of her domineering husband, as well as of marginalisation (despite her Ph.D. from Oxford University), manifests a vibrant spirit and a desire to write herself into history through her autobiography. As Kathleen Woodward puts it, '[t]o have a life means to possess its narrative'.[30] In her life story, the authorial narrator uncovers intimate details of her life, and liberates age from the constraints of compliance, stoicism and erasure normally associated with other ageing women such as the old woman in Alia Mamdouh's *Mothballs*. The narrator of Khalidy's work embraces an assertive, forceful and scandalous self that is not intimidated by social rules and restrictions or 'prescribe[ed] behaviors and obligations',[31] underscoring the basic instability and diversity of the ageing experience.

I explore points of affirmation and resistance to normative conceptions of ageing and old age in the Arabic novel, and how individuals of certain ages are supposed to behave and how they are positioned and categorised. In addition to works that insist on old age as static and predictable, I also dwell upon other works that reveal the incongruities of the ageing process owing to rapid sociocultural, demographic and economic changes that have transformed family relations. I consider the historical and social moment and the situatedness of the ageing individual within gendered and cultural contexts, 'community standards and beliefs, local culture, and kinship networks', without underestimating the specificity and singularity of individual experience,[32] what Calasanti refers to as 'the experiences of particular groups on their own terms, rather than through the lens of unquestioned standards'.[33]

Cultural and Religious Norms

In 'Anthropological Approaches to the Arab Family', Young and Shami assert that traditionally, the Arab family is 'extended, patriarchal, patrilineal, patrilocal, endogamous, and occasionally polygamous'.[34] Cultural and religious norms within the extended Arab/Islamic family have traditionally conferred respect and honour on the old, which is acknowledged as a natural and taken-for-granted phenomenon. The old are viewed as a sacred obligation figured in the Bible and the Qur'an, establishing the strength of a stoic tradition of accepting divine will, retreating into religious life and resigning oneself from the world. Longevity, in accordance with the Bible,[35] is the Lord's reward for faithful service, and the fifth commandment demands respect for elders where the 'hoary head' is 'a crown of glory'.[36] Similarly, Raghib al-Isfahani maintains that in the Qur'an, and within Islamic law, Abraham is said to have been the first person to have grey hair. When he asks the Lord what it signifies, the Lord responds that it means '*waqar*' (dignity), and Abraham beseeches God to 'increase him in dignity',[37] a trait that has become directly linked with old age. As a result, *shayb* (grey hair), which was generally associated with age, was directly linked with restraint from objectionable behaviour. In many instances, age was measured not so much by the number of years one had lived as by the sheer appearance of white hair. In his Diwan, vol. 1, Abu Nuwas, whose hair was turning grey, mocks the concept of dignity associated with *shayb* – 'but mine, thank God, is free from dignity'[38] – since grey hair is irreconcilable with the youthful pleasures that Abu Nuwas was constantly in pursuit of.

The Qur'an instructs the believer 'to be dutiful to your parents. If one or both of them attain old age in your life, say not to them a word of disrespect, nor shout at them but address them in terms of honour' (Chapter 17, verse 23). Hasan Shuraydi maintains that filial piety, which 'figures prominently in the Koran', points to the respect and caring that children owe their parents in old age, and refers to the 'Prophetic traditions' that 'give precedence to taking care of one's parents over military jihad'. For instance, 'Umar ibn al-Khattab, following such prophetic traditions, had to recall a young man from an expedition to Iraq and order him to stick to his two old parents'.[39] Similarly, when a young man consulted with the Prophet about joining a military campaign, the Prophet asked him if his mother was still living. When he affirmed that she was, the Prophet asked him to 'stay with her and serve her, for Paradise is at her feet'.[40]

The Traditional Family and the Male Patriarch

In Arab/Islamic culture the family is the pre-eminent institution, headed by the father who represents authority, which is closely bound up with patriarchal power, what Yount and Sibai refer to as the 'patriarchal bargain',[41] with the male as head of the household. Halim Barakat sees a close link between family and identity, where the individual's 'success or failure' is inextricably bound up with 'the family as a whole'.[42] The position of strength, and wisdom attributed to the elder of the family, generated a mixed sense of love, awe and fear on the part of the other members, coupled with conformity and deference. Since the patriarch is viewed as a repository of wisdom and knowledge, demanding no further need for learning, the family must submit to the inevitable. One must add here that women are denied the growth in wisdom attributed to men, who are supposed to accumulate knowledge and experience. Since within Arab/Islamic societies all the norms governing marriage and the family are seen as 'expressions of God's will',[43] the images of God and the father have become analogous with the father's position as '*rabb al-usra*' or 'lord of the family'. As Barakat puts it, 'the father and God in Arab culture are a promise and a threat (*wa'd* and *wa'id*), grace and suffering (*rahma wa 'adhab*)', while punishment is described as ('*iqab al-rahma*) or mercy punishment.[44]

The attempt to de-gender old age can be seen in family 'relations of dominance and subordination',[45] such as the focus on the struggle between young and old like the one between father and son in Jordanian writer Taysir Subul's *Anta Mundhu al-Yawm* (1968), and in Rashid al-Daif's *Dear Mr. Kawabata* (*Azizi al-Sayyid Kawabata*, 1990). These novels, set in the 1960s and 1970s, focus on inter-generational conflicts, where old and young are placed in oppositional roles and where the younger generation feels the dire need to struggle against the father's oppression. The younger members consider the knowledge disseminated by the older generation as obsolete at a time when Western cultural hegemony has started firmly establishing itself worldwide. In Taysir Subul's *Anta Mundhu al-Yawm*, the protagonist, whose name is Arabi, lives in the shadow of political and familial oppression. He describes his father as vicious, aggressive, belligerent and abusive, with eyes like a hawk', and sums up the latter's relationship with Arabi's mother as 'angry, screaming, subservient and weepy'.[46] The father, seen by his son as an obsolescent remnant of the past, insists on remaining a formidable stronghold of power, and proves his hardiness by subjugating and battering his wives, whom he whips with a thick leather belt. His rigidity, arrogance and unwillingness to admit vulnerability or emotional weakness turn him into a symbol of ruthless and absolute authority that the son has to contend with and displace. Arabi tells us that during Ramadan, his father viciously killed a cat and severed its head from its body for eating a piece of the meat that was reserved for the *iftar*. He rules over his family, expecting stern submission and reminding them that his power and influence are 'grounded in punishment'.[47] Expecting all members of the family to be subservient, he harasses and strikes his son Arabi in the same way that his neighbour beats his son Ali. When Arabi asks Aisha how old her brother Ali is, she tells him that he is 25, and Arabi responds sarcastically: 'a very suitable age!'[48]

Similarly, in al-Daif's *Dear Mr. Kawabata*, the narrator views his native background as damaging to his agenda of achieving progress for his country and rejecting an insular, pre-modern world that is gradually becoming peripheral. He soon clashes with his own father, and is accused by the latter of betraying his own culture. His foreign ideas about secularism, socialism, individual freedom and scientific and technological progress grate on the ears of his father, who is angered by his son's new Marxist ideology, which he views as an evil that threatens a stable order. His persistent use of the word 'viper', when it comes to his son, points to his father's fear of being dragged out of an earthly paradise that he had considered eternal and unchangeable. To control his son and ensure his paternal and absolute will, he resorts to violence by scorching his son's finger with 'a red-hot iron rod'.[49]

The exact age of the fathers in both novels remains unknown, in line with pre-modern societies that attach no importance to dates in contrast to industrial societies that are 'haunted by numbers'.[50] In line with Western colonial systems of retirement, the official age of retirement is 65 in most Arab countries, regardless of personal achievement or ongoing vitality and competence. However, for the majority of people who have no schooling, employment or retirement benefits, age remains a fluid category. In mainstream Arab/Islamic society, the ageing process is seen as ranging from the forties until the eighties, and in certain situations earlier than forty for women. Such a lengthy stretch of time justifies the haphazard lumping of the old into one predetermined lifestyle. This approach, that treats old age as a static phenomenon, leads to over-generalisation and an attempt to downgrade elderly people, place them within restrictive moulds, force them to withdraw from earlier activities, and erase any subjective experiences. The chronological mode of ageing rejects continuing development after age 65 and endorses the sanctioned cultural notion that entry into old age demands disengagement from earlier commitments and actions. This perspective is 'legitimised' by the view that decline is a numerically 'determined point of closure', which explains why age in many of the novels under study is measured by chronology which emphasises similarities rather than differences among ageing individuals.[51]

In multi-generational families, the old are viewed as a duty, which demands care, respect and differential treatment. The old man is valued for his wisdom and status within the extended family, and for the sense of history and rootedness that he inculcates within the family. The elderly mother, on the other hand, is supposed to receive the same care and protection from her children that she had received from the father in terms of economic support, in her role as housewife and her service inside the home space. In other words, older individuals are seen as a distinct category that demands special treatment; they are disconnected from the rest of the world, where their position falters and shifts from 'integration to segregation, from involvement to disengagement',[52] and from caring to being cared for.

The Disruption of the Family Hierarchical Structure

Since the family is the entity in charge of the elderly, the number of older people living in institutions in the Arab/Islamic world is low. However, it is gradually increasing owing to demographic, geographical and global factors, which have attracted the young to the cities, breaking down the hierarchical structure of the extended family in favour of the nuclear conjugal unit. The growth of mass education and literacy in the 1950s and 1960s began gradually erasing the 'mystique of age'[53] which gave older men power and cultural esteem, disrupting their time-honoured supremacy and respect within the family, thus eroding family support for them and gradually displacing communities structured on religious and social norms and based upon traditional hierarchy, and filial obligation.

The growing number and proportion of older people in the Arab/Islamic world can be attributed to a variety of factors such as urbanisation, modernisation, changes in fertility patterns and increased levels of longevity owing to medical advancement and changing lifestyles. Shifting attitudes to older people are linked to the pressures of globalisation, information technology, the media, television, socio-economic and political factors and youth migrations, causing significant transformations in family structures and further denigration of old age. The greying of the villages is a consequence of modernisation, which encouraged a marked migration of young people from the rural to the urban areas to seek better opportunities outside their environment, thus destabilising the traditional household. Such changes have dealt a serious blow to the level of care normally accorded to elderly members by their families. In the Arab world, the situation accelerated in the 1960s when the new generation began embracing modernisation and secularisation that swept the area with the rise of Gamal Abdel-Nasser, who propagated a homogeneous pan-Arab secularised identity. Another factor was the rise of the Palestine Liberation Organization (PLO) and the Palestinian struggle against Israel, where the young *fidayeen* were idolised, turning the old into peripheral and virtually irrelevant beings. In Jabra Ibrahim Jabra's *In Search of Walid Massoud* (1978), the Palestinian intellectual and political activist Walid Massoud is devastated when he learns that his son wants him to limit his military operations against Israel to financial support. Walid bangs his head against the wall and sobs and moans because as an old man of fifty he is supposed to disengage himself,[54] leaving the arena for his son.

While wisdom and physical power may have been effective weapons of control in the past, they no longer serve as useful standards with which to judge old age. As a result, older individuals are downgraded in a modern world that privileges youth over age, and 'the patriarchal contract is beginning to erode'.[55] In such an atmosphere it is not surprising to come upon novels that make no bones about describing the vicious massacre by young male fighters of old men and women, as seen in Elias Khoury's *White Masks* (*al-Wujuh al-Bayda'*, 1986) in the gory massacring of an old man and the rape and murder of his old wife. In a similar vein, the old man stringing his way through the streets in René al-Hayek's *Beirut 2002* (2003) is viewed by Raja, a young university student, as an obsolete image that is no more than a discordant sight. Watching elderly men eating and drinking in a traditional all-male café makes Raja feel all the more alienated and unable to understand an archaic culture that he thought had vanished forever. In Elias Khoury's *The Journey of Little Gandhi* (*Rihlat Gandhi al-Saghir*, 1994), ageing is often associated with a reduced ability to maintain homeostasis, as in the case of the Protestant minister who ended up wetting his pants.

Women in Traditional Settings

Despite the ungendered image attributed to older persons, 'older people are not just old, they are either men or women'.[56] As Barbara Myerhoff maintains, 'aging, if it is to be adequately studied, must be understood as a gendered process'.[57] The works reveal that men and women experience ageing differently, owing to a long history of gender differentiation where men's sense of self-adequacy differs from that of women. Although the ageing individual is rooted in corporeality, where the body takes centre stage as the principal signifier of ageing, it is bad taste to display older bodies, particularly woman's bodies. The female-authored works that focus on traditional societies highlight family support networks, rather than romantic or sexual relationships, while male writers tend to focus on sexuality and performance. These works reveal that older women de-prioritise physical appearance and place more value on non-somatic abilities such as moral, ethical and religious qualities, and upon women's 'emotional intelligence',[58] which makes them retain a sense of power and control within the household, and serve as protective shields against anxieties related to the body and physical appearance.

Other traditional women, like the two grandmothers in Aliah Mamdouh's *Mothballs* and Inaam Kachachi's *The American Granddaughter*, engage in the liberating social role of mothering their grandchildren. As for less privileged women who have no children or occupation, they wind up either as servants in their father's or brother's home or as destitute and deprived. One example is the bag lady walking the warring city of Beirut in al-Daif's novel 'Tactics of Wretchedness' (*Taqaniyyat al-Bu's*, 1989); another is the prostitute in Mahfouz's *Sugar Street*. The study also deals with Fuad al-Takarli's *The Long Way Back*, a novel that centres on female ageing characters as marginal figures, and presents them within traditional precincts and normative ideals.

In Tayyib Saleh's *Season of Migration to the North*, the old woman Bint Majzoub is well-known in the village, and her language is daring and licentious. As an old woman, she is sexually and reproductively irrelevant. She joins the group of old men who tell dirty jokes and obscene stories about women, enjoys the stories, and joins the other men in laughter. She is seen as no different from men, especially when she asks Wad Rayyes: '"What's come over you? . . . For two years now you've contented yourself with a single wife. Has your prowess waned?"'[59] Bint Majzoub serves only as a link between the village and the westernised narrator. She tells the latter that she is thankful to God that when abroad he did not marry an 'uncircumcised' woman and informs him of what goes on in the village. She has no power of her own, but simply follows the rules prescribed by a male-controlled society, and male-inscribed customs and traditions.

The Menopausal Woman

The trajectory for educated urban older women in Arab culture is different from that for men. Ignored by society when old, they achieve a measure of freedom and independence in old age, the kind of autonomy normally denied them during their years of fecundity. In these works, I explore the changes that surface at mid-life and anxious worries about deterioration, death and the finitude of all things mortal. As such, ageing is viewed by many of them as a perilous stage where traumas and anxieties are intensified owing to changing physical appearance, ailments and lethal maladies. In fact, women bear the brunt of '"the double jeopardy"' or the '"double stigmata"' of ageism and sexism,[60] which disadvantage them and make the ageing process all the more problematic, as seen in Sahar Khalifah's *The Inheritance* (*al-Mirath*, 1997).

Although educated women tend to be more independent, self-sufficient and sexually active than traditional women, they are more conscious of the stakes involved in ageing, as in Haifa Bitar's self-reflexive novel 'A Woman of Fifty'. Feeling degraded in their relationships with men, they become more fixated upon beauty and physical appearance in an attempt to look younger and to attract men. Other menopausal women decide to free themselves from the tyranny of the body and from male sexual control associated with it. As a result, they make the decision to abandon men altogether and join older women's groups that focus on the exchange of ideas, personal experiences, awareness campaigns, and other activities related to women.

Feeling disadvantaged by menopause incites some women to prioritise nurturance over physicality, and to create a buffer zone against corporeality, as seen in Haifa Bitar's novel 'A Woman of Fifty'. Others, like the fifty-year-old Nahleh in Khalifah's *The Inheritance*, manifest an obsession with youthfulness and a dread of age, which spurs them with a strong sense of urgency and a desire to refurbish the body through cosmetic creams and other procedures. Unlike men, who are supposed to age much later and with far more freedom, women have to contend with stereotypes of sisterhood and menopause. As modern Western industrial societies and consumer culture associated with social transformations within modernity and late modernity are disseminated worldwide, the new technology that focuses on youth, health and beauty and degrades the ageing body pushes the female body into the limelight as an object of vision and revision.

The Older Man

In addition to the destabilising effect of globalisation, the modern Arab nation states have also contributed to the disruption of old family traditions where not only women are affected, but also older men are swamped by images of disengagement, unemployment, retirement, obsolescence, physical debilitation and a morbid sense of a dreary, repetitive and marginal existence.

Far from the 'teleological' male narratives of the life cycle where achievement and success[61] privilege men over women, modern fiction and autobiography are taking a different turn. Under the influence of consumer culture, the body is taking on increasing significance and the 'traditional male immunity to middle age' is being eroded [62] as the gap between men and women begins to narrow. Wyatt-Brown and Rossen see the importance of looking at older men as gendered beings. They maintain that it is important that ageing men are analysed as well as ageing women in order not to further 'the myth that men are exempt from the influence of aging'.[63]

Because men's sense of personhood has depended upon their physical power, dominance and sexual exploits, age robs many of them of their selfhood, as seen in Hassan Daoud's brilliant novel titled *Ayyam Za'ida* (*Borrowed Time*, 1990) woven around the author's old grandfather. The old man is subordinated especially in relation to his children and family and is ridiculed and ignored by them. Accordingly, he is isolated from family and friends, particularly because he is unable to maintain any friendship networks, rejecting the village friendships his children try to impose on him. When he joins a family gathering, his children and their friends stop talking, and view him as 'other', an intruder into their youthful circle. Because his sense of personhood has always depended on dominance and physical power, he is seen as a threatening presence that needs to be neutralised and is left alone to clean his own dirty space, increasing his chances of occupying a feminine space.[64]

Gha'ib To'mi Faraman's short novel titled 'The Pains of Mr Ma'ruf' (*Alam al-Sayyid Ma'ruf*, 1979) deals with a middle-aged man who is in the tumult of what Hepworth and Featherstone refer to as 'the male menopause',[65] defined as 'a midlife crisis which in itself is less of a hormonal change *of* life than a change in life mostly related to work, status, cultural expectations, sexuality'.[66] Instead of reaping the rewards of past efforts and sacrifice, as in the case of traditional fiction on ageing, the protagonist has to contend with demotion, ridicule, corrupt exploitation, and young men's mockery of an older eccentric man. Ma'ruf lives in a twilight world of dream and fantasy that he garners from watching the sunset every evening, which disconnects him from a dark empirical reality outside. He looks after a disabled mother and two spinster sisters, suffers from neurotic, psychosomatic and hypochondrial complaints, and maintains that he would have ended up an alcoholic had the pain in his stomach allowed him to drink.

In a world where wisdom in old age is becoming irrelevant and where older men are beginning to occupy inferior positions in relation to younger men and women, I focus on works that trivialise the role of complacent knowledge in old age and reveal anger, frustration and dissatisfaction, as seen in al-Daif's 'O.K. Good-bye'. According to Woodward, 'a moratorium on wisdom' when it comes to ageing men allows for an ageing experience tinged with anger, which is 'a sign of moral outrage at social injustice, at being denied the right to participate fully in society'.[67] Such a devastating sense of defeat has the tendency to make age 'multidimensional',[68] thus problematising the idea of what it means to be old, especially when it comes to men.

Narrativising the Ageing Process

Other works focus on ageing men and women who attempt to revive memory through writing, telling the past and the present, and contemplating the finitude of all things mortal. These individuals negotiate family relationships, engage in social activity, and acknowledge the need for agency, and for embodied presence in the outer sphere in a heightened artistic productivity often associated with 'late style',[69] as seen in Randa Khalidy's 'An Unheroic

Autobiography', Nazik Yared's *Improvisations on a Missing String* and Abbas Baydun's 'The Album of Defeat'. The investment in language that literary forms necessitate provides fertile ground for the revision of the strong cultural narratives that rigidify ageing. These writers link past and present, and scramble time and render it cyclical and spasmodic, through the use of digressive and fragmented narratives that correlate past and present and disrupt the linear pattern. The works make use of flashbacks and flash-forwards, offering a multi-directional pattern and a dialogic world that resists closure.

I also take into account works on ageing by older and younger writers. For instance, some of these authors, like al-Daif, Yared and Baydun, started writing at an early age and continue to work through their old age and depict their experiences with age. Other works are represented from a younger person's perspective. The study makes a distinction between old-age writing and writing about old age by younger authors. These works represent age from a variety of perspectives, affirming the diversity of the ageing experience in fiction. In addition to themes related to ageing, literary and artistic merit is taken into consideration, including in works by established writers and others by lesser-known authors.

This monograph is a first critical attempt to look at fictional works written by Arab male and female writers through the lens of ageing. It centres on ageing as it is understood, practised and problematised in the modern Arabic novel. It counters the critical corpus that reads the modern Arabic novel as predominantly a political discourse and focuses on achievements made in youth and adulthood, while discounting any accomplishment in old age. Through close consideration of sixteen fictional works by sixteen different male and female writers, the study addresses an age span that covers mid-life, late middle years, and older individuals of both genders. Having struggled to find texts that feature ageing individuals as major protagonists, I can say that there is an increasing preoccupation with older individuals in the modern Arabic novel, and a gradual change of their role in society as more people live longer, and remain healthy in their old age. The first chapter considers ageing individuals within traditional societies. Chapter 2 explores the impact of urbanisation and change on older men and women. Chapter 3 examines menopause and how women respond to this biological phenomenon. Chapter 4 analyses the impact of ageing on men, and Chapter

5 considers the significance of autobiographical writings by older men and women. The study shows how individuals navigate old age, the stereotypes they encounter and the manner in which they subvert them. It also focuses on precariousness and transience, which represent major problems to ageing individuals who are confronted by an unstable identity that encroaches on a self always thought to be fixed and stable, demanding religious faith and surrender to the inevitable.

For many years, most novelists, poets and playwrights have not made older characters their central characters, since in a region where the young prevail such works do not attract many readers. The elderly have received little attention, because as creatures close to death they are relegated to the margins of society and their actions and thoughts are taken for granted. Focusing on characters in experiential relations, fictive creations are valuable sources with which to define, analyse and understand the experience of ageing in the modern and contemporary Arabic novel, and even to challenge the traditional, negative stereotypes and prejudices associated with it. Although the writers selected come from Lebanon, Syria, Palestine and Egypt, the inclusion of a novel from Tunisia aims to convey awareness of an overall devaluation of ageing male individuals by younger generations, and the gradual erosion of the controlling role of the male patriarch within Arab societies. The novels also reveal that practices within Arab societies differ not only from one Arab country to another but also internally, from city to village, and across family, nationality, religion, sect, class and geography. The texts reveal that there is no single model of old age and that in many cases ageing individuals are more differentiated. Even in works where people share local, religious, cultural and family paradigms, each individual's experience is distinctly singular and private. Without falling into the trap of essentialism, my study demonstrates how men and women are physically and psychologically disadvantaged by age. In looking at ageing from a gendered perspective, I do not see each category as exclusively homogeneous, and focus instead on the idiosyncrasies of each experience within each category.

The study will show the gradual move from a traditional ideology of ageing into a more diverse and fluid representation of elderly individuals in their daily experiential lives. The selected works range from tropes of elderly men and women within paternalistic and hierarchical family structures which revere older individuals, to more open-ended models generated by social and demographic factors, leading to a more self-reflexive awareness of ageing. Male and female writers are gradually subverting the earlier tenets and inventing new modes of narratives of ageing to show that there is no standard female or male experience of senescence, and that the ageing process is multiple and inconsistent rather than homogeneous and uniform.

The texts cover physical and psychic pain, alienation from family and youthful society, self-doubt, feelings of uselessness, grief over the loss of friends, but also mental acuity and physical energy – all of which present the old in a position of power or powerlessness or both. The work deals with the realities of ageing as a stable, contextual, historical, contingent and subversive entity, with old people continually destabilising the meanings attached to the physical realities of ageing.

The study focuses on ageing as a biological and social formation. If it tells an individual story about ageing, it articulates simultaneously combined political, social and economic discourses, underlining the pivotal importance of history and location in the articulation of an ageing subjectivity. As Cole puts it, ageing and old age 'are certainly real, but they do not exist in some natural realm, independently of the ideals, images and social practices that conceptualise and represent them'.[70] Accordingly, the process of ageing can be viewed as 'polysemic'[71] in its capacity to reinforce traditional gender identities, but also to interact with the cultural forces outside it.

Notes

1. Sibai and Yamout, 'Family-Based Old-Age Care in Arab Countries', pp. 63–76.
2. Powell, *Social Theory and Aging*, pp. 23–8.
3. Gullette, *Declining to Decline*, p. 3.
4. Fiedler, 'Eros and Thenatos', p. 236. See also his Fiedler, 'More Images of Eros and Old Age', pp. 37–50.
5. Bytheway, *Ageism*, p. 362.
6. Grosz, *Volatile Bodies*, p. 84.
7. Powell, *Social Theory and Aging*, p. 48. See also Cumming and Henry, *Growing Old*, and Havighurst, 'Successful Aging', pp. 8–13. For Disengagement theory as opposed to Activity theory see Powell, *Social Theory and Aging*, pp. 47–50.
8. Deats and Lenker, *Aging and Identity*, p. 5.
9. Gullette, *Declining to Decline*, p. 212.

10. Featherstone and Wernick, 'Introduction' in *Images of Aging*, p. 3.
11. Butler, *Gender Trouble*, pp. xv–xvi.
12. Rich, 'Notes toward a Politics of Location', pp. 210–31.
13. Katz, *Cultural Aging Life Course, Life Styles, Senior Worlds*, p. 189.
14. Gravagne, *The Becoming of Age*, p. 35.
15. Powell and Longino, 'Towards the Postmodernization of Aging', p. 203.
16. Andrews, 'The Seductiveness of Agelessness', p. 311.
17. Laz, 'Age Embodied', p. 517.
18. Hazan, 'The Social Trap', p. 17.
19. Friedan, *The Fountain of Age*, p. 51.
20. Andrews, 'The Seductiveness of Agelessness', p. 313.
21. Chivers, *From Old Woman to Older Women*, p. xi.
22. Cole, *The Journey of Life*, 5.
23. Katz, *Disciplining Old Age*, 136.
24. Marshall and Katz, 'The Embodied Life Course', p. 222.
25. De Beauvoir, *The Coming of Age*, p. 284.
26. Woodward, 'Performing Age, Performing Gender', pp. 167, 163.
27. Featherstone and Hepworth, 'The Mask of Ageing and the Postmodern Life Course', pp. 371–89.
28. Gravagne, *The Becoming of Age*, p. 29.
29. Le Gassick, 'The Faith of Islam in Modern Arabic Literature', p. 97.
30. Woodward, *Ageing and its Discontents*, p. 83.
31. Calasanti and Slevin, *Age Matters*, p. 5.
32. Laz, 'Age Embodied', p. 506.
33. Calasanti, 'Feminist Gerontology and Old Men', p. S307.
34. Young and Shami, 'Anthropological Approaches to the Arab Family', p. 11.
35. Deuteronomy 4:40, 5:33.
36. Proverbs 16:31.
37. Shuraydi, *The Raven and the Falcon*, p. 9.
38. Ibid., p. 9.
39. Ibid., p. 15.
40. Quoted in Sibai and Yamout, 'Family-Based Old-Age Care in Arab Countries: Between Tradition and Modernity', p. 65 n.
41. Yount and Sibai, 'Demography of Aging in Arab Countries', p. 291.
42. Barakat, *The Arab World*, p. 98.
43. Ibid., p. 131.
44. Ibid., pp. 132–3.

45. Millet, *Sexual Politics*, p. 3.
46. P. 10.
47. Sharabi, *Neopatriarchy*, p. 41.
48. P. 29.
49. See Aghacy, 'Modernization without Modernity', p. 569.
50. Sontag, 'The Double Standard of Aging', p. 31.
51. Deats and Lenker, *Aging and Identity*, p. 9.
52. Hazan, 'The Social Trap', pp. 22–3.
53. Friedan, 'Denial and the "Problem" of Age', p. 42.
54. Aghacy, *Masculine Identity*, p. 65.
55. Olmsted, 'Gender, Aging and the Evolving Arab Patriarchal Contract', p. 54.
56. McMullin, 'Theorizing Age and Gender Relations', p. 37.
57. Kaminsky, 'Introduction' *in Remembered Lives*, p. 77.
58. Small, 'The Double Standard of Aging', p. 211.
59. Saleh, *Season of Migration to the North*, pp. 76–7.
60. Quoted in Pearsall, 'Introduction' in The *Other Within Us*, p. 5.
61. Smith and Watson, 'Reading Autobiography', p. 150.
62. See Hepworth and Featherstone, 'The Male Menopause', pp. 276–301.
63. Wyatt-Brown and Rossen, 'Introduction: Aging, Gender, and Creativity', p. 1.
64. Meadows and Davidson, 'Maintaining Manliness in Later Life', p. 297.
65. Featherstone and Hepworth, 'The Male Menopause', pp. 235–46.
66. Marshall and Katz, 'From Androgyny to Androgens', p. 84.
67. Woodward 'Against Wisdom', pp. 63–4.
68. Moody, 'Toward a Critical Gerontology', p. 20.
69. Said, *On Late Style*.
70. Cole, *The Journey of Life*, p. xxii; quoted in *Images of Aging*, p. 30.
71. Katz, *Disciplining Old Age*, p. 40.

1

Ageing in Traditional Neighbourhoods: Conformity and Transgression

The focus in this chapter is on ageing within traditional families and local communities. The emphasis is predominantly on ageing women who dominate the scene and live from day to day, relying on social mores and religious values as well as on the support of family and kin. These are generally sedentary women who are virtually unsexed and who place no priority on appearance, but on service to family and community. While the degree of freedom these women possess varies, each one attempts to achieve agency within her own family and environment.

The Iraqi writer Fuad al-Takarli's *The Long Way Back* (2001) (*al-Raj' al-Ba'id*, 1980) is about a household full of women of different generations. While the emphasis is on women, it also includes the ageing patriarch whose looming presence in the background keeps the household in order. He only appears on the scene when talking to his son; otherwise he is absent from the affairs of the house and women. Since family support is high in a traditional, pre-industrial society, the two elderly women in the family 'recede into invisibility',[1] being confined to a room within the domestic space and entirely dependent on the family for food and care. Their role in the narrative is the minor one of comic relief when the conflict among younger characters intensifies.

The Iraqi writer Alia Mamdouh's *Mothballs* (1986) (*Habbat al-Naphtalin*, 1986) is a narrative that centres on a grandmother who becomes head of the family after the death of her husband. She upholds the values of society, abides by the teachings of Islam and raises her two grandchildren when their mother dies. In the text, more attention is given to her actions than to any concerns about growing old. What matters is the public side of her life and her role as sustainer and caretaker of the family. Her poise and philosophical calm show her to be a proud and enduring old woman who represents backbone and courage and safeguards the values of her community. She prevails over her son and daughter and supports the family from her husband's pension.

The Iraqi writer Inaam Kachachi's *The American Granddaughter* (2010) (*al-Hafida al-Amirikiyya*, 2008) is a novel of conflict between grandmother and granddaughter. The Christian grandmother lives alone in Mosul after the death of her husband and the emigration of her children and family. She survives from day to day through prayers and a strong bond with her Shi'i housekeeper Tawoos and the latter's sons, who take care of her. But more importantly, her power comes from her national consciousness, zeal and rootedness in the land of Iraq. For her granddaughter, who comes back as an interpreter to the American army that had invaded Iraq, she represents tradition mingled with national consciousness that views the American invasion with suspicion.

Elderly Women on the Margins

Al-Takarli's novel *The Long Way Back* focuses on a family living in the Bab al-Shaykh area of Baghdad in a period of political instability after the toppling of the monarchy in 1958 and the seizing of power by military officers headed by Abd al-Karim Qasim, and his eventual overthrow in 1963. This lower-middle-class Shi'a family lives in a central area of old Baghdad 'situated around the famous mosque of old Abd al-Qadir al-Kilani (al-Jilani), with its big dome, minarets, and chiming clock'.[2] Amid the political upheaval, the family continues to uphold a hierarchical structure where the father is head of the family and the major provider who expects compliance from all members of the family, who are supposed to safeguard the prevalent customs and moral and religious values. This is a patrilineal, multi-generational household where sons remain in the family household together with their wives and children.

Living close to the famous mosque, the family upholds Qur'anic principles that demand veneration of elderly parents: 'you be dutiful to your parents. If one or both attain old age in your life, say not to them a word of disrespect, nor shout at them but address them in terms of honour.'[3] Within such a context, kinship bonds ensure economic and religious ties, family obligations and community interests.

At the core of the novel is a household full of middle-aged and elderly women, although it is not clear how old they are. Nuriyya, the patriarch's wife, attends to the needs of her two sons (Midhat and Abd al-Karim), and takes care of her daughter Madiha's children, while her daughter Madiha (who has been abandoned by her husband) cooks and takes care of the kitchen. Nuriyya is still on her feet and appears to be younger than her husband, the hajj; however, the two characters that are considered old are Aunt Safiya, the hajj's sister, and Umm Hasan, Nuriyya's mother. The two elderly women are represented as continuously 'squabbling' about food and are reduced to their eating habits, biological functions, and the petty details of their daily exchanges.

They are minor characters who are generally outside the main action of the novel. They are on the margins of the plot and are rarely listened to or credited with knowledge. Their characters, far from being well-developed, cannot be known in any depth, and their inner lives are unmapped and shrouded in mystery. The third-person authorial male narrator speaks for the old women rather than letting them articulate their own subjectivity. He trivialises them and presents them as comic figures and innocent children, underscoring the hegemony of adulthood represented by the narrator and the younger members of the family.

The conventions and taboos of society upheld by the family are imposed upon the two elderly women, restricting their behaviour to what is deemed appropriate. In the novel old age is cast into a marginalised space and inhabited by women who are relegated to the margins of the plot. Owing to the limits age imposes on them, they are doubly marginalised as women and as old.[4] They are confined to their room and deprived of active participation in the affairs of the household, which causes them to fade away into a shadowy existence and remain invisible. In addition to being belittled and infantilised, old age being seen as 'a form of second childhood',[5] they serve as comic props whose function is to give the reader momentary relief from the tragedy that is taking place, the ramifications of the rape of Munira (Madiha's niece) by her own nephew, and her catastrophic marriage to her cousin Midhat.

For lack of other pleasures, food becomes the old women's sole enjoyment, and their childish exchanges are mostly related to food. These provide comic relief and lighten the gloomy atmosphere. For instance, Aunt Safiya ensures that all the food given to them is eaten before Umm Hasan wakes up.

Deprived of any other occupation, they fix their attention on food and each of her own accord entreats 'Karumi' (nickname for Karim), their nephew and grandson, to buy her pastries, and they surprise each other with bags of pastry. Umm Hasan is spotted by Safiya 'holding two pieces of sesame pastry in her fingers'. The sight is so overwhelming that it seemed to Safiya that 'Umm Hasan only had to wave her hand and they descended on her like manna from heaven'. Responding to Safiya's inquiries about the source of the pastries, Umm Hasan asserts facetiously: ' "The Lord looks after His own." '6 The two elderly women are generally infantilised, and presented as dependent, helpless, garrulous, frivolous, pathetic and dependent on the generosity of the family. What they have in common is a repetitive brand of life; they are confined to their beds, although Aunt Safiya is still in full control both physically and mentally, while Umm Hasan has reached the fourth stage of ageing where she is generally confined to bed. The two old women recognise that it is lunch or supper time from the *Idhan* (the call to prayer from the nearby mosque) and are overjoyed as it is time to eat. Conscious of their dependence on the charity of the family, Safiya entreats Madiha not to ' "forget us, Madiha, dear. We're at your mercy. Collapsing with hunger." '7

They continue to pester Madiha about smelling 'kebab' or 'mutton broth' and are seen by her as a nuisance. During Ramadan, the two elderly women become more demanding and more importunate about food, and Madiha interjects to stop their pestering: ' "Patience is a virtue. You ate two hours ago. Everything will soon be ready . . . There are people who've been fasting, you know." '8

Madiha is irritated by the unrelenting old women, who are taxing her nerves with their demands and abhors their decrepitude and disability, but is afraid to speak her mind. She views dependent old age as a liability, but if this is God's wish she must obey. Despite her impatience, she adheres to social and religious values that demand respect, care and protection for the elderly. Her brother Midhat, an intellectual and sensitive young man, appears more sympathetic and sums up his grandmother's and aunt's predicaments: 'They had passed through life, nothing more. They would never be able to say they had known it'9 – being eternally confined to the inner communal space and not given the privilege of a full personal life.

Despite the fact that they are trivialised, and viewed as puerile and frivolous, Aunt Safiya challenges the family's views of old age as a static phenomenon divorced from the dynamism of everyday life by breaking barriers, immersing herself in the day-to-day problems of the family and trying to offer her opinion. Umm Hasan, on the other hand, is generally bedridden and apathetic, having fallen into deep old age. Safiya is alert and inquisitive and tries to keep abreast of what is going on downstairs through Sana, Madiha's young daughter, who provides her with 'some snippets of news'.[10]

Safiya suspects that Adnan, Munira's nephew, is pursuing Munira for a reason and remarks that Munira looks ill and that her '"face is as yellow as turmeric"'.[11] She wonders why Adnan, her nephew, came to see her and did not even bother to greet his own grandmother, Munira's mother. When Munira learns that her aunt Safiya thinks that the former looks ill, she responds irritably: '"I'm not ill. There's nothing wrong with me, but I'd be better if you weren't so nosy, Auntie."' She tells her aunt that they are '"not hiding anything from you, but you shouldn't interfere all the time . . . Don't talk to me about it, and don't interfere in my business. Leave me alone. Do you understand?"'[12] The patronising attitude of the younger women in the family reveals the extent of discrimination the elderly suffer at the hands of the young people, who intend to banish the older women to the margins of the family.

In effect, Munira's panic and harsh words spring from her realisation that her aunt is more insightful than she had assumed. Munira is struck by Safiya's insight and tells her mother that she '"wasn't scared of Aunt Safiya as a person, but of her instincts. She sprayed us with bitter truths like polluted rain . . . I found it strange how much truth there was in her pronouncements."'[13] Described by Munira as her aunt's 'instincts', it is clear that Safiya possesses a sort of hidden and unrecognised wisdom. Despite her shock at Munira's offensive words, Safiya generously tries to justify Munira's behaviour, as she had 'a vague feeling that something broken, something abnormal in the girl's life had provoked her harsh words'.[14] Although she has no experience in life apart from that related to the internal space, Safiya is sharp, intuitive and quite capable of grasping any hint. She voices her own opinions on various issues. On learning that Munira's mother is going to rent a flat in Baghdad, she responds fervently: '"Why shouldn't she? Her daughter's a teacher with a salary, and she's not married. I didn't have her luck. God have mercy on all those who made me suffer."' She maintains that they' "left me to sit and stare at the walls. Every time a nice boy approached them they said he wasn't good enough. As if they were the only ones with no flaws."' She blames her family (perhaps her own brother) for blocking her chances for marriage, turning her into a spinster, and asks God to exact ' "his revenge on them"'.[15]

Despite her wrinkles she still retains lingering traces of beauty and remains aware of her physical appearance. She dyes her hair with henna every week and finds pleasure in looking younger as one way of compensating for the wasting away of her youth and life. She subverts the cultural dictates of ageing women that strictly determine her behaviour and ensure that she remains passive and uninvolved, and insists on playing a role in the family. Despite the family's attempt to neutralise her, she continues to give her opinions on issues pertaining to the family and to matchmaking. Safiya notes that her nephew Abd al-Karim is not suitable as a husband for Munira since he is several years her junior, and she sets out to watch Munira's behaviour more closely. She also warns Midhat, her other nephew, against marrying her, but he does not comply.

When Midhat abandons Munira on discovering she is not a virgin, Safiya recalls the numerous times she had warned him against marrying her: 'and these walls are my witnesses: "My dear Midhat, this isn't for you. Everyone must go his own way."' When Umm Hasan tells her that she too had warned him, Safiya responds: ' "You? You'd be better off keeping your mouth shut. You sleep day and night and don't know whether it is 'sunrise or sunset'." '[16] Feeling downgraded, Safiya wants to play an active role in the family by adopting the role of the traditional matriarch who upholds social and religious mores. Safiya is also concerned about her brother's limited means and believes that Munira and her mother must leave because they are draining the finances of the family. Her brother is poor and has to look after his daughter Madiha and her two daughters. Despite the rigidity of the normalising social and religious structure when it comes to old women, Safiya continues to support, and paradoxically disrupt, the system by remaining visible and active.

Madiha's frustration with her marriage, and the burden of responsibility for her two daughters, make her life a series of repetitive actions that bring no hope or expectations for the future. Nuriyya, her mother, notices with dismay that her daughter is ageing, and that in 'among the waves of her black hair'[17] threads of white hair were clearly visible. Unlike Aunt Safiya, Madiha has lost hope and no longer pays any attention to her body and general appearance after having been abandoned by her husband and becoming a burden on her father. Her disappointment and helplessness make her wonder why Aunt Safiya, who is unmarried and has had no man, bothers to dye her hair.

While his sister is seen as the other, the inessential, the lack, Abu Midhat is the epicentre of the house; everything begins and ends with him, although he is generally absent from the household, which appears to belong to the women. His memories are abundant and he has plentiful stories to tell about his past and a long meaningful life. When reminiscing, the old man has an audience, such as his eldest son Midhat, who listens with awe and respect. Abu Midhat is himself an old man but, unlike Aunt Safiya, he is revered for his experience, economic support and general sagacity. His prestige increases as he grows old, while Safiya's value decreases as traits such as incompetence, helplessness, triviality, senility and passivity become attached to her. The debilitating ageing process has a stronger effect on Safiya and Umm Hasan than on Abu Midhat, who is viewed as judicious, competent, respectable and pious, and he commands more respect and deference than the old and young women in the family. As the receptacle of wisdom, history, tradition and achievement, he is revered by all members of his family.

When Midhat, the eldest son and heir, leaves the house after discovering that his bride Munira is not a virgin, Abu Midhat suddenly submits to an incapacitating old age. Feeling close to death, he surrenders himself stoically to God's will. With a stifled sob, he decides to send a message from the Qur'an to his estranged son:

> In the name of God the Compassionate the Merciful . . . a burdened soul shall not bear the burden of another. That Man shall have only that which he has striven for. That his strivings shall be seen, and thereafter he will be fully rewarded. That with your Lord is the end of all things. That it is He who causes people to laugh and to cry . . . That it is He who causes people to live and to die.[18]

The father's way of dealing with this problem represents a Muslim man's retreat into a passive and contemplative religious life where he distances himself from the ways of the world and surrenders to death, having lived vicariously through his own son and children. As a devout Muslim, he accepts the infirmities of ageing and puts his trust in God. However, when Midhat reads his father's message, he is shocked at a 'decrepit' old man's absolute submission to death. Midhat is angry at this surrender to 'nothingness' and feels the need to confront death rather than capitulate. Despite the fact that Midhat does not approve of his father's submission, he takes his words seriously and responds accordingly:

> What was this decrepit old man doing? Why, now of all times, was he evoking these reminders of death? Was it because he thought there was no escaping it, and it was prudent to train yourself to accept it? Why should anyone accept death, nothingness?[19]

The novel suggests that the extended family structure is a shelter for the elderly from the privations of life, although it does not apply to all elderly people in close-knit communities since not everybody is protected by family support. The system is disrupted from within, by old men and women who are not protected by family ideology since it intersects with other factors such as class, positionality, family conditions and location.

For instance, Midhat tells of an old man who, so unlike his own father, was depraved and hardened, and who lived in the same house of Husayn (Madiha's estranged husband). The decrepit old man tried to drag Midhat by the ear and throw him out of the house, but Midhat bribes and neutralises him with food and money. Midhat describes the old man's 'small dirty eyes with no lashes, the caved-in mouth, the henna stained beard and moustache and the deformed language, profound impotence, thinly veiled by a childish ferocity and hardness'.[20] Similarly, Midhat's father tells the story of an old woman who was neglected by her family. As a result, she was forced to work in a house of 'ill-repute',[21] but her nephew, contrary to his traditional obligations to protect and take care of her, murdered her for tarnishing the reputation of the family by working in an infamous place. The experience of ageing that appears to be homogeneous in traditional societies is disrupted by social and economic factors and the daily realities of each individual. While Umm Hasan and Aunt Safiya find refuge under the roof of the extended family, the old impoverished and destitute woman finds release only in death.

A Nurturing Grandmother

While *The Long Way Back* centres on marginalised old women within the family space, Alia Mamdouh's *Mothballs* concentrates on the grandmother as the centre of the family after the death of her husband. The novel is preoccupied with the daily lives of a poor Iraqi family in the A'dhamiyya neighbourhood of Baghdad during the 1940s and 1950s. The narrative is focalised through the granddaughter Huda's nostalgic memories, which are transformed into a sort of eulogy, a hymn of praise and devotion to her grandmother. Huda focuses on the period when she lost her mother and was raised by her grandmother in an extended three-generation family. The old woman is seen as the embodiment of the maternal ideal in her caring function, sacrifice and services to her children and grandchildren. The narrator's reminiscences are dominated by linearity as she centres on a particular period of time when the two children (Huda the child and her brother Adil) witness the sickness and death of their mother, and the desertion by their father, who takes a second wife. As a result the children are raised by their grandmother, who is regarded as a sacred presence and viewed 'as if she were created only for worship',[22] far removed from the more prosaic world around them, although paradoxically she is fully immersed in the mundane everyday functions. Her spirituality is inextricable from her quotidian experience as the only supporter of the family. She is the one who does the shopping, pays the bills and rents a new and cheaper house, all from her husband's tiny retirement pension, which she hopes will increase if Jamouli, her only son, is willing to assist them financially. Through her emotional intelligence, cool judgement, nurturing qualities and stoic disposition, the old woman is the central power and potent presence in this traditional family.

While the narrator tells a personal story about her grandmother, who collapses the role of mother and grandmother, she also tells the story of the social and economic reality of growing old in a particular time and place. After the decease of her husband, the old woman takes over and acts in conformity with social and religious values. For her two grandchildren, their grandmother is associated with tropes of sacrifice, family bonding, domestic comfort and unceasing care. Viewed by members of her family as maternal, docile, reticent, dignified, insightful, religious and upright, she is the perfect image of the grandmother in a traditional society. Her identity is produced through repetitive performances of what Pam Morris calls 'a citation of the norms that is not simple reiteration but insubordination'.[23] As a surrogate mother, she takes upon herself the task of raising and educating her grandchildren with love and prayers, transmitting moral and religious values, and commanding respect and deferential treatment from the whole family.

Using a second-person point of view the narrator, Huda, addresses her younger self as 'you', while her older present self is referred to as 'I' to underline the forces that have shaped her present identity. She remembers her parents' room at the end of the corridor, and her aunt's, her grandmother's and the children's room situated at the entrance. Huda describes her mother as tall and slender, with brown chestnut hair and fair skin. She is repressed and submissive, and whenever she laughs she asks God's protection from Satan, her facial features becoming tense as she remembers that 'laughter is a sort of sin'.[24] If she appears in action it is only fleetingly, and the only time she reacts is when she learns that her husband has taken a second wife. She tears his clothes, but spits blood immediately afterwards, ceding to defeat and death as she laments: '"He'll kill me for tearing his clothes. I don't care! I'm dead! I don't even have any blood left!"'[25] Although she is no longer able to look after her children, the narrator and her brother, she is 'omnipresent, haunting the novel (and her children) like a ghost'.[26] The children are terrified by 'her sharp coughing [that] travelled through walls and windows' and hear their grandmother 'reading prayers to her'.[27] However, she remains an idealised presence without any internal life save a blind devotion to her husband, and exasperation and collapse on hearing about his marriage.

The grandmother embraces the living and the dead members in a strong family bond with its own rules and obligations. She is a model of 'generational continuity' that embraces three generations through a legacy of care.[28] The narrator recalls the stories that her grandmother told and retold and the verses she read from the Qur'an. In the presence of the children she prayed for their deceased mother, and for their aunt Farida to be directed to the right path and to be reconciled with her husband. She read verses from the Qur'an to calm Aunt Farida's 'hell', and Huda is sympathetic as she believes that Munir, her aunt's husband, is possessed by an evil spirit. She tells us that he disappears for a long period of time and returns home whenever it suits him. To nine-year-old Huda and eight-year-old Adil, Munir 'looked big and scary'. They learn that he was about forty while their aunt ' "only came of age a few years ago" '.[29] To top it all, there is a suggestion that he was paedophilic. The little boy was afraid of him, especially when he always 'looked for him' and opened the door of the bathroom when Adil was there.

In Huda's eyes he is a slimy subhuman creature who belongs to the gutter: '[He] mocked and ridiculed. He laughed and winked. He jumped like a field locust and scurried like the cockroaches in the cesspool.'[30] Huda's grandmother watches silently like a wise overseer, and only takes action later when Farida, her daughter, retaliates by suddenly and unexpectedly attacking her husband physically. Although the grandmother is idolised by the narrator there is a slippage in her presentation, her willingness to sacrifice her daughter in the name of kinship and tradition. She marries her young daughter to an older man solely because he is a rich cousin. Although she is dismayed at Munir's irresponsible behaviour, she is also aware of her daughter's flaws and maintains that Farida is ' "vain and sour, and her tongue cuts like a saw. When she opens her mouth about anyone, God help them!" '[31] As a result, her daughter needed to be pacified, meaning controlled through prayers and nurturance.

Within the family, the grandmother is the only source of income. At the end of the month she dresses up in her best clothes, 'the new cloak . . . along with the only silk dress, with its design of graceful trees. The high-heeled slippers . . . taken out of their box hidden in the bottom of the closet.'[32] She combs her hair carefully and goes to the General Retirement Directorate in the crowded Baghdad neighbourhood of Bab al-Mu'azzam to collect her husband's retirement pension, and in her new outfit she looks like a 'princess'.[33] After receiving the pension, she goes to the market and pays her debts without bargaining or delay, and the shopkeepers open up their new sacks of merchandise. Her religious devotion tinged with her routine responsibilities and services represent a particular brand of lower-middle-class elderly woman shaped by 1940s Arab/Islamic semi-rural communities and discourses. She is in full harmony with prescribed social behaviour and acts in full conformity with it where spirituality is inextricable from quotidian experience. Through the example of her words and deeds she imbues her grandchildren with her own religious and stoic philosophy, so much so that they are sure that '[if] she prays over a wound, it heals'.[34]

Through her performative role, the reiterative practice of regulatory norms that stabilise identity in accordance with the norm,[35] the old woman controls and sustains her own family and neutralises any conflicts. She possesses moral acumen, spiritual wisdom, and understanding that touches the hearts of the children. When she tells the children of their mother's terminal illness, Huda 'kissed her and hugged her, burying my head beneath her ribs. I felt her belly, her soft breasts, and her long, narrow neck. I raised my face to her calm, sorrowful, inspired face.'[36] Such a swift reaction reveals that Huda knows that the most fitting surrogate mother is her own grandmother.

After Iqbal's funeral, she takes the children home and tells them:

> Cry for your precious mother. Cry your tears out here. When we go downstairs I don't want to see any tears in your eyes. This is the way the world is. We come and we go. Others come and carry on. No one remains. Even the Prophet, the beloved of God, was taken, to be with Him. Only Almighty God remains.[37]

She gives them reassurance through religious devotion and the example of the Prophet to ensure that they act in conformity with social and religious mores.

Her stories gleaned from the Qur'an stood out, especially the story of Joseph: ' "My dear, it was he who was the death of Potiphar's wife" ', who was ' "like Lucifer himself, but Joseph pushed her away" '.[38] She is subdued and paradoxically enlivened by her passionate religious convictions, which enable her to imbue the children with her own values: 'if you steal, your corpse will not be laid open, and if you lie, God is forgiving and merciful'.[39]

She achieves meaning in the context of family and community, and her brand of religiosity is an amalgam of religious conviction and superstition. Huda recalls that her grandmother sprinkled water behind her and her brother after every meal in order to wipe out their footprints and protect them from Satan. She also warns the children who sleep on the roof about the crows: ' "If a crow settles near your head, and caws, it's a bad omen." ' Despite the grandmother's attempt to keep the children within the constraints of superstition nurtured by her gullible understanding of Islam, Huda is not intimidated by the crows since they always 'flew so close to my head that I could hear their wings beating'.[40]

The old woman's world consists of the home, the street and the cemetery. On religious holidays, the whole family went to the cemetery behind the mosque, where the old woman

> read aloud and her voice rang out, painfully sharp. It floated over the expanse of the cemetery, moving the women to sob. You used to watch her as she filled your head with the dark side of death, as if she were opening up all the holes in all the heads, the land, and souls.[41]

Huda's grandmother is a sort of female orator whose sermons centre on prayer and death, she having surrendered completely to the social and religious norms that she accepts without questioning. Standing in the cemetery after Iqbal's death, she prays as if she were all by herself addressing Iqbal alone. Like a wise orator who embodies maternal wisdom and nurturing, she stands before the grave without crying or wailing, and mutters verses from the Qur'an asking God's help:

> Lord, You are all-knowing. You are the protector. Oh Lord, take her from my heart as You have taken her from my path. Every day You test me, Lord. Almighty God, I do not oppose Your will. God is great! . . . Why? Why? Dear Iqbal, this too is a test. God is constantly testing his servants. Rest there in the gardens of grace. I prayed the sura of Yasin forty times for you, and it will do you some good there in Heaven. It will relieve you of some of the pain of this dirty world. A thousand mercies to your soul![42]

When she completes her speech, she kisses the Qur'an, and rises slowly oblivious of those around her even though their shouts fill the air, pronouncing her a source of comfort to the community and a maternal and spiritual presence. On a second visit to the cemetery, she covers Iqbal's grave with her tears and asks the children to:

> 'Pray the *fatiha*. Huda, breathe on your mother's soul. Adil, my boy, don't make any mistakes as you pray; send them to her pure soul. The soul can hear and feel, and get upset as well. This is where we will all be buried.'[43]

The cemetery rituals help her release her frustrations so she is able to cope with endless problems and a strong sense of abandonment and worry about her daughter's collapsing marriage and the family's financial problems, especially that her son has forgotten them. However, she keeps going, fortified by her stoic fatalism and acquiescence to God's will, which give significance to her spiritual, maternal and social life.

She informs the children that they are going to Karbala 'to see the absent ones' and 'to weep in the presence of the Lord of Martyrs, Hussein, may God honour his face. We will ask him to soften Jamil's [her estranged son] heart and heal him, and I will ask him for patience.'[44] Feeling vulnerable and unprotected by her own children, she prays to God to help her need no one and to take her to him before she becomes disabled. The narrator tells us that her tears were so dry with grief that she feared that she might be going blind.

Even the children's roguish father is pacified by her silent and commanding presence and stops beating his daughter Huda for dancing and singing in the streets and being hugged by children. Huda maintains that the moment 'your father saw her, he changed; he calmed down. He loved and honoured her, and weakened in her presence.'[45] She being a model of virtue and formulaic principles, the only unstable feature in her physique were her eyes, which 'were honey-coloured [in the morning], and by the time we came home in the afternoon they were blue. But at night they were grey.'[46] Her outer appearance is a 'model of propriety' with her modest outfit, and the 'narrow black band round her head, whose ends dangled by her thin braids which were white'.[47] Although we do not know how old she is, she is a prototype of the old woman in a traditional Shi'a community. Removed from any signs of sexuality or desire and the 'unspeakable subject'[48] of the body, she is an image of unsullied chastity. In her stoic acceptance of age, since '[a]nger in the old is outlawed',[49] she generates awe at her religiosity and stability and exercises power over her children and grandchildren.

In addition to stories from the Qur'an, she 'dazzled' the children with a story about their father, who went through a special ritual that transformed him into a man. The story was told and retold, to the elation of the children. The narrator's father was trained for two weeks by his father to ride a horse and he returned a changed man: '"his skin became tight, his voice had changed – he was like a beast of prey"'. In other words, he was transformed into '"a [real] man"'.[50] Ironically, he fails in all his male endeavours, and when it comes to women, male chauvinism, cruelty and egoism are clearly manifested, especially when he took a second wife after learning of his first wife's illness.

As for the old woman's relationship with her own husband, she remained generally reticent about it. She showed the children an old picture book, at the beginning of which was a photograph of their grandfather. The children learn that he was 'venerable, terrifying, handsome, harsh, sceptical', but also jealous and uncommunicative. He had a 'superior air, like an Ottoman pasha', and when 'he went to work everyone scuttled out of his way'.[51] The grandfather is 'constructed implicitly and through allusion ... and even absence' and retains his 'familial and economic' power[52] even after his death. Although the grandmother seldom spoke about herself or her life with him, it is clear what she might have had to go through with such an authoritarian husband. It is clear that she achieves a measure of freedom and independence denied her when her husband was alive. This explains her love of and high esteem for justice, especially when it comes to her son's fierce treatment of his children. She is asexual, but complete in herself and secure in her beliefs. In other words, her character is shaped by ideology, which gives her a strong sense of rightness and belongingness.

Strongly assured of the stable biological and social differences between men and women, she teaches Huda that ' "a girl's beauty is in her silence and modesty" ',[53] which is in sharp contrast to a man, who should be bellicose and self-confident. Ironically, Huda projects her younger self as insolent, aggressive and masculine, and her brother as timid, introspective and feminine. Huda and Adil exchange roles, challenging the 'fixity' of their grandmother's values, and the 'discursive constraints' imposed by traditional culture.[54]

Nevertheless, despite the grandmother's traditional views about the superiority of men, she stands firm on the side of the children's victimised mother against her son's new wife. When her son, Jamouli (nickname for Jamil), marries 'one-eyed Nuriyya', his mother vows that in honour of the children's mother, the second wife will never set foot in her house. Her son defends his new wife by telling his mother that she 'loves' him and is 'afraid' of him, and also alludes to her mother, who 'used to read prayers for Imam Hussein'.[55] While accepting her son's second marriage as religiously lawful, she reveals her protest by focusing on his first wife's tragic death, that transcends any legal marriage contract. In her role as nurturing grandmother she insists on maintaining ties with Iqbal and the maternal. Despite her traditional/religious views, she is ready to see that human values sometimes take priority. She is convinced of the justice of her decision not to receive her daughter-in-law in her house, as it is her own way of sanctifying the memory of Iqbal. When her son's second wife sent sacks of luscious Karbala dates in the summer, and baskets of oranges in the winter, along with chicken and cheese, and loaves of bread fresh from the oven, the whole family ate except the grandmother, who remained strongly committed to her principles and compassionate values, which transgressed social and religious sanctions.

Despite her countless stories of the past, and of the various family members, she herself remains enigmatic, and her restraint gives her an air of poise and composure. She does not talk about herself or reveal any of her feelings. The gaps in the plot can be seen when she tells the children about her husband, or when we learn from the narrator that she had lost four children and is left with Jamouli and Farida, with a difference of fifteen years between them. This old woman's tragedy remains hidden in the folds of her concealed body, raising questions and speculation without answers. Despite her tragic history, she is, as her granddaughter describes her, 'strong without showing signs of it, mighty without raising her voice, beautiful without finery'.[56] As a widow, she is patronised by no one and can easily communicate with her children, and particularly with her grandchildren. Her identity remains strongly enmeshed in relationships within a situated context. Hers is a familial and spiritual self, tinged with personal ethics in particular situations, but 'her only passion was for God'.[57] Her prescribed ethics fostered by her religious faith, and a protracted experience, give her the revered status she enjoys among all the members of her family, particularly the children. The narrator avows that her grandmother 'explored herself with prayers that never ended . . . divulged no secret' and 'contrived no tricks . . . stirred up no scandals, or played with anyone's nerves'.[58] She remains the archetype of the wise woman possessing emotional insight, righteous ideas and spiritual wisdom.

A Grandmother's Coping Strategies

Like the grandmother in *Mothballs*, who upholds social and religious values, Rahma in Kachachi's *The American Granddaughter* is another elderly woman who attempts to survive in war-torn Iraq after the death of her husband and the emigration of her children. The novel begins with the narrator Zeina, who recounts her disenchanting experience in Iraq as an interpreter in the American army during the Second Gulf War. Zeina's family had emigrated to the USA when she was a child, but she still retains a strong tie to the homeland and to her roots. Now that she is in Iraq, she wants to tell her friends in the American army how proud she is of her country: 'I wanted to flaunt my kinship in front of them, show them that I was a daughter of the same part of the country, that I spoke their language with the same accent, I wanted to tell them that Youssef Fatouhy, assistant to the chief of army recruitment in Mosul in the 1940s, was my grandfather.'[59] For Zeina, Iraq is represented by her grandmother Rahma Girgis Saour, who lives in Mosul: 'How could I not love Mosul, when everyone there spoke with my grandmother's accent?'[60] Zeina's grandmother Rahma was born in Mosul in 1917, and during the American invasion she was in her early eighties. The novel focuses on the political, economic and social reality of growing old in 2003 Iraq, revealing that old age is a cultural construct with shifting boundaries.

When Zeina visits her granddaughter in Mosul, Rahma tells her that when she was born, her grandparents had already crossed over into an empty and depressing old age. Zeina was like a 'beautiful adornment' to their lives: 'They raised her from the time she was still in nappies, watched over her with prayers and sheltered her under their watchful gaze.'[61] Grandmother Rahma's nicknames of fondness aimed at pampering and spoiling Zeina were overwhelming: Zein, Darling Zayouna, Zuweina, Zonzon. Like the Muslim grandmother in *Mothballs*, the old Christian woman has similar values. For this traditional Christian Iraqi grandmother, family and care are the highest values that give meaning to existence. As a child, Zeina descended upon them like a ray of light, like 'confetti', and they took upon themselves the task of raising her and watching over her. But when Zeina's parents emigrate to America, the grandparents feel 'like orphans'.[62] As a retired old man, Rahma's husband becomes more feminised despite his military background. Without this pivotal nurturing role, ageing becomes a terrifying period of inertia, barrenness and decline for Rahma and her husband. Like orphans, the elderly couple have lost their source of sustenance, and the roles of parent and child are reversed.

Living alone after the death of her husband, Zeina's grandmother Rahma retains a stoic attitude to ageing and death nurtured by her Christian faith and acceptance of divine will, a pervading trope of coping in the face of infirmity and the war raging in Iraq. Her faith is not about withdrawal into an inert existence and state of decline, but about engaging with the world around her in an energetic and spirited manner that gives her self-worth and agency. Her prayers focus on her own personal needs and those of her family; she asks the Virgin Mary to preserve what is left of her health, prevent her from falling, and have mercy on her dead. She prays for the Virgin to bless her children and grandchildren, naming a few and asking her not to forget the others ' "whose names I forgot to mention but whom you know one by one" '.[63] The narrator's facetious playfulness when it comes to her grandmother's religious rituals exposes her view of her elderly grandmother as infantile, while simultaneously uncovering Zeina's deep affection for the old woman.

The narrator maintains that after the death of her husband, Rahma's saints are her daily companions. She addresses them in a casual manner, focusing on prosaic matters and involving the saints in her mundane quotidian actions inside the house during a time of instability and war. She expects them to assist her and give her power and self-worth, and her communication with them depends upon contingency and her own agenda. Her prayers, tinged with the political, military and personal situation, are characterised by randomness and unpredictability. The morning prayer could be held in the evening, especially when there is no television owing to electricity cuts. When the light is cut suddenly, she reproaches the Virgin for not keeping it running for five more minutes for her to finish her massage, and she tries unsuccessfully to recall the name of the patron saint of electricity. Her daily rituals reveal the inextricable link between the domestic and the commonplace and the sacred and the revered. Such incongruity accentuates the comic situation and the narrator's awareness of the tragedy behind it.

Rahma's style of worship is devised to suit her different moods, her preoccupations and the state of her health. She sees no harm in saying her 'Hail Marys' while she rubs her arthritic hands with almond oil, or massages her feet, 'whose big toes curled on top of the others'.[64] While the grandmother's body in *Mothballs* is transcendent and invisible, Rahma's body is visible only as a misshapen ageing body, in line with the current discourses of ageing as a body in decline. The text denotes the various ways in which age, gender and politics intersect to shape the multiple dimensions of the old woman's experience in a war situation and the way in which her ageing body copes with a ruthless and changing world of war. Rahma is presented in a debunking comic style that veils agonising anomalies that govern her tragic situation and shape her life despite her unflagging attempts to deal with it.

We are told by the narrator that the family's attitude to Rahma is forbearing, tolerant and patronising. They put up with her, oblige her and accept her eccentricities. The love and respect attributed to old age is maintained, but not taken seriously. At times, they trivialise her religious rituals when they refer to her saints as the 'Cabinet of President Rahma', with Saint Anthony in the lead.[65] Rahma gives orders to her saints, raising their status when her prayers are answered and blacklisting them when she gets no response. Since her family has moved away and is no longer under her wing, her saints are her sole companions and source of power, and her first priority is to look in her prayer books for the name of the patron saint of immigrants, but she is not able to find it.

Rahma provides 'employment' for the idle saints, and decides to keep them busy and relieve them of boredom as they sit on the clouds with their halos around their heads. Among these saints is Saint Christopher, the patron saint of travellers, who she always invokes reproachfully for scattering her family all over the wide world. In her angry moments, she begrudges her husband for leaving her behind, blames the Virgin and the saints who are slow to grant her death wish, and reproaches her children who had left her behind. When her granddaughter Zeina shows up unexpectedly in Iraq, she responds: '"I kiss your hand Virgin Maryam, for these good tidings."'[66] Religious ritual is a recurrent trope used to reveal her way of dealing with the barrenness, unpredictability and anxieties of a septuagenarian during a time of war. Within the regularity, order and predictability of religious ritual, she provides a semblance of order to a life that is coming to an end. Faced with the incongruities of war and the aloneness of old age, she manifests a robust vitality and geniality as her way of resisting war and death.

In addition to religious rituals, another of her coping strategies is (like that of the grandmother in *Mothballs*) her strong social relations with the community. She possesses no internal subjective life, and her identity and source of agency are embedded in social, communal and time-honoured associations such as her relationship with Tawoos. Her sturdy patriotism, rooted in her native land and situated within interactional communities, is another major source of agency and empowerment.

When asked by her granddaughter whether she is afraid to be alone in a war situation her answer is: '"Who would I be afraid of? Tawoos [a Shi'a housekeeper] comes to me every day, and the people of the street have known me for forty years."'[67] Besides, Tawoos's son Muhaymen, who has joined the Mahdi army, has ensured her safety. Tawoos is the seamstress and general caretaker of her house: '"All our clothes, all our handkerchiefs and scarves, sheets and pillowcases, come from the work of her hands."'[68] Tawoos is indispensable, as she is responsible for endless chores inside the house such as 'tidying up Rahma's cupboards; washing and changing pillowcases; ironing sheets and tablecloths; picking oranges from the garden, making juice' to be kept in the fridge, and 'making *kibbeh* balls and half-cooking them for freezing . . . [and] sprinkling cockroach repellent in the corners and drains'.[69] Despite the war, Rahma insists on retaining the earlier pre-war normality of life.

In addition to doing the housework, Tawoos plays a role in beautifying Rahma by dying her hair with henna in a culture where old women were expected to be sexless and to focus on spiritual rather than corporeal issues. Rahma's pretext for dying her hair is to prevent headaches, although Tawoos also threads Rahma's eyebrows and upper lip. When it comes to her appearance, Rahma, an educated middle-class Christian woman, while going by the rules of society, subverts the rules from within, underlining the complex relation between the individual and society and the intersection of social, religious and educational factors, allowing 'spaces for resistance'.[70] She stretches these rules to appear to coincide with prevailing social mores in order to preserve a self in line with the behaviour prescribed by society. Since an elderly woman is supposed to think solely of spiritual matters and forget her corporeality, Rahma covers her white hair with henna under the pretext that it is supposed to cure headaches.

Rahma proclaims her 'lifelong kinship' with Tawoos. When Zeina asks about the gold and jewellery that used to adorn the frame of the Virgin's picture, the old woman reacts by asking '"Did the Virgin, bless her name, need the gold when we were suffering under the sanctions? I sold it to pay for Tawoos's dentures"',[71] affirming her resourcefulness and successful engagement with the community. In addition to her reliance on religious faith, Rahma also survives on her strong nationalistic political views that she gleans from television, and her knowledge of English that enables her to watch CNN. Unlike the apolitical grandmother in *Mothballs*, Rahma has strong opinions regarding the American invasion of Iraq, which save her from the weariness of routine and give her a sense of agency that she achieves through political commitment. In a playful and facetious manner, Zeina admits her amusement on hearing Rahma expounding her views on politics, and sounding like a CNN commentator or an expert on strategic affairs using expressions such as 'communist tide', 'American plot', 'Zionist conspiracy', 'Kissinger's plan' and 'the charisma of Nasser'.[72] On her side, when Rahma learns that her granddaughter is working with the Americans, she decides to educate her; to win her over; to put her on the right track (the Iraqi viewpoint as opposed to the American); to transmit the traditions, cultures and values; 'to nourish my roots, to bring life into the branches of my belonging';[73] and to drive away the evil spirit that has possessed Zeina and has returned her to her grandmother in a distorted form. Consequently, her grandmother gives her a lesson in the genealogy of her family. She tells her stories about the family and homeland, and her characters are 'perfumed with the scent of Iraq, and her education program took no shortcuts'. But Rahma's prescription does not impress her granddaughter, who remains sceptical about whether her grandmother's patriotic stories will have any effect on her, particularly since the stories appear too hyperbolic and extravagant. For instance, Zeina wonders why there was no one in her family 'who was idle or corrupt'.[74]

Rahma's commitment and nationalistic spirit create a rift between her and her granddaughter. According to the narrator, her grandmother 'preserved in the folds of her wrinkled skin, all the heritage of generations brought up with a strong sense of justice'[75] and unreasonable nationalistic feelings. Rahma tells Zeina that the history of her family, her blood group and her ancestors' bones are 'here' in the homeland, and that is why she should act like a 'true' Iraqi and reject the Americans. On the occasion of Iraq's Armed Forces Day on 6 January, Rahma hangs her husband's military suit, the source of his power and distinction, in the house and is full of pride and high esteem for her patriotic husband's services to the army. She stands by her husband through thick and thin, and when Zeina tells her that the Americans are doing a good job in Iraq the old woman reacts contemptuously: '"Don't you dare say these things in the room where your grandfather's soul ascended. Have some respect for his memory at least." '[76] She insists that it was a mercy from God that he died before witnessing the occupation and the shameful role of his granddaughter. Despite her attempt to control her own life and cope with a contingent reality, like the grandmother in *Mothballs*, she remains fixed in the past and within the precincts of her husband's religious, moral and political arena.

Rahma is proud of her husband's feats in the army and his commitment, discipline and high ethical standards. He was always seen in the early hours of the morning proudly polishing the stars on his military suit, and his veneration for the army was such that when he drank arak with his companions, or when he was in a fight, he always took off his military suit. As a traditional and nationalistic old woman, Rahma is in full adoration of her husband's military masculinity. When he retires, Rahma takes his old military suit to the dry-cleaner's and brings it back packed in white paper. The younger members of the family refer to it sarcastically as '"the groom's outfit"'.[77] The more cynical Zeina looks at her grandfather's military suit hanging in front of her like 'a crucifix without a head'[78] and wonders why her grandmother wants to carry this cross up until the last days of her life.

Convinced of the rightness of her views, Rahma remains loyal to her national and political convictions. When she visits her granddaughter at the American headquarters, Zeina lies to her and tells her that she is a UN representative observing the operations of the US Army among Iraqi civilians. Being sharp-eyed, alert and able to '"see through thick Yoghurt"',[79] Rahma asks her granddaughter distrustfully whether she receives her salary from 'Bush or Kofi Annan'.[80] At the American base, she refuses to eat or drink anything, as if 'our [American] water was poisoned'.[81]

Rahma wanted to bring Zeina back to the path of righteousness, modesty, propriety and tradition, while Zeina maintains that her grandmother's partial views spring from a delimited existence and narrow horizons that make her naively firm in her conviction that those values belonged exclusively to her and to her nation. According to Zeina, hers was a kind of 'blind Bedouin patriotism'[82] that celebrated with gunshots when a man took his brother's side against his cousin's, and his cousin's side against the outsider, regardless of whether they are right or wrong, and she wonders if Rahma has heard the expression '"citizen of the world"'.[83] In Zeina's view, her grandmother is traditional, inflexible and resistant to change.

Rahma's political commitment and nationalistic zeal create a rift between them. She knows that Zeina is working with the Americans and seeks the assistance of Tawoos's son Haydar, Zeina's 'milk brother', to '"bring her [Zeina] up from scratch, this ignorant girl . . . We won't leave her to her ill manners."'[84] Her attempt to transmit traditions, culture and values to her granddaughter is a communal undertaking rather than a personal endeavour. She reassures Haydar that his mother's milk is 'pure', but 'the girl has been led astray'[85] and needs help. As a transmitter of values and culture, she insists on rescuing Zeina from the opposing trench.

After learning from Tawoos that Rahma had cursed her granddaughter before her death, referring to her as '"that slut who was raised in the gutter"',[86] Zeina suspects that her grandmother died from the shame she felt within her predominantly Shi'a community. Tawoos tells her that Rahma drank the whole bottle (of her husband's arak) the day she saw Zeina wearing an American military suit and riding a tank. She spent the whole night wailing as if she were mourning the death of a beloved daughter. With the failure of the American project in Iraq, Zeina recalls her earlier simplistic attitude, thinking naively that the Americans have come to bring salvation to the Iraqi people: 'They [the Iraqis] won't believe their eyes when they finally open onto freedom. Even old men will become boys again when they sup from the milk of democracy and taste of the life I lead here.'[87] Now Zeina describes herself as a 'squeezed rag', a squashed woman 'who bears a cemetery inside her chest'.[88] She recalls the old woman who, like the fortune-tellers of Babylon, shook her head once and murmured, '"The worst is yet to come. We can only ask God for protection."'[89] Unlike the narrator with her adulterated identity, she notes that her grandmother and her friends 'remained pure Iraqis, like pure gold. Their patriotism was not tainted by a dual nationality, and their blood raced in their veins when they heard the name Iraq, their unique glimmering planet in the midst of dark galaxies.'[90] Zeina comes to the conclusion that despite her age, her grandmother's views regarding the fate of Iraq rang true. The struggle between youth and age, tradition and modernity destroys the grandmother and leaves Zeina in a state of liminality.

Conclusion

According to Kate Millet, 'Patriarchy's chief institution is the family',[91] which is the focus of the first chapter, which has centred on ageing individuals within the traditional, circumscribed family sphere. Cultural and religious norms in the Arab/Islamic world have traditionally conferred respect and honour on ageing men and women, where the ageing patriarch retains his familial and economic position, while the woman is relegated to the margins of the narrative. The ageing process within the family is shaped by paternalistic and hierarchical structures, which guarantee a high level of integration of their elders in the family and community. The texts discussed, which are dominated by linearity and closure, show that in old age the emphasis is on the cultivation of the spirit where the ageing individual achieves 'a sort of divine maturity'[92] by retreating into a meditative existence of tranquillity, composure, and a pious wisdom that is a token of the desired smooth path to eternity.

The gender issue is pivotal in traditional and religious cultures where old women (unmarried aunts, ageing grandmothers and mothers), such as Umm Hasan and Safiya in *The Long Way Back*, are dependent on their families. They are confined to their rooms and remain outside the daily goings-on of the family, although Safiya is physically and cognitively fit. Notwithstanding, these women are taken care of by younger women, such as daughters and granddaughters. Other ageing women are empowered only after the decease of their husbands, as in the case of the two grandmothers in *Mothballs* and *The American Granddaughter*.

Although there are minor differences among women such as those related to class, education and religion, 'the master narrative of aging'[93] takes centre stage, where the values of modesty and socially and religiously sanctioned performances of ageing remain the same, and where the female body is generally absent. The nurturing grandmother in *Mothballs* is an idealised image of old age who pays no attention to her personal needs, and acts in conformity with society that 'proscribe[s] appropriate behaviours and obligations '[94] where the female body is 'significant only in terms of its absence'.[95] She is the exemplary grandmother, who is the embodiment of care, sacrifice and service to the younger generation, but who remains an idealised icon of reverence devoid of any idiosyncratic traits. Other women achieve agency through communal and political solidarity, such as the Christian grandmother in *The American Granddaughter* who embraces strong nationalistic and political views that enhance her role in the community.

While the novels in this chapter perpetuate the dominant norms regarding ageing, minor gestures of resistance are discerned under the cover of religious piety, supplications and minor physical ailments. For instance, the grandmother in *The American Granddaughter* dyes her hair with henna pretending that it is supposed to cure her headaches. Despite such transgressive actions, these women achieve meaning exclusively within the framework of family and community. The three novels explored in this chapter shed light on the situation of elderly women in traditional Arab societies, who within the confines of numerous and divergent restrictions manage to achieve agency within the parameters of traditional society, while their inner selves remain wrapped up in mystery.

Notes

1. Woodward, 'Introduction' to *Figuring Age*, p. xii.
2. *The Long Way Back*, p. v.
3. Chapter 17, verse 23.
4. Bouson, *Shame and the Aging Woman*, p. 3.
5. Featherstone and Wernick, *Images of Aging*, p. 140.
6. *The Long Way Back*, p. 41.
7. Ibid., p. 277.
8. Ibid., p. 276.
9. Ibid., p. 111.
10. Ibid., p. 51.
11. Ibid., p. 47.
12. Ibid., p. 48.
13. Ibid., p. 208.
14. Ibid., p. 48.
15. Ibid., p. 135.
16. Ibid., p. 274.

17. Ibid., p. 12.
18. Ibid., p. 292.
19. Ibid., pp. 362–3.
20. Ibid., p. 306.
21. Ibid., p. 58.
22. *Mothballs*, p. 1.
23. Morris, 'Women's Writing: An Ambivalent Politics', p. 58.
24. *Mothballs*, p. 5.
25. Ibid., p. 43.
26. Hamdar, *The Female Suffering Body*, p. 80. For the impact of disability on women, see Ibid., pp. 75–81.
27. *Mothballs*, p. 5.
28. Woodward, 'Inventing Generational Models', p. 152.
29. *Mothballs*, p. 2.
30. Ibid., p. 2.
31. Ibid., pp. 68–9.
32. Ibid., p. 34.
33. Ibid., pp. 33–4.
34. Ibid., p. 53.
35. Butler, *Gender Trouble*, pp. xv–xvi.
36. *Mothballs*, p. 32.
37. Ibid., p. 95.
38. Ibid., p. 12.
39. Ibid.,
40. Ibid., p. 99.
41. Ibid., p. 22.
42. Ibid., p. 95.
43. Ibid., p. 101.
44. Ibid., p. 68.
45. Ibid., p. 28.
46. Ibid., p. 30.
47. Ibid., p. 29.
48. Hillyer, 'The Embodiment of Old Women: Silences', p. 53.
49. Woodward, 'Against Wisdom', p. 63.
50. Ibid., p. 30.
51. Ibid.
52. Featherstone and Wernick, *Images of Aging*, pp. 102, 127.

53. Ibid., p. 30.
54. King, 'Discourses of Ageing in Fiction and Feminism', p. 172.
55. *Mothballs*, p. 46.
56. Ibid., p. 29.
57. Ibid., p. 12.
58. Ibid.
59. *American Granddaughter*, p. 7.
60. Ibid., p. 5.
61. Ibid., p. 68.
62. Ibid., p. 102.
63. Ibid., p. 53.
64. Ibid., p. 52.
65. Ibid., p. 53.
66. Ibid., p. 55.
67. Ibid., p. 104.
68. Ibid., p. 41.
69. Ibid., p. 42.
70. Powell, *Social Theory*, p. 79.
71. *American Granddaughter*, p. 103.
72. Ibid., p. 43.
73. Ibid., p. 44.
74. Ibid., p. 92.
75. Ibid., p. 65.
76. Ibid., p. 102.
77. Ibid., p. 80.
78. Ibid., p. 77.
79. Ibid., p. 59.
80. Ibid., p. 63.
81. Ibid.
82. Ibid., p. 117.
83. Ibid., p. 130.
84. Ibid., p. 64.
85. Ibid., p. 67.
86. Ibid., p. 165.
87. Ibid., p. 10.
88. Ibid., pp. 2, 1.
89. Ibid., p. 103.

90. Ibid., p. 117.
91. Millet, *Sexual Politics*, p. 33.
92. Wada, 'The Status and Image of the Elderly in Japan', p. 57.
93. Rubenstein, 'Feminism Eros, and the Coming of Age', p. 4.
94. Calasanti and Slevin, 'Introduction', p. 4.
95. Woodward, 'Performing Age', p. 162.

2

Hoary Monuments, Residual Bodies: Senescence in the City

This chapter focuses on the way in which older generations react to demographic and architectural transformations in the city. It centres on the cities of Cairo and Aleppo, whose features are disappearing because of modernisation, regime change and the rise of the modern nation state, but are resurrected in the memories of the older generation. In memory, the old city and its edifices come to life again in the midst of an unstable and chaotic present invaded by modernity and by new forces from the countryside and from rural areas. For the elderly inhabitants of the city, the past is predominant and is poignantly juxtaposed with their present situation. In the streets of the city, the ageing individual is an odd presence in a youthful and bubbling city, and a sign of the past. However, the past remains clearly visible, and the elderly person feels strong identification with the aged edifices that are seen peering through the cracks of modernity.

Naguib Mahfouz's *Sugar Street* (1993) (*al-Sukariyya*, 1957) traces the old patriarch Hajj Abd al-Jawad's attempts to deal with senescence and the tropes of lost strength, energy, sexuality and control through the power of reminiscence. Like the ageing man, the old Cairene edifices still relentlessly resist the passage of time despite decay and disuse. While the hajj and his ageing friends lament the past in their comfortable room, the old prostitute (Sultana Zubayda) roams the streets and laments her fate of being rejected by her lovers, who force her 'to face abjection'.[1] As a declining old woman, she is 'anchored in visuality', where her body is 'both hypervisible and invisible'.[2] Having lost her youth and her past attractions, she leads a tattered existence as an old, decrepit and petrifying sight for anyone who looks at her.

The Egyptian writer Alaa al-Aswany's *The Yacoubian Building* (2004) (*Imaret Ya'qubyan*, 2002) focuses on a sixty-five-year-old man, Zaki el-

Dassouki, who walks the streets of Cairo and notes the decaying edifices and a new brand of inhabitants who have moved to the city from rural areas and who continue to live their lives as they did in the villages. Although the city is losing its intelligibility, he compensates by resurrecting the past through memory. Although the remaining old haunts have declined and diminished they retain some of their old charm, and despite all the hurdles Zaki is determined to stay in touch with the present.

The Syrian writer Khalid Khalifa's *No Knives in This City's Kitchens* (2016) (*La Sakakin fi Matabikh hadhihi al-Madina*, 2013) introduces a group of lonely men and women in Aleppo, some of whom grow old and incarcerate themselves behind their shuttered windows, while others continue to resist by participating in the activity outside. However, the past remains predominant and is poignantly juxtaposed with their current life and present situation. The focal point of the narrative is the mother, whose inability to accept the filth and smells of the new Aleppo with its vulgar rural inhabitants drives her into a world of dreams and fantasy away from the material reality outside.

Crumbling Bricks and Bodies

Mahfouz's *Sugar Street* centres on the ageing of a traditional family within a transitional period in Cairo between 1935 and 1944. The novel begins with images revealing the inevitability of senescence and death: 'The January cold' enough to 'freeze water', and the 'long-standing lantern' without oil and no longer functional, to be replaced by 'electric light'.[3] The upper storey of the house has been moved downstairs to accommodate a new situation where al-Sayyid Ahmad Abd al-Jawad, suffering from heart disease, is too frail to climb the stairs. The commanding and authoritative father is weakening, while the mother is described as 'disappearing into old age'.[4] Their eldest son Kamal notes the debilitating effects of age on his father [not his mother] as he 'sat hunched over his ledgers . . . his grey moustache almost concealed by his large nose, which looked bigger now because of the thinness of his face'.[5] The same applies to Abd al-Jawad's shop assistant, who at seventy looks even more pitiable after serving a customer. The linear style of reporting brings home to us the inevitability of decline and death.

Despite the general debilitation, the old traditional quarter of Cairo is infiltrated by modern structures that threaten to expunge the past. The old barber, the bean seller and the milkman have no choice but to look enviously at Uncle Bayumi's new store that stands in stark contrast to their 'dilapidated premises'.[6] The latter's old ice cream and confectionery store is renovated: 'It has lots of mirrors and electric lights, with a radio playing day and night.' Aware of the threatening invasion of modernisation manifested in the tearing down of old houses in the vicinity and their replacement by modern buildings, Abd al-Jawad and his friends become all the more attached to the good old days when life was 'worth living, and hearts had been carefree'.[7] However, despite Abd al-Jawad's partiality for the past, the family has acquired a radio 'which brings entertainment, news, and even religious services',[8] but what the old patriarch and his friends look for in particular are the old songs as their way of clinging to a vanishing past.

Despite the hajj's antipathy to change, other members of the family have different opinions. Conscious of the fact that the world is changing and her father's views are growing out of date, Aisha, the hajj's daughter, regrets the fact that her own father the hajj prevented her daughter Na'ima from going to school when many of her classmates were pursuing their studies. Her father was unwilling to abandon his ideas on the education of girls within his family. The general sense was that education belongs solely to women who cannot find a husband because of their looks. In a similar vein, the hajj's daughter Khadija is critical of her son's educated fiancée: ' "So she's a journalist too! What kind of girl works outside the home except an old maid, a hag, or a woman who apes men?" '[9] She gazes at her daughter-in-law scornfully and disapprovingly, and wonders how she has the guts to join the conversation and discuss politics shamelessly.

Even with the changes that are taking place, Abd al-Jawad's authority within the family remains paramount. The tap of his walking stick is enough to make the whole family stand up 'politely'. The father who dominates the family scene remains a figure of control and absolute veneration, and the result is unproblematic subservience to a sacredly held paternal authority where there is no room for generational conflict. The only members of the family who have the courage to challenge him are his grandchildren, affirming that the world is changing and that the system of hierarchy represented by the patrilineal family is being undermined from within.

In spite of his age and illness, the hajj is always elegantly dressed in his 'broad cloth cloak, striped silk caftan and silk scarf'.[10] He never goes out without wearing cologne, taking 'full advantage of the charm and dignity of old age', and leaning on his stick that had been a symbol of virility and elegance, as well as absolute control.[11] By upholding his elegant style, he maintains continuity with the cherished past despite health complications.

Considering his disengagement from customary activities, al-Hajj does not compensate by focusing on the next world and embracing spirituality and ascetic piety. He leaves that to his wife. His appetite for the pleasures of life remains voracious, and he resents having to avoid alcohol, replace it with a bowl of yoghurt and orange, and go to bed early to preserve his failing health. Even the cold shower that reinvigorated him is forbidden: '"God have mercy on us," he thought, "when everything good becomes harmful."'[12] Likewise, his ageing friends lament their old 'ecstatic intoxications' and resent the fact that they are relegated to '"the point of envying one glass"'.[13] These men regret their waning health and sexuality and yearn for the days of youthful vigour and potency, and begrudge their present state of lethargy and impotence.

These are pleasure-loving old men who remain youthful in spirit. Ahmad Abd al-Jawad, the '"court jester"'[14] as his friends refer to him, does not repent of his old licentiousness, adventurous spirits and towering passions, and considers them a 'blessing'.[15] This is a group of men who counter rigid images of old men as bastions of tradition, old men who capitulate to current views of ageing men as stoic, religious and asexual. Instead, they yearn for their old ludic selves which demonstrate that, even in traditional societies, old men are not a homogeneous group, and that ageing is not a stable and uniform phase.

The only uplifting feeling entertained by al-Sayyid Ahmad to cope with a debilitating situation is a cherished homosocial relation with his old friends. Sensing that their brand of life is becoming obsolete, the old men cling together as a distinct group separated from the new world, and find refuge in male bonding as a coping strategy. Despite their loss, the old men do not lose their sense of humour. They joke about Abd al-Jawad's serious, dignified and cerebral son Kamal visiting the same brothel his father used to frequent. They facetiously attribute such visits to a possible existence of a '"branch of the National Library"' in Jalila [the prostitute]'s house, where he supposedly reads '"ribald classics like *The Sheik's Return*"'.[16] They go as far as envisaging Kamal walking '"into [Jalila's] establishment as solemnly as if entering the holy mosque in Mecca"'.[17] Jokes and ribaldry are their way of coping with a lethargic and uneventful present.

Forced to close his store, which was 'the hub of his activities' and 'the meeting place for his friends and lovers, and the source of his renown and prestige',[18] al-Sayyid Ahmad feels bitter and views it as a '"shattering experience"'.[19] He laments that the time-inflicted changes have made him dependent on his cane even when he goes to the bathroom. In his present condition, he remains predominantly confined to the inner space, or 'house arrest',[20] as he refers to it. As an incapacitated old man, he finds his temporal horizons beginning to shrink, making him all the more conscious of mortality. He spends his time at home, and his space is restricted to the balcony and his bedroom, while Amina, his wife, achieves freedom through religious faith and spends her time outside, visiting al-Husayn mosque and other holy sites and praying for her ailing husband: 'Amina was off on her spiritual tour of the mosques of the Prophet's grandchildren al-Husayn and al-Sayyida Zaynab.'[21] As al-Sayyid and Amina age their roles are reversed, and the hold al-Sayyid had on his wife relaxes as his situation becomes more vulnerable with his deteriorating health, idleness and boredom.

Seated in a large chair on the balcony and listening to the radio, newly acquired by the family, al-Sayyid Ahmad Abd al-Jawad gazes at the street. This is the same spot as where Amina watched the carriage bring her husband home on his return with his friends from their night revelries. Despite the fact that Amina appears to have more freedom in her old age, she continues to define herself in relation to her husband and to conform to the ideal of wifely submission and adoration.

Unlike Abd al-Jawad who has the time to look back at his life, evaluate it and think about illness, ageing and death, Amina's religious ethic and stoic attitude give her courage to accept death as the happy route to eternity. Her newly acquired freedom to go on her spiritual tours around the city enables her to contemplate the spiritual life, accept death and remain blindly submissive to her husband. Her passive unquestioning attitude, adherence to a culturally fixed identity and acceptance of her husband's brand of authority as the norm underline a futile freedom that ensures her marginality. She has a sudden attack of paralysis and pneumonia and dies within three days. As Hamdar rightly puts it, while Abd al-Jawad is 'afforded the space to articulate and reflect upon his own physical decline', Amina 'disappears at the moment she becomes ill'.[22] Amina is a non-person, erased, mystified and constructed in terms of lack. She lives and dies voicelessly, like a shadowy phantom without trace.

Unlike Amina, who is economically dependent on her husband, where marriage is her refuge from poverty and rejection, other unmarried women are in severe straits despite having worked hard all their lives. Sultana Zubayda, the entertainer and vocalist, al-Sayyid's favourite mistress, is hardly recognisable in her old age, that exceeds seventy. The sight of the poverty-stricken entertainer roaming the streets in threadbare attire and a painted face strikes Kamal, al-Sayyid's son, as uncanny. Addicted to cocaine, wearing 'an ankle-length shirt like a man's', and a 'skullcap' that covers a 'bald or diseased scalp',[23] she incurs revulsion and horror, and situates her body in the position of the 'abjectedly grotesque',[24] especially when exposed to outsiders.

At seventy, she is transformed into an old hag because of her body, the sole marker of age. Having lost her youthful attraction and being financially deprived, she rages against her present situation: ' "In my glory days, they [men] vied to kiss my slippers, but now if they spot me on the street they cross over to the other side." '[25] As an old woman, she is 'hyper visible', bearing 'the visible signs of aging', and is 'socially and sexually invisible', and her life is 'devalued and discredited'.[26] She appeals to al-Sayyid for money, but he rejects her. Since her value as a female depends on her youthfulness, she becomes a target of mockery and neglect. Kamal describes her as 'bizarre, outlandish, unhinged'.[27] As an old woman, Sultana is doubly oppressed in a social environment where relations of power and inequality cut across age, gender and class.

In his present condition, Ahmad Abd al-Jawad goes out only once a week for Friday prayers, assisted by his son Kamal. The novel abounds with tropes of lost strength and vitality, diminished desire and fatigue, where ageing is perceived 'as a pathological problem tied to discourses of decline and dependency'.[28] Because his sense of personal adequacy has depended upon his dominance, physical prowess and sexual exploits, age is seen as depriving him not solely of his masculinity, but of his identity. He laments the loss of the good old days in a world that is rapidly changing: 'Everything's been modernized. The roads have been paved with asphalt and illuminated with streetlights. Every shop has electricity and a radio. Everything's new, except me, an old man of sixty-seven who can only leave his home once a week. Even then I'm short of breath. My heart! It's all the fault of my heart that loved, laughed, rejoiced, and sang for so many years.'[29] The alienating present has 'othered' him and turned him, like the old edifices of the city, into a remnant of a bygone past.

As losses begin to accumulate around him, he finds himself coming closer to death. Many other friends and acquaintances had died, leaving him deprived of friendly visits or sick calls, and he begins to sense that there 'would not be a single friend to see him off at his funeral'.[30] The increased unreliability and dependency of his body, and an idle and passive existence, make him feel downgraded and reduced to a feminine state, but what he fears most is disability and total dependence. Conscious that his body has betrayed him and expecting a dreaded decline, he ' "pray[s] that God will favor me with death before my strength gives out" '.[31] He finds himself alone, receding into invisibility as his fear about deep old age takes hold of him. He discovers that the younger generation has ceased to identify with him. Even his own son Kamal joins him and 'sits with me for fleeting moments, as if he were a guest'.[32]

Kamal, his son, who is approaching middle age, is nostalgic for a past that he continues to cherish, especially his unrequited love for the daughter of the rich Shaddad family. When he learns that the Shaddad mansion will presently be demolished and that the whole area will undergo rapid change, he asserts dejectedly, ' "my heart is buried in its rubble?" '[33] Unlike his father, who remains absorbed in his own extended family and spends his life chasing prostitutes, his son's love of one woman coincides with his preference for a nuclear family and an egalitarian relationship. Such an attitude is fostered by education and modernity and remains unchanged. His earlier experience has turned him into an 'emotionally crippled'[34] and reclusive middle-aged bachelor whose life is divided between teaching at a school and walking around the streets of Cairo. He visits the house of Jalila, the prostitute, and feels guilty for not being able to curb his appetites. Walking towards al-Husayn mosque, he notes that this sacred district is losing its articulacy and coherence. The ageing of the city intersects with the ageing of its inhabitants, and both are fast disappearing. As the modern penetrates the old surfaces and communities, it brings about uncanny disparities, and disorienting ruptures.

Ageing as a Continuum

The incongruities brought about by modernisation in Mahfouz's *Sugar Street* are amplified in al-Aswany's *The Yacoubian Building*. The novel features a number of ageing individuals such as Zaki el-Dessouki, who is 65, Hagg Azzam, a man in his sixties, and Zaki's older sister Dawlat. The Yacoubian Building where a great deal of the action takes place is itself over seventy years old, having witnessed many events since the 1930s up until the present. After the Nasser 1952 revolution and the overthrow of King Farouq, the demography of Cairo began changing. Many of the rich foreigners who lived in the building had left and were replaced by lower-class military officers who came from rural backgrounds. The roof of the ten-storey building, which originally served as a storage area consisting of fifty rooms, is taken over by migrants from the countryside who moved to Cairo seeking employment. The roof has been transformed into a slum neighbourhood bursting with naked, scruffy and noisy children of the working classes. As a result, the protagonist, Zaki Bey el-Dessouki, has to contend with a new, urbane and more prosaic Egypt.

Zaki is the son of Abd el Aal Basha el-Dessouki, the renowned pillar of the Wafd party who also served as prime minister of Egypt on several occasions. Zaki studied engineering in Paris, but his hopes for a thriving and successful career are dashed by the revolution. Despite all drawbacks, Zaki is not a sickly, decrepit, ostracised or bitter old man; he is healthy, energetic, friendly and outgoing. On his way from his house to his office in the Yacoubian Building, he stops to greet a vast number of people such as clothing store owners, waiters and waitresses, cinema staff, doorkeepers, shoe shiners, beggars and traffic cops.

Making his way through the streets of Cairo, Zaki is a sign of a past that is being overpowered and displaced by rapid demographic changes and an anarchic urbanisation. To the residents of the street where he lives, he is a 'folkloric' figure in 'his three-piece suit', his 'carefully ironed handkerchief always dangling from his jacket pocket and always of the same color as his tie', and the 'Cuban deluxe' cigar which he smoked in the old days and 'is now of the foul-smelling, tightly packed, low-quality local kind'.[35] At 65, Zaki is described by the younger narrator as an old man with wrinkled face, false teeth, thin black hair and thick glasses. In other words, he is viewed as a formulaic old man representing deterioration and decline.

Zaki is also a figure of hilarity in his obsessive carnal lust. Learning that his major preoccupations in life are women, and hearing about his wide knowledge in the field, young men of the neighbourhood consult him about sexual matters solely for the fun of it, but Zaki takes it seriously and 'draw[s] on his vast and encyclopaedic knowledge of the subject', fixing on 'the most subtle sexual secrets' without hesitating to make use of pen and paper to illustrate 'some curious coital position'.[36] He is possessed of comic energy in his unrelenting pursuit of passion and sexual gratification. Contrary to the traditional religious, devout and genderless old man, Zaki is a worldly man whose physical and psychological health, autonomy, social class and economic independence determine his lifestyle and the horizons open to him.

His apartment, which was originally his engineering office, is now the place where Zaki spends his free time and receives his mistresses. Women for him constitute 'an entire world of fascination that constantly renews itself in images of infinitely alluring diversity'.[37] Before any rendezvous with a woman, Zaki goes through a preliminary ritual, which consists of an injection of 'imported Tri-B vitamin supplement' roughly administered in the buttock by his crippled servant, causing Zaki to 'pour curses on that "ass" Abaskharon for his heavy, brutish touch'. This is followed by 'a cup of sugarless coffee made of beans and spiced with nutmeg' as he melts a small piece of opium in his mouth,[38] his way of keeping desire visibly alive, and sustaining the sexual potency of youth. In a playful style and with corrosive irony, the authorial narrator makes fun of the farcical ritual and the old man's attempt to enhance his masculinity in order to continue to function in this alienating world. His repetitive preparatory acts are his defence weapon against a disorienting contemporary Cairo, and his prescription for survival in the face of looming extinction.

Zaki is particularly attracted to the ' "vulgarity and provocativeness" ' of women who belong to the 'common people' and who remind him of a maid who worked at his father's house: 'Do you remember that maid at home who used to beguile your dreams when you were an adolescent? And of whom it was your dearest wish that you might stick yourself to her soft behind . . . as she washed the dishes at the kitchen sink? And that she would bend over in a way that made you stick to her even more closely and whisper in provocative refusal, before giving herself to you, "Sir . . . It is wrong, sir." '[39] Rabab was that kind of woman whom Zaki first met at the disreputable Cairo Bar in Tawfikiya Square where she worked as hostess. It was a 'dirty, cramped, badly lit and poorly ventilated place' with 'suffocating smoke', deafening clamour and vulgar songs accompanied by 'foul-mouthed arguments and fistfights'.[40]

Zaki invites her to his office, but he is shocked to discover when he wakes up that his 'beloved Rabab' had stolen all the precious items in his possession: his gold watch, five hundred pounds, a set of gold cross pens, a pair of Perol sunglasses and, most importantly, 'the diamond ring belonging to his elder sister Dawlat el-Dessouki'.[41] Lying naked on the couch with his frail body and empty, misshapen mouth (he had removed his false teeth so as to be able to kiss the beloved), he looked like a deflated figure of indulgence and excess. The narrator's derisive mockery and his exposure of Zaki's oddities and excessive libido are a visual illustration of the consequences of violating the norm, which cause him to wind up as the comic butt of the younger narrator and a young and designing prostitute. It also reveals the deep sense of disorientation that Zaki has to contend with as a downgraded old man in an anarchic, incoherent and unmanageable new world, and the comedy resides in the deflation of Zaki's prodigality and over-indulgences.

Perturbed by this scandalous deed, Zaki screams, '"I've been robbed, Abaskharon! Rabab robbed me!"' Shocked and excited like 'a locked-up dog', Zaki's elderly servant, Abaskharon, panics and starts to hit the ground with his crutch and 'pace the room in every direction'.[42] The bizarre and senseless movements manifested by the crippled servant trivialise Zaki's tragedy and turn the comedy into farce. The interweaving of the humorous with the monstrous represented by his servant is not only a joke at Zaki's sexual transgression, his abuse and cuckoldry, but also a step towards further manipulation by Abaskharon of his master.

Abaskharon is an old man who has been in Zaki's service for twenty years. With 'his hoarse, phlegmy, panting tones',[43] his torn *gallabiya*, his crutches and his amputated leg and twisted physique, he represents a grotesque image of spectral ageing and abjection, evoking a general sense of denigration, distortion and ontological diminishment. Such deprivation dramatises the plight of this old man trapped in his own disability, and his brutal attempt at coping with social aberration to protect himself from a hostile world that rejects his grotesque otherness, his beggarly appearance, his amputated leg, and his crutches.

The narrator maintains that when Abaskharon emerges out of the dark and damp corners of the house with his crutches, his dirty *gallabiya*, his hoary countenance and his grovelling smile, he seems like a creature functioning in its natural surroundings, 'like a fish in water, or a cockroach in the drain'. In the street under the sunlight, he is an uncanny and shrivelled presence miserably disoriented 'like a bat in daylight',[44] and only dilates and revives the moment he returns to his familiar habitat. He has spent all his energy trying to rob his master and hide the large number of banknotes he had accumulated behind a picture of the Virgin Mary that he had hung in his room, using his religious faith to cover up his fraud, unlawful deeds, manipulation and blackmail of his master and anyone who comes his way.

Zaki dreads a confrontation with his sister Dawlat, an ageing, embittered and ill-tempered old woman who begrudges his delinquent behaviour and his inappropriate pursuit of women. She is described as an old woman with chestnut-dyed hair wrapped on her '*boucles*',[45] heavy make-up on a wrinkled face, her '*pantoufles*' shaped like white rabbits, and her mechanical knitting, disclosing an enforced domestication and defeat in the face of a progressive ageing process and a threatening new world outside. Convinced that Zaki must leave his possessions to her children, she decides to turn him into a domesticated and immobile old man awaiting death. On his side Zaki wonders how a great pianist like his sister, who married Air Force Captain Hassan Shawkat, who had close relations with the royal family, could have been transformed into a vile, spiteful and bossy old woman who interferes in his affairs and tries to control and rob him.

Feeling alienated from a country she no longer recognises as her own, and conscious of all the political, personal and financial losses she had endured, she intends to compensate by seizing whatever is left of her ageing brother's money. Believing in a stable age identity, she insists that a delinquent man like Zaki must be tamed into adopting a lifestyle befitting his age. As a result, she kicks him out of his own house claiming that her father's house has been 'defiled' by his '"filth"'.[46] Zaki possesses a feminine temperament nurtured perhaps by being predominantly in the company of women, but also by the fact that after the revolution his natural softness is augmented, especially, with the setting of old age, which in itself is a 'subtle continuum'[47] of his earlier lifestyle. Even Busayna observed how peaceful, compromising, 'kind and well-mannered'[48] he was.

Over the years, Zaki had developed sensitivities in himself that he had once known only in women, while his sister is hardened and emasculated. In her adherence to family traditions and her resistance to change, while paradoxically robbing her brother in the same manner that Abaskharon robs him, she exposes a divided self that fully rejects the present but does not hesitate to make use of its tools to regain lost power and control. She bribes the police and sends them to Zaki's place in order to humiliate him. When they arrive and find him in bed with Busayna they address him jokingly as 'Valentino' and the 'Drinking Sheikh'[49] and assert mockingly: '"Have some shame, man! One foot in this world and the other in the next! Someone your age ought to be spending all his time at the mosque, not being brought in naked on top of a prostitute."'[50] The bawdy comedy is generated by the disgrace that Zaki endures for his sexual transgression and failure to maintain cultural, social and religious values pertaining to the sexuality of older individuals.

The ten-storey Yacoubian Building on Suleiman Basha Street was built in the high classical European style where the select Egyptian elite – ministers, pashas, businessmen and millionaires – lived. But the 1952 revolution drove the residents out of the country and replaced them with officers of the revolution and their working-class families, who found no problem raising rabbits, ducks and chicken in the building and leaving their children 'barefoot and half naked'[51] on the roof. Their women cook, gossip, and when they disagree exchange 'the grossest insults as well as accusations touching on one another's honor', but their actions are not taken seriously by the men since it is 'one more indication of that defectiveness of mind of which the Prophet – God bless him and grant him peace – spoke'.[52]

If the Revolution had failed, Zaki would have had a bright career. He would have become minister for sure, perhaps prime minister, leading a life that is appropriate for him instead of the present depravity and humiliation: 'A prostitute drugs him and his sister throws him out and exposes him to scandal',[53] and he ends up sleeping in his office with Abaskharon. In this new Cairo, a crude and predatory locale, that endlessly gnaws at the remaining edifices of the past, Zaki is no more than a human relic alongside other artefacts interspersed around the city and standing against the surrounding monstrous constructions of urban Cairo. Among such remnants is Maxim's restaurant that transports Zaki to the magical past with its stylishness and elegance, reminding him nostalgically of the accomplished owner Madame Christine who sings, and plays the piano and violin to entertain her friends, who also enjoy the pure and commanding voice of Edith Piaf which transports them into an exotic past. Another locale is the Automobile Club, the haunt of the Western-educated Egyptian aristocracy before the revolution, where 'they would spend the evenings accompanied by their wives in revealing evening gowns, sipping whisky and playing poker and bridge'.[54]

The present-day surrogate for the Automobile Club is the kebab restaurant at the Sheraton, where policies are made 'at the tables groaning beneath the weight of grilled meats'.[55] The Sheraton regulars are men from the lower echelons of society who drink no alcohol, but have voracious appetites for good oriental food such as kebab, *kofta* and stuffed vegetables, and a strong religious orientation, which is manifested in adherence to the 'outward forms of religion'.[56]

Since nostalgia for the past is Zaki's predominant tenor, he takes Busayna around Cairo to introduce her to the old haunts. After Maxim's, they stop in front of a few closed shops, and an old bar adjacent to a hairdresser's salon and a restaurant. He tells her that the goods on display in these shops came from London and Paris, but these familiar sites are now infiltrated by an unfamiliar present, creating a rift between an unadulterated past and a contaminated present.

As the oldest resident in a time-worn Yacoubian Building, Zaki maintains that the day it is ' "demolished or something happens to it, that'll be the day I die" '.[57] According to Zaki, the remarkable architecture of the Yacoubian Building was copied to the last detail from a building he had seen in the Quartier Latin in Paris. Zaki does not pay any attention to Pharaonic and Islamic architecture and prefers a facsimile of the Quartier Latin; his Cairo is the one that looks like Europe. The old city was ' "clean and smart and the people were well-mannered and respectable and everyone knew his place exactly"'.[58] Present-day Cairo, on the other hand, is an urban slum with dirty streets, and 'chickens and ducks running around outside the houses, small children playing barefoot, and veiled women sitting at the doors'.[59] It is an anarchic and unpredictable place fraught with unemployment, housing shortage and open sewers, a place hospitable to militancy and corruption.

Despite this ghastly metamorphosis of the city, Zaki succeeds in striking a balance between the two places. He cherishes his sojourns around the city and his moments of reminiscence in the company of Busayna, which allow him to be in the past and present at the same time. Zaki tries to retrieve a vanishing past and sustain his youthful sexual pleasures, without expunging a nascent but threatening present. Destabilised by urbanisation and modernisation, the city staggers on, dragging its 'Janus-faced' present into an uncertain future of radicalism and violence. But Zaki does not retreat; he marries Busayna, the offspring of the new city. Such a decision is a sign of his strong and meaningful engagement with the present and an attempt to reconcile his nostalgic narrative with the counter-narrative of a slippery and chaotic present. He abandons the polarity between past wholeness and present degeneration by reconciling an abiding past with a candid receptiveness to a new world.

Hagg Azzam is another man past sixty who serves as a foil to Zaki. He is a self-made millionaire, a Saidi migrant from the countryside who made his money from drug dealings. To cover up such activities he pretends to be pious and religious and always consults with his sheikh on important matters. He attributes his success to 'his uprightness and avoidance of anything that might make God angry'.[60] Now that he has accumulated enough money, he intends to serve in the people's assembly. His power is embedded in wealth and deception that allow him to manipulate the social, political and religious systems without batting an eyelid. Despite his belief that at his age he is supposed to be sexless, he begins to suffer from wet dreams and a resurgent sexuality. His friends reassure him that at his age it is just an 'ephemeral phenomenon',[61] and his wife reproaches him and reminds him that they are old and that they have grown children.

Having deep confidence in his spiritual leader, he seeks his opinion, and abides by his advice that comes directly from God: '"Glory be, Hagg! Why, my brother, make things difficult for yourself, when God has made them easy for you? Why open the door for Satan, so that you can fall into error . . .

God has made marriage to more than one wife lawful for you as long as you behave with justice. Put your trust in God."'[62] Following the advice of his sheikh, he believes that he is entitled to a second wife who would satisfy his lust, especially if he chooses a disadvantaged woman who must be indebted to him for dragging her out of deprivation. Accordingly, there is no need for any kind of communication between them apart from sex. His selfishness, inflexibility and a strong sense of entitlement sanctioned by his sheikh put his mind at ease. Preoccupied with relationships in which exploitation prevails, he represents the monstrosities of modern Egypt.

His choice of Souad is based on her youth, physical appearance, and stipulations to the effect that she follows his rules and does not get pregnant. He describes her 'as a light-skinned woman, full-bodied, beautiful, who covered her hair, which was black and smooth and flowing, the tresses peeking out from beneath her head scarf'; her eyes were an enchanting black with full and sensual lips, but what he liked best about her is 'the meekness that poverty and a hard life had left her with'.[63] However, her major attraction to him resides in his ability to dehumanise and commodify the younger woman.

Being in dire need, she marries a man as old as her father, and their relationship is based on fake deceit. Souad, who resents his treatment of her, launches a scathing attack on the man who has deprived her of her son (who should remain in Alexandria) and prevents her from having any children, and her role is to submit to his narcissistic sexual needs. She is disgusted with his ageing body, his dyed hair, 'wrinkled skin, the few, scattered hairs of his chest, and his small, dark nipples',[64] that repelled her whenever he touched her. She feels nauseated whenever he touches her body, likens his grotesque body to a 'lizard or a revolting, slimy frog'[65] and yearns for the youthful and firm body of her former husband. Souad pours out her scorn, outrage and moral indignation on the hajj, and her invective is concentrated on his age and his flagging manhood. The hajj represents all the cultural negativity, prejudice and 'aging lechery'[66] attributed to older men who pursue younger women. Unlike the humorous and forbearing presentation of Zaki, the hajj is savagely derided by the narrator. The intrinsic viciousness of his character and his way of life is manifested in forcing Souad into a brutal miscarriage and throwing her out. The grotesque and abrasive derision aimed at the hajj is epitomised by physical exposure, ageism, and cynicism based upon sexual lack, religious hypocrisy and deception. Julia Kristeva refers to it as the 'laughter of the apocalypse' in which absurdity, ferocity, denigration and physical dissipation generate a sort of mesmerising abjection.[67]

Gender and Old Age in the Inner and Outer Spaces

If Zaki reconciles past and present and adjusts to a new Cairo, the characters in Khalifa's *No Knives in This City's Kitchens* are unable to survive in modern Aleppo. This is an autobiography of the demise of Aleppo's old aristocratic families, notably the narrator's own family which suffers from the bruises of the past and the uncertainties of the present in the wake of the 1963 Syrian Baath revolution. The novel begins with the death of the mother, the focal point of the family, leaving an unmarried ageing daughter, a gay brother and two ageing unmarried sons behind, all of whom live in the shadow of Aleppo and are socially, politically and economically marginalised. Using an episodic and digressive style, each story generating more stories, the narrator tells the history of Aleppo from the First World War up until the few years before the 2011 war.

The novel is focalised through an unnamed participant male narrator who reflects on his mother, who dies just before she reaches 65, but when she passes away he feels relieved as she had suffered over the past ten years from 'lack of oxygen',[68] both physically and metaphorically, within the stifling atmosphere of present-day Aleppo. The narrator reports what his mother and other members of the family say and do and is sometimes transformed into an omniscient narrator who enters the minds of the characters and reports their thoughts and feelings, so that a great deal of the narration is shaped by the narrator's own views. Before his mother dies, the narrator maintains that his uncle told him that she got out of her rancid bed and wrote a letter to an unknown lover or old female friend who represents the past that she had lost. Her attachment to the past is her own revenge on her present humiliating existence, and her strong feelings of apartness and exile. His mother yearns for those beautiful times when 'lettuce was more tender and women more feminine'.[69] She longs for the days when she sat by the window watching the lettuce and cherry trees, listening to her son Rashid play the violin.

The mother's hysterical condition springs not only from their present economic problems, but also from the drastic political and social changes in Syria, and the cultural shifts that have worsened her physical as well as psychological situation. The narrator describes his mother as a dreamy woman with soft long hair, big black eyes and an elongated white face. After the revolution of Hafez al-Assad (who is not mentioned by name), she finds herself trying to cope with a ruthless regime that tortured her nephew in prison causing his death. The last time they saw the young man was in the morgue. His face was 'charred', his fingers were severed and his body bore the marks of electric shocks and knife wounds. After a quick prayer, his body, which looked like 'a lump of flesh wrapped up in a dirty shroud',[70] guarded by six paratroopers, was hastily buried.

The mother loathes the president and his supporters who have ruralised the city and erased its original inhabitants and its august features. The new settlers spend their time frying aubergines and cleaning up their children's runny noses. At night they make a huge racket with their Party songs and the blaring sound of the tape recorder which transmits the speeches of the president. As a result, the mother insists on safeguarding her family and their 'civilized home' from the thugs who 'cannot distinguish between the smell of Iris and that of turnip pickle'.[71] Soldiers and farmers, who have come from the surrounding villages and who have transformed the city into a place where the sewers stink of excrement, now encircle her house, that was once surrounded by lettuce gardens and cherry trees. Feeling paranoid, she goes as far as declaring that the birth of her son (the narrator) on the eve of the Assad revolution is 'a sign of bad luck for the boy'.[72]

Insisting on juxtaposing a flawless past with a defective present, she shuts all the doors and windows against a threatening new world that stands like a rampart against her antiquated world that is shrinking and on its way to extinction. She spends her time walking 'like an old tortoise'[73] around the house and wondering how the rancid smell of decay outside has not yet killed them. She sees herself as a woman of breeding and education confronted by subhuman rural intruders who have invaded her city in an attempt to expunge all that it stands for. With her fears, insecurities and delusions she is trapped within the claustrophobic confines of her house and the rapidly changing city. The brutal reality outside drives her to seek refuge in her romantic illusions, but this is a struggle that she cannot win as she is old and physically and psychologically frail, confronting a young, tough, palpable and audacious new world.

She is particularly frustrated with her own friends and colleagues at school who have decided to support a dictator who takes over, bans freedoms, closes newspapers, dissolves parliament and imposes a new constitution that gives him absolute power. Having joined the Baath party, her colleagues at school record in their copybooks words uttered by the leader, and learn all the songs that glorify him. They wear similar clothes and the same cheap perfumes. The majority of her colleagues also write reports about the narrator's mother and her friend Nariman, accusing them of reactionary bourgeois haughtiness. Shocked by the disappearance of the geography teacher at school, the mother warns her children that informers live in the leaves of trees and instructs them to be reticent and not challenge anyone or anything as 'mice' cannot do anything ' "when they are surrounded by traps" '.[74] Her paranoid dread of the despotic president was such that when he died, in 2000, she refused to believe it, thinking that it was a trick set up to separate his friends from his enemies.

When she learns that at school her children sing songs that glorify the president, she buys a violin and asks her brother to teach them 'real' music. She dreams of her children becoming engineers and doctors, with a taste for classical music and expensive ties and shoes. The mother's bourgeois pretentions prompt her to stop her son from inviting his friends since they belong to a class that will dirty the couch and the furniture, although her house is in a state of disarray, her paintings are fading and her sofas are crumbling. Nevertheless, she is convinced that everything outside is contaminated, and that the smell of rural people has befouled the air in the city.

The signs of mental decline become more noticeable with her loud voice, fragmented speech and barefaced contempt for her colleagues. As a teacher, she starts going to school in an old, unkempt, threadbare dress with mice-bitten lace, a fetish that represents youth, beauty and sexuality, and leaves the school without permission. Reluctant to cut the umbilical cord joining her with the past, she plunges into a world of fantasy and make-believe. In her anachronistic appearance, she wanders around the streets looking for her husband who had abandoned her many years before, and for the famous painter who had asked her to visit his atelier. The political and personal pressures have augmented her regressive behaviour and her 'senile fragility'.[75]

She suffers from sporadic attacks of comatose stupor that reduce her to a vegetative state. When she wakes up from her coma, she talks about the past with a power that amazes her brother Nizar. She refers to her nights with her husband and his elopement with an American woman thirty years his senior. This new power and rejuvenation testify to a strong sense of resistance triggered by the past represented by old Aleppo, her wealthy family and her love affair with her socially inferior husband. Brother and sister sit together and try to settle their scores with the past and conclude that although the past was beautiful it gave them nothing but misery. She admits that her life has consisted of a series of disappointments with her husband, and a mentally disabled daughter who makes her feel shame and humiliation.

Ironically, she had married an ambitious employee and rural man against the wishes of her family, and they cut all relations with her. Her family despised her husband and her new brand of life, and her sister referred to her children as '"the summer bugs"'.[76] As a result, she lived like a farm woman and put up with the contempt of her own family. She visited them only once when her father died, and her trip home with her four children was on a slow train smelling of buffalos and of leather treated with the nauseating smell of chemicals. It was her desire for her husband that overpowered her bourgeois pretentions. However, in her old age, she is swept off by the deluge of vulgar rurality that had once allured her and is now threatening to engulf her. The menacing city is transformed into an uncanny double mirroring the grotesqueness of her own self.

Seeing her lying in bed in a comatose trance, the narrator describes her as a living decay, her breath smelling of 'sourness like the smell of old hollows full of disintegrating animal cadavers'.[77] Unlike her son's macabre allusions, her brother refers to her as a '"perfumed breeze"' from the past with its enchanting graces, captivating refinements and magical beauty. Haunted by visions of the past, she populates her dreams with erotic phantoms and girlish dreams. She revels in her eccentricities and fantasises about a sea voyage in the company of a man who dances with her under the moonlight. He '"weaves from the sea foam a white bed for her to lie on it like a *Huri* . . . he strips her naked and kisses all parts of her body talking as if he were "weaving a huge carpet from the tears of elephants"'.[78] This pre-lapsarian paradise is where she seeks refuge from loss, deprivation and a pugnacious present, where the line between fantasy and reality, sagacity and senility, become blurred and where 'the tension between *eros* and *thanatos*, carnal love and physical death . . . determines the basic rhythms'[79] of this woman's life.

Her desires continue to haunt her even into her old age. Her old creams, hairstyle reminiscent of young women in the 1960s, and her silk nightgowns trimmed with lace (kept safely in a wooden arabesque box she had bought from an antique shop) were enough to inflame her desires and resuscitate her. Her imaginative powers, creativity and rituals of sexual self-possession revive her spirits and energy, but in her attempt to recapture the past, she finds herself in a surreal world. The novel contrasts the prosaic present with a haunting past suffused with youth, sensuality and romance, revealing the disjunction between her emotional adolescence and her ageing body. This is a rarefied woman committed to the ideal past, but living in an antagonistic present that has scorched her by the incendiary explosion of a new Aleppo. Nevertheless, the residual fragments of her romantic personality can no longer survive in the drab and unpolished prevailing order. As the delicate last remnant of an archaic age and a declining class, she finds herself stranded in a predatory new world that seals her fate and speeds her headlong descent into decline and annihilation.

The mother is viewed by her family as an individual and symbol, and as the loving and terrible mother. She draws contradictory feelings from her children, a mixture of devotion and distrust, admiration and fear, love and hate, creation and destruction. She is a complex amalgam of life-force and death-force, fulfilment and denial, sympathy and hostility, nurture and denunciation, dominance and defeat, escape and defiance, fecundity and sterility, desire and deprivation. Her distinctiveness and unpredictability attest to an individually unique ageing woman, a fecund and sumptuous woman confronting a bleak and barren city which is a trope of her own sundered psyche.

As the signs of cognitive impairment and senility become more visible, her actions assume an unpredictable and dangerous pattern, especially when she starts going out of the house in the morning leaving the door open behind her and returning at night looking like a beggar. As a result, the narrator and his sister Sawsan take upon themselves the task of accompanying her around a city filled with the nauseating smell of open sewage and crammed with slums that have devoured the fields of lettuce. Her agitation, restlessness and rage are overwhelming as she sees herself and her city fading away in the glare of a hostile present. Her double marginality as an old woman, and her attraction and repulsion to a peasant husband and the boorish new world that surrounds her, magnifies her sense of otherness, causing her to retreat into silence and death.

In one of her comas, she suffers from unrelenting hallucinations of coffins criss-crossing the living room, and her spectral appearance produces an uncanny sense of the macabre, and the ephemerality of human existence. When she awakes, the narrator compares her moans to that of 'an old horse whose skin is specked with fungus'.[80] The decaying house, the rot and the surrounding squalor attest to the decline of a particular class of people, notably upper-middle-class Aleppo.

Unlike the narrator and his sister who begrudge their mother, their brother Rashid kisses his mother's hand, and devotes himself to her. He carries her to bed after changing the sheets that have turned yellow with her perspiration smelling of tranquillisers. He washes his mother's body and sprays it with cologne, selects a jacket for her whose ends have not been nibbled by mice, and sprays the corners of her room with a cockroach killer. Rashid's attachment to his mother is based on filial obligation and strong moral values, which are closely linked to a sense of duty and indebtedness to an ageing parent.

When the mother dies, the family places ice cubes around her dead body and covers her with blankets. The narrator describes her as 'an old heap of scraps emitting dirty water',[81] which they wanted to dispose of the following morning. Such words of revulsion reveal the narrator's deeply engrained feelings of resentment against his mother. While he bears a grudge against her, and describes her as 'drowned in her own rot'[82] and smelling of disease and decay, he also harbours sympathies towards her. He admits that she was irresistible, and that she put a spell on all those around her. Following in his mother's steps, he gives up teaching 'ignorant' students who will write reports about you to the *mukhabarat*. He devotes himself to the retranslation of texts such as T. S. Eliot's *The Wasteland* and 'The Love Song of J. Alfred Prufrock', poems that reflect his emotional sterility and his estrangement and retraction, and the city's deterioration and decline under the Baath regime.

After the mother's funeral, Rashid opens her wardrobe that was still full of her once-stylish clothes that were the envy of many women. Although the wardrobe is full of mothballs, he is surprised to find dead and dried-up mice inside the wardrobe, a sign of a pervading diminution and death. Unlike Rashid, the narrator and his sister Sawsan seem rather remote, although they continue to fulfil their filial duties towards their mother.

At forty, the narrator's sister Sawsan decides to contact an Armenian photographer who had pursued her earlier to take a photo of her sensual naked body and face, to be exhibited in Paris. However, after noticing wrinkles and 'a small protuberance around her stomach',[83] he no longer believes that her body is worth the money he is going to spend on her. When a group of thugs attack her and try to rape her for defying tradition by wearing a short skirt, even the women living nearby open their windows and begin to curse her and call her a whore. As a result, she returns home with dishevelled hair, and a torn shirt. The new Aleppo is antagonistic to women who venture into the public spaces in revealing clothes.

If sexuality at the mother's age remains within the framework of dreams and unrequited desires, her ageing queer brother Nizar stays sexually active until the end. While Nizar is marginalised by his homoerotic sexual identity, his gendered identity remains anchored in the sociocultural order that still grants him the prerogatives of men while repudiating his sexual orientation. At seventy, Uncle Nizar was still elegant and full of energy. Returning from work in the cabaret, he prepares food and spends hours cooking complicated meals, preserving pickles and cheese, and having ephemeral love affairs with men, the last of whom is the thirty-year-old Midhat, an employee in the ministry of finance whom Nizar picked up one night at the cabaret. At seventy, desire has not abandoned him, and he is not ashamed to talk to his sister about it and tell her of his craving for the taste of kisses of men with thick moustaches.

Unlike other members of their family, who blamed Nizar for being apprehended for sodomy and being raped by an *imam* inside the prison, his sister and her children never abandon him and seek love and companionship by his side. After all, he was their financial saviour, and his generosity and care make him the redeeming sanctuary of the family. Despite his age, Nizar is not a serene and passive old man who surrenders to death. After his sister's death, he retires with his new lover into a sequestered rural locality away from the oppressive and claustrophobic world of the city.

As the narrator and his siblings reach fifty, like their mother, they begin to feel marginalised in a place where their social class is considered an aberration and where an elderly appearance is almost synonymous with invisibility and erasure in a world of spirited and uncouth youthfulness. Having entertained fearful associations of old age with deterioration, infirmity, dependency and fixation on the past, they find themselves denied the possibilities of a future. The narrator is surrounded by images of mortality and the fleetingness of life inside the house and outside it, and, like his mother, he feels trapped within this prison. The political and social changes place them in a liminal zone, oscillating between the cloying residues of a vanishing past and the present world of the Baath regime and of Islamists, the men with beards, and knives under their arms. As a result, and like their mother, they choose disengagement, vegetating in a vanishing past, and spending a great deal of time looking at a patchwork of old family photographs as they watch the final collapse of their world.

Conclusion

In the face of demographic, social and economic realities, inter-generational systems of care and support within cohesive families are under threat,[84] especially for those who live in the cities. The Arab city has two opposing effects on ageing individuals: one that alienates them, limits their movements and drives them to the safety of the inner space, and another that empowers them and gives them the freedom to challenge prescribed values and norms. The novels in this chapter centre on the invasion of the city by migrants from the countryside, causing the place to lose its legibility, and the elderly to lose their sense of direction externally and internally and become 'culturally residual' and 'alien in the new world to come'.[85]

Rapid demographic changes and an anarchic urbanisation have destroyed the old terrain of childhood, and these old men and women bemoan the old traditional quarters that have been infiltrated by an erratic modernity that threatens to expunge them and abolish the familiar surroundings. Al-Sayyid in Mahfouz's *Sugar Street*, a patriarch with absolute authority, finds the ground shaking under his feet. The alienating present has 'othered' him, and turned him, like the city, into a remnant of a bygone past where, in a world of vigorous youth, an elderly appearance becomes synonymous with invisibility and erasure. These ageing male and female individuals witness despondently an antiquated world on its way to extinction and seek safety in withdrawal. Denying a befuddling present, the ageing mother in *No Knives in This City's Kitchens* is transported into a space of absolute otherness and monstrosity, where she mutates into an alien figure, a caricature of senile senescence. Similarly, women who have no family support end up in tatters roaming the streets, grotesquely hyper-visible and begging for sustenance, as in the case of Mahfouz's prostitute, revealing that the city is more merciful to men than to women. However, those who survive within such unanticipated transformations are characters, like Zaki, who succeed in reconciling the old and the new and embrace a hybrid identity, in which Zaki engages with the new world without abandoning the past that he continues to perceive as his model of existence.

In addition to the feminised Zaki and his positive interaction with the modern city, modern Cairo has fashioned a new species of older men who have displaced the traditional patriarch with another from a rural background, one that is dishonest, deceitful, ruthless and greedy, masquerading in the guise of religious piety. As a misogynistic patriarch, Hagg Azzam uses money and religion to achieve political power and practise violence against women in the name of religion.

Notes

1. Segal, 'Forever Young: Medusa's Curse and the Discourses of Ageing', p. 49.
2. Woodward, 'Performing Age, Performing Gender', p. 167.
3. *Sugar Street*, p. 1.
4. Ibid., p. 9.
5. Ibid., p. 12.
6. Ibid., p. 1.
7. Ibid., p. 2.
8. Ibid., p. 225.
9. Ibid., p. 249.
10. Ibid., p. 6.
11. Ibid., p. 130.
12. Ibid., p. 7.

13. Ibid., p. 35.
14. Ibid., p. 38.
15. Ibid., p. 35.
16. Ibid., p. 38.
17. Ibid.
18. Ibid., p. 130.
19. Ibid., p. 154.
20. Ibid., p. 182.
21. Ibid., p. 178.
22. Hamdar, *Female Suffering Body*, p. 53.
23. *Sugar Street*, p. 224.
24. Russo, *The Female Grotesque*, p. 55.
25. *Sugar Street*, p. 15.
26. Bouson, Shame *and the Aging Woman*, p. 1.
27. Ibid., p. 224.
28. Powell, *Social Theory and Aging*, p. 19.
29. *Mothballs*, p. 155.
30. Ibid., p. 131.
31. Ibid.
32. Ibid., p. 155.
33. Ibid., p. 233.
34. Ibid., p. 185.
35. *Yacoubian Building*, p. 3.
36. Ibid., p. 4.
37. Ibid., p. 5.
38. Ibid., p. 8.
39. Ibid.
40. Ibid., p. 10.
41. Ibid., pp. 62–3.
42. Ibid., p. 63.
43. Ibid., p. 30.
44. Ibid., p. 25.
45. Ibid., p. 64.
46. Ibid., p. 79.
47. Woodward, *Ageing and its Discontents*, p. 6.
48. *Yacoubian Building*, p. 159.
49. Ibid., p. 211.

50. Ibid., p. 212.
51. Ibid., p. 14.
52. Ibid.
53. Ibid., p. 112.
54. Ibid., p. 145.
55. Ibid., p. 144.
56. Ibid., p. 145.
57. Ibid., p. 162.
58. Ibid., p. 161.
59. Ibid., p. 196.
60. Ibid., p. 51.
61. Ibid.
62. Ibid., p. 52.
63. Ibid., p. 53.
64. Ibid., p. 126.
65. Ibid.
66. Segal, *Out of Time*, p. 42.
67. Kristeva, *Powers of Horror*, p. 204.
68. *No Knives*, p. 7. All translations are mine.
69. Ibid., p. 8.
70. Ibid.
71. Ibid., p. 117.
72. Ibid., p. 18.
73. Ibid., p. 80.
74. Ibid., p. 154.
75. King, *Discourses of Ageing in Fiction and Feminism*, p. 29.
76. *No Knives*, p. 120.
77. Ibid., p. 193.
78. Ibid., p. 72.
79. Fiedler, 'Eros and Thanatos', p. 2.
80. *No Knives*, p. 231.
81. Ibid., p. 220.
82. Ibid., p. 201.
83. Ibid., p. 155.
84. Sibai and Yamout, 'Family-Based Old-Age in Arab Counties: Between Tradition and Modernity', p. 63.
85. Russo, 'Aging and the Scandal of Anachronism', p. 27.

3

Menopausal Tremors: Refurbishing the Body

This chapter deals with urban women whose education, professional lives, and other modern lifestyles, have given them agency and self-awareness. Reaching middle age, they are exposed to the panic that signs of ageing generate on their bodies. The impact of the ravages of time diminishes their self-esteem, sets them face to face with unwelcome processes of physical change and forces them to experience invisibility and neglect. Unlike traditional women such as the grandmother in *Mothballs*, they are acutely conscious of the cultural and biological forces that draw the line between youth and age, particularly for women who have reached menopause, a period described by Silver as a 'deep Narcissistic wound'.[1] These novels reveal the demoralising effect of the menopause on women, which invalidates them and renders them irrelevant. As a result, they deal with their degradation through concealment via cosmetic products, and withdrawal from public life.

In the Lebanese writer René al-Hayek's 'An Abandoned Winter' (*Shita' Mahjour*, 1994), the narrator, who has not yet reached fifty, finds succour in resignation, disavowal and withdrawal, and in transcending sexual needs, especially after being abandoned by her lover. She notes the discrepancies between an unchanging inner self and an eerie image reflected in the mirror, and begins a struggle with a changed physical form seen as an uncanny double, both outlandish and unfamiliar. Kathleen M. Woodward refers to the 'mirror stage' of old age as 'the inverse of the [Lacanian] mirror stage of infancy' which leads 'from sufficiency to wholeness', while 'the mirror stage of old age is the feared trajectory from wholeness to physical disintegration'.[2] The narrator's inner sense of wholeness 'is felt to reside *within*, not *without*'.[3] After she has returned from her only daughter's wedding, the life that appears to be open before her brings her disappointment. Although she is freed from all shackling responsibility after the marriage of her only daughter, she is no longer able to live up to this freedom, and surrenders to a life of looming ineffectiveness and decline.

In the Palestinian writer Sahar Khalifah's novel *The Inheritance* (2005) (*al-Mirath*, 1997), the protagonist, who had spent her life working as a schoolteacher in Kuwait, is alarmed about remaining single at age 50. This situation causes her panic, a strong sense of urgency that time is running out and that she needs to find a husband. Living in a small village near Nablus, she engages in improving and enhancing her looks, and finally meets a man in his seventies who is married and has ten children. Even though he is old, illiterate and disagreeable, he is still eligible, while she, as a woman, feels her time is running out. As a middle-aged woman, she has two options: ending up as a servant to her family, or marrying a common, illiterate and uncouth man. She chooses the latter.

'A Woman of Fifty' (*Imra'a fi al-Khamsin*, 2015) by the Syrian writer Haifa Bitar features a middle-aged woman who tries to defy convention and engage in sex with a man who despises older women. Her aim is to impress him with her young-looking and attractive figure, viewing her body with his own eyes. However, she soon discovers that her relationship with him is no more than a humiliating experience. Despite the fact that he himself is in his fifties, he attributes all ageing signs exclusively to women. He measures them by the moistness of their vaginas and despises them for 'impersonating youth'.[4] As de Beauvoir puts it, woman defines herself in relation to man, but 'he does not in relation to her; she is the inessential in front of the essential. He is the Subject; he is the Absolute. She is the Other.'[5] Her lover's attitude reveals the 'double standard of aging'[6] since society is permissive of sexual activity in older men, but more severe and fanatical when it comes to the older women's sexuality.

In the Lebanese writer Lina Kreidiyyeh's *Khan Zada* (2010), ageism is rooted largely in the narrator's personal fears of ageing and death. She is conscious that she no longer draws the male gaze and that her body is a reminder of death itself. As a menopausal woman, she is seen as useless and 'abject',[7] having lost both procreative power and sexual attraction. The narrator reacts by transforming her body into a 'project'[8] to be monitored and improved through diet, exercise and cosmetic restoration. Despite all such attempts, she feels disappointed and depressed, and begins to evaluate her situation by looking backward in time and trying to compare her situation with her mother, who has a fulfilling senescence, and her virginal aunt Khan Zada, who had succumbed to God's will by clinging to the safe haven of tradition, religious values and norms.

The Unnerving Image in the Mirror

Al-Hayek's 'An Abandoned Winter' is preoccupied with menopause, seen by the narrator as the main sign of ageing. The novel is rendered through the consciousness of the narrator, Mona, who is divorced and is approaching fifty. After her only daughter's marriage ceremony she returns home to an old building and an empty house in disarray, empty glasses and cigarette stubs all over the place in the ashtrays and on the floor. Her daughter's marriage brings her face to face with the signs of ageing that are beginning to assault her body. Her sense of obsolescence is further amplified by the time-worn objects surrounding her: the fading colour of the curtains, the couches and the old furniture, all tropes that mirror her feelings of atrophy on a gloomy winter night with heavy rain and lightning.

Feeling trapped within her space, and conscious of approaching old age, she is filled with a pervading sense of failure and pointlessness. Although she has not yet reached fifty, she feels old. She decides not to go to work the following day, and has arthritic pain in her joints. Abandoned and lonely, she switches the TV on to disperse the chilling silence, but soon retires to a cold bed and cold sheets, thinking of the hot water bottle that her mother used to put in her bed whenever she had tonsillitis. Feeling isolated, she yearns for her old bed, her sister Mary and her childhood home.

She has a relationship with an unpredictable man who appears for a short while and disappears for months. After her daughter's wedding, he makes a short stopover, but when he leaves, 'something inside me was crushed, turning into an abyss, a dark well, and I started to cry'.[9] The end of the relationship marks the onset of old age and biological decline. Since she is approaching fifty, a date that concurs with the onset of menopause, the 'biological marker of decline',[10] she envisages herself growing old alone, trying to deal with the ravages of time on her ageing body. She sees herself outside youth and desire and assumes that as an ageing woman, she is no longer a desirable object to be gazed at. Consequently, she turns her gaze upon herself,[11] and the creeping wrinkles on her body. Aligning herself with corporeality, she develops a strong dread of ageing that she sees in the mirror in 'a perpetual striving to meet an ideal configuration of body and selfhood'.[12] Even though she lives a free and independent life, she realises that freedom at her age is manifested in 'self- hatred',[13] emptiness and limited possibilities.

Since Mona is an educated professional woman and a by-product of modernisation, her awareness of ageing is amplified as she enters into old age alone, without a man and outside the realm of desire. In other words, she internalises the circulating cultural discourses that produce, and stabilise, the meanings attached to her ageing body.[14] The space in which she circulates shrinks, and she becomes restricted to her apartment and to weekly visits to her ageing parents in the mountains.

On her way to the village, accompanied by her friend Colette, the narrator notes the protruding 'thick blue veins' on Colette's hands compared to her own hands that look less 'tired'.[15] Yet, she notes that her finger knots are more creasy and consoles herself by attributing this to the cold, and to the need to use hand cream to deal with the dry skin. If her friend's hands look like 'the hands of an old person',[16] she too notices the lines on her wrist and wonders how her hands have aged 'when I was not paying attention'.[17] Age takes her by surprise as it creeps into her body suddenly and unexpectedly. As she ages, she notes that her body is gradually taking centre stage and losing resilience, and that the depredations of time on her body will soon diminish her self-esteem and decrease her social expectations.

On their way to the mountain, Mona thinks of the limitations and repetitiveness of her parents' lives and is conscious of more deprivation in the offing. She knows that she is going to have the same exchanges with her parents down to the exact words, and that her mother will focus on her ailments: the pain in her knees, joints, and the medication that hurts her stomach. The narrator's conversation with her parents centres on their health problems; her mother and father represent stereotypical images of traditional ageing which Mona subscribes to, and which reveal an obsessive preoccupation with the body and its vicissitudes. She envisages her ageing father sitting in the winter room drowned in silence and coughing from time to time. She observes that his green eyes have lost their colour, with the redness and the fine congested veins clearly visible, and that he acts as though he were her son not her father. Her internalisation of ageism accentuates her father's infantilisation and the reversal of roles between father and daughter. When she holds her mother's hand she perceives the dry desiccated skin covered with brown spots, and the cracks in her palms. Her mother complains that her husband sleeps all the time and does not give her a hand in the garden, but the old couple soon tire of talking and fall asleep.

Mona does not tell her parents of her daughter's marriage as they live in the past and still think that she is still a child. The amount of desperation about change and the ruthlessness of time are confirmed on their way back from her parents' house when they pass by her old house, which is now occupied by a new wife. She notes that the colour of the curtains has changed and that the vegetable seller is no longer there, his shop having been replaced by a tall building. The clothes shop is now a butcher's shop and the chocolate place is closed. The world she knew no longer exists, and she is unable to recognise any faces. She is surrounded by images that reflect the fleetingness of life and her own transitory existence.

In her struggle with a changing physique, the trope of mirror gazing permeates the narrative. In the mirror, she confronts the 'horror of the mirror image'[18] in the image of an intruder with wrinkles that have gathered around the eyes and the corner of the lips. Since she defines herself in terms of corporeality, she experiences ageing as a process of abject deterioration. As a woman in proximity with old age, she develops the 'age gaze', which, through her 'learning appropriate practices and a set of knowledges guiding the age gaze', enables her to determine whether she has crossed the threshold into decline. [19]

Conscious of the tyranny of the ageing body, she is stunned to see her mother's image reflected back to her in the mirror, destabilising her own sense of identity, blurring the boundaries between daughter and mother and producing an uncanny double in the mirror. This uncanny encounter with her own ageing in the image of her mother haunts her, to the extent that she imagines that she is using her mother's words and general demeanour whenever she cleans the windows or dusts the house. Her rejection of her mother's lifestyle is what Adrienne Rich calls 'matrophobia' or the fear of 'becoming one's mother'.[20]

Mona notes that her lover looks pallid and skinny, which she views as signs of ageing. Equally conscious of the onset of age, he informs her that he had decided to escape the noise pollution in the city and withdraw into a peaceful life in the village. As an ageing man, he seeks a static rurality and a sedentary existence. He tells her about his grandfather's house, how he sits at dusk on the stone seat over the terrace and watches the fog that covers the valley. He disengages from all activity and surrenders to a traditional, cultural and institutionalised view of a static brand of ageing that erases agency and resistance. While middle-aged men are considered functional and still very attractive to women, Youssef, Mona's lover, is more feminised and the gap between them as middle-aged individuals is narrowed. He too feels the burden of age and, like her, capitulates to a lonely old age.

Like Mona, Youssef too is having nightmares. He dreams of being his grandfather, a man with white hair and bent back, who stands on the *mastaba* and remembers that he is alone after the death of his wife. He starts crying and goes to the winter room, approaches her bed and removes the blankets, only to come face to face with her old cold clothes that 'crack'[21] when he touches them. In the mirror of his mind, Youssef assumes the shape and character of his own grandfather, and they become one and inextricable, revealing that the disorienting mirror image is not gender-specific.

The performance of age is the narrator's way of understanding a debilitating future, although she is still in her late forties and has no reason to grouse over what might happen to her when she reaches her mother's age. However, since youth and age are understood in binary terms instead of in gradations, the general view is that age is natural and coherent, making the elderly identifiable and predictable. In line with such views, Mona fixates on a future of decline, lives increasingly at home, in the shadows, unwilling to accept any new challenges. Her essentialist view of ageing and her internalisation of the ideology of decline expose her total reliance on the prevailing hegemonic social forces that fix ageing in a particular mould and invoke images of physical decline and social downgrading. Hers is a narrative of a coercive biological, psychological and social decline that views older individuals as biologically determined. This is a narrative that erases differences between older people and views them as a predictable and uniform group.

Her mother is Mona's projected image of herself as an elderly woman irrespective of time, place and situatedness: 'If I reach the age of my mother,

I would look smaller, shorter; I will have her grey hair, and my father's eyes, but I will not lose my teeth the way they have.'[22] Mona also assumes that she will end up like her mother in a rural house with a *mastaba* full of flower-pots that she would water daily, and tend the house and her little garden. When she tells Colette about her desire for a rural abode, her friend responds: '"What are you going to do? How are you going to spend your time?"'[23] In other words, she draws her attention to the fact that unlike her mother, she is a professional who is urbanised and independent. Similarly, Mona recalls her mother's obsession with cleanliness and her attempt to resist and free herself from her mother. Unlike her mother, and as a woman living alone, she neglects the housework and discovers accidently that the source of the putrid smell in her apartment is three rotting potatoes in her kitchen. As a working woman, she can no longer cope with housework and only realises that the gas cylinder has been empty for days when she switches on the heater.

Mona is aware of her difference, and of the fact that her 'model' is both depressing and terrifying, but she is at a loss as to what awaits her as an old woman since she has no other model. As Woodward astutely puts it, 'aging is understood through the concept of identification – visual identification – with a member of one's family and one's mother at that, as though how we look were everything, as though maternal biology were absolute destiny'.[24]

Mona recalls scenes and incidents from her childhood, her father's Christmas tree, and the family's sense of wholeness and unity. These recollections represent her perception of the past as opposed to the present sense of instability and fragmentation, and her realisation that the two cannot be reconciled. Her cold house and the stale smell that pervades the rooms testify to a strong sense of defeat and capitulation in the face of the ravages of time. She exhibits an unsettling sense of withdrawal, lethargy, marginalisation and invisibility, represented by her own mother, with the added problem of being an ageing woman living alone without family support. While she focuses on the changes taking place to her physique, she is also aware of the stigma surrounding old age and her failure to fight back.

The stale smell of her neglected apartment and the cold rooms speak to the spectral world that surrounds her. Her house, and the area where she lives, have also succumbed to obsolescence and a general sense of loss. She recalls her landlady's story of the Armenian family that used to live in her apartment.

During the war, the children emigrated to Canada while the mother stayed on in the flat throughout the war until one of her children returned, put her in a home, and went back to Canada. Mona identifies with the old woman and is worried about a similar fate awaiting her since, as Segal puts it, when it comes to ageing it is 'the future that haunts the present, and not the past'.[25]

Disciplining the Female Body

Khalifa's *The Inheritance* focuses on Nahleh, an unmarried woman who has reached the age of fifty, and who lives with her father and brothers in Wadi al-Riha in the West Bank. When the female narrator, a cousin who comes to visit from America, first sees Nahleh, she describes her as a small woman with bold eyes and a dignified smile, with curlers in her hair. On arriving at her uncle's house, the narrator observes her cousin Nahleh holding a broom and a garden hose, washing, and sweeping the floor. This image sums up her role inside the house as a sort of a family servant and domestic caretaker serving her father and brothers. At fifty, Nahleh passes her time embroidering, knitting, and weaving an empty life of sterility 'without a husband, without a house, and no one to call me Mama . . . a forgotten cow in a barn, now that her breasts are dry'.[26] Nahleh tells the narrator, her American cousin, that she woke up one day and found herself old: ' "Now I find myself doing nothing but housework, sweeping and cleaning, washing and making pickles! I'm about to explode; this kind of life is killing me." '[27] Surpassing the age of childbearing, and realising that biology is the sole marker of femininity, she ends up marginalised and relegated to the trivialities of housework and subservience to the family.

As a teacher in Kuwait for many years, she manages to exceed her subordinate role, and be viewed with respect by her brothers; however, this is all short-lived. At fifty and without a job she is downgraded, reduced to powerlessness, and expected to be a submissive elderly woman who is of no value to anyone and who is restricted to the family home space. She tells the narrator, her cousin Zeina, that her brothers enjoyed their lives when she was slaving away in Kuwait and sending them money. She paid for her brothers' education, while she remained a mere schoolteacher teaching the same lessons, receiving the same salary, and leading a repetitive and uneventful life, which ironically is curiously reminiscent of her present domestic work at home, although the latter is without a salary.

She complains to the narrator that none of her brothers cares that she has wasted her youth in the heat of Kuwait, living alone in a foreign country: ' "Is this what I get in life, is this what I spent my youth for – living in exile!" '[28] She tolerated this situation because she believed that her brothers will be by her side when she needed them – ' "I could become ill; I'll grow old, become senile, and they'll be there for me in my old age" '[29] – but she was wrong. Even though she sustained the family economically by appropriating the male role of breadwinner and reversing gender roles, her situation as an unmarried woman in the West Bank puts her at the mercy of her brothers and the cultural forces that privilege manhood and ensure an unmarried woman's subjugation.

She maintains that her brothers only think of her when they need money. Her revolutionary brother, Mazen, is unemployed, and instead of finding a job he is going around with a woman, writing bad cheques and waiting for her to cover his debts as usual. Feeling exploited, she decides to resist. When her brother Said asks her for 'a few bucks' she responds, ' "Well brother, no more of this talk. I'm not a stupid girl any more, leave me alone, you've bankrupted me. Get off my back. You've milked me like a cow." '[30] Her sister-in-law blames her for irritating her husband and putting him in a sullen mood when she, a childless woman, is sitting ' "on a treasure" ' and leaving her family ' "at the mercy of the sun and the rain" '.[31] In her sister's view, menopause is proof enough that Nahleh is outside 'the gendered norm of true femininity',[32] and that her role should consist of service to her family. In line with King's contention, 'age is a cultural construct its boundaries shifting with changing demographics'.[33] In this context, one could say that within Palestinian culture in the West Bank, menopause for many implies that a woman can no longer produce men to resist the Israeli occupation, and needs to engage in service work whether inside the family or nationally, if needed.

Nahleh's brothers have married and have children while she remains single with no children, no husband and no home of her own, keeping in mind that, as a woman, she is supposed to remain virginal and utterly self-sacrificing. She complains to her American cousin that her brothers have ' "squeezed me like a lemon" '[34] and left her contending with a strong sense of sterility and irrelevance. She suffers from fears of ageing, low self-esteem and menopausal social exclusion, and envies American women, who, like men, take jobs, have boyfriends, marry, and divorce without problems. The 'double jeopardy'[35] of being a woman and being old further complicates her situation. Her fear of ending up as a stunted, dried-out 'spinster' devoid of sexual fulfilment and of a husband to define her and grant her the social status of marriage places her in a particularly problematic position.

Since spinsterhood is perceived as 'a deviance from the gendered norm of true femininity',[36] it causes her trepidation and anxiety. Her devalued, menopausal, dysfunctional body and her terror of inevitable biological degeneration, together with the loss of youth and physical attraction, which is 'grounded in a nostalgic view of the body',[37] force her to take hasty measures against decline, and embark on a process of physical modification intended to restore a youthful self. Accordingly, she heads to Nablus weekly to buy face and body creams and many other items that claim to restore her youthfulness. This action makes her forget her fifty years, greying hair, hot flushes, changes in her body, and worries and sleepless nights. Having no choice but to integrate her culture's meanings, values and norms about ageing, she is convinced that her physical, social and psychological fulfilment all depend on her ability to attract a man.

Feeling particularly vulnerable, and complying with cultural representations of feminine beauty, she is determined to restore the beauty and freshness of a youthful look, which constitutes her 'cultural capital'.[38] Accordingly, she makes use of her own money to beautify herself and rebels against her family's attempt to neutralise her, take her money away and place her under their control. With the cosmetics industry expanding, she heads to Nablus to purchase creams, mascara, eye shadow and lipstick, as well as clothes and trinkets. Her destination is a shop always packed with veiled women observing the vendor, who like a magician produces the mysterious products: '"This is for firming the skin, this is for blood circulation, this is meant to open the pores, and this is to whiten the skin; they will make your skin feel like velvet."'[39] Back home, she would spend hours in her room, trying numerous face and body creams as well as clothes and trinkets she had purchased in an attempt to erase the signs of ageing. She would also spend time on other embellishing interventions such as exercise in order to lose weight. Her intensive pursuit of youthfulness releases suppressed erotic desires for an old man who starts pursuing her.

Determined to resist family tyranny, a creeping fear of decline and a sense of lowered self-esteem and existential sterility, Nahleh starts a relationship with a seventy-year-old cousin, an illiterate broker and a married man with ten children, who wants to take her as a second wife. When she first sets eyes on him, she is shocked at the sight of a stocky old man, with a bloated paunch and puffed-up eyes, using appalling foul language. Nahleh attributes his coarse behaviour to the fact that he grew up among grapevines like a goat, and grazed like sheep in the midst of grass, radishes and shrubs. His crude rural background can be contrasted with Nahleh's urban and middle-class family that looks down upon this class of uncouth farmers.

Nahleh's sudden unorthodox behaviour is depicted as interchangeably tragic and comical. We are told that when the old man looks at her she has the same sensations she experienced when she listened to her favourite romantic songs. That was the time she dreamed and woke up with a beating heart, dazed looks and sweating body. She sings, with Umm Kulthum, ' "Give me my freedom, release my hands, I have given everything and did not hold back" ',[40] and listens to other romantic songs that capture her nostalgic craving for the dizzy thoughts, visions and sensations of youth. Surprised at the persistence of her desire and her awakening sexuality, she decides to marry and have a husband and a home. Her only regret is that, had she been ten years younger, she could have become pregnant and given birth to a baby 'boy': 'Well, what could she do, this is better than nothing, as the proverb goes.'[41] She knows that as a woman determined by biology, she becomes 'sexually ineligible'[42] much earlier than the old man, who is free to marry at any age. As a result, she decides to marry the old man, her last chance to escape her ordeal and the misery of repression, loneliness and a squandered life.

Despite the broker's crudity and vulgarity, he possesses an aesthetic appreciation of beauty and an admiration for technology, cosmetic surgery and progress. Watching the Arab singer Warda on television, he comments on her youthful beauty, rosy face, slender neck and general radiance after the facelift and weight loss: ' "How lovely Warda is, looking so young and energetic. That's the way to live, that's life for anyone who understands what living means, not like my life, worthy of cows." '[43] His image of the desirable woman is youth, or the appearance of youthfulness, sexiness and class, and his beloved [meaning Nahleh] is ' "a city woman, well born, educated, and composed, with two twinkling eyes, white skin, without a moustache or a double chin.

She is fashionable, with legs that look like cheese under the nylon stockings, a behind as soft as butter"', [44] and a coquettish laugh and soft talk.

In order to attract Nahleh he too makes an effort to embellish his looks, and when he looks in the mirror he is pleased with his new look. He dyes his hair and is enthralled by the smell of the 'first class cologne' that he has bought from the barber's shop near the mosque. The barber showers him with compliments:

> this cologne came directly from Rome . . . a mixture of orange and European jasmine blossom . . .. look how young you look after the coloring . . . people in civilized countries live to be ninety, and you being only seventy . . . you're prosperous and healthy, you're youthful, even younger looking than your children.[45]

On the other hand, her family sees Nahleh's uncharacteristic behaviour as irrational and psychologically unstable. For them, she has changed and is transformed into a hysterical, stingy, stubborn, overbearing and querulous woman whose attitude is absurd and depressing.[46]

As an ageing woman, she has no existence outside the general familial consent, and no autonomy apart from the family. Her brothers Saeed and Mazen believe they have a transgressive promiscuous sister whose dangerous sexuality and *fitna* (seduction and chaos) need to be contained since she has failed to manage her behaviour according to normative standards of respectability. As a result the whole family becomes involved in determining Nahleh's destiny.

Her uncle expresses dissatisfaction with her unanticipated behaviour: '"Nahleh has changed, changed very much. She has become cruel and stubborn and says strange things. She even wears strange clothes, laughs loudly, and chews gum! . . . This isn't like her."'[47] For her family, Nahleh is a 'biological text',[48] which they read, revise and rewrite in accordance with the ideology of chastity which sustains their masculine authority. They watch her breaking social and religious inhibitions by indulging in vain pleasure-seeking practices, and decide to put an end to such behaviour. The general ageism and sexism of a male-dominated society demands that Nahleh be relegated to a corner where she is supposed to lead a life of imposed virginity, self-effacing spinsterhood and domestic servitude.

On a visit to Nahleh's family, the old man spots Nahleh in the bathroom surrounded by 'Perfume bottles, small bars of soap like pieces of Turkish delight, and a basket full of small elegant towels . . . displayed on a marble table in front of her'. Having removed her scarf to comb her hair, which 'rolled like spirals over her shoulders' like a 'black waterfall', and shaking her head 'in an elegant manner akin to a gazelle or a mare',[49] he attacks her. Her brother Mazen appears on the scene, grabs the old man and hurls him into the terrace, where he lands like a sack in front of the guests. The slapstick trivialises the infatuated old man, a man who colours his hair, has a partial denture in his mouth and 'doesn't know his head from his heels',[50] and turns him into the laughing stock of Nahleh's family and friends.

Her brothers Mazen and Said are furious and consider her a source of shame and dishonour. Viewing her as a minor, they are determined to manage her life. Her brother Said calls her 'whore' and threatens her with a kitchen knife. While Mazen wants to protect her virginity and ensure that his sister remains submissive and peripheral in accordance with social mores, his eldest brother, who had lived in Germany for a period of time, wants to take her to Germany and let her live her life rather than marry a pygmy and an old ignorant broker.

When she marries the old man, she is also harassed and kidnapped by his sons, and the old man runs off to Amman fearing for his life after having been threatened by his sons, who want to keep their share of the inheritance. They have no problem with the old man marrying a younger woman, because it is his legal right. One of his sons tells Nahleh:

> Listen to me, woman, stepmother, we can't grant you a divorce because it doesn't depend on us . . . what's happened, has happened; our father took a second wife, so let him get his fill. The man wants a younger wife and it's his right. God gave him wealth, what can we say? However, our assets are our right – the land, the villa, and the shares all belong to us. As for you, shari'a law gives you what is rightfully yours.[51]

But Nahleh is defiant and insists that the shares in the company belong to her as part of her dowry. The women in her husband's family are infuriated and refer to her as the 'whore' who seduced their 'sick and half senile' father by exposing her ' "merchandise in the street" '⁵² and stripping him of the little brain he had left.

They are certain that their father was simply seduced: ' "It is well-known that men are small-minded and their eyes dazzle at the sight of flesh, painted nails, and blonde hair." ' The old man's daughter accuses her of being a witch who ensnared her father by using such ' "powerful magic" ' that ' "even the Sumerians were unable to undo it" '.⁵³ As a shameless woman, she is seen as a monstrous curse on their father and the family.

When Nahleh's brothers urge her to divorce a cowardly old man who has chickened out and left his bride in the lurch, she insists that the marriage was ' "according to the sunna, according to God's law and that of His Prophet" '.⁵⁴ When they insist that divorce is the best solution to the problem, she reacts: ' "If I'm insulted while married, what will you do when I'm divorced and single? . . . If I were divorced and went back home, you would use me as a doormat." '⁵⁵ Despite her inner disappointment with the imbecilic old man, Nahleh prefers a disastrous marriage to the stigma of spinsterhood.

The Female Body as a 'Project'

Lina Kreidiyyeh's *Khan Zada* (2010) focuses on three females who move from a disappointing revolutionary pan-Arab ideology and headlong immersion in public/political events into a private narcissistic concern with body maintenance through constant monitoring in order to fight the signs of ageing on their bodies. The narrator is a woman who has reached middle age and who spends a great deal of time reflecting on her own life, her female and male friends, and the history of her family. Being in her fifties she decides to move out of Beirut, the city of her childhood, as it is a place that no longer offers her any succour and drives her into the mountain town of Suq al-Gharb, a semi-rural setting that overlooks the city.

At her age she enjoys autonomy and personal agency, especially since she is an educated, working and financially independent woman who has more choices and more freedom than other women, like Nahleh, who do not have similar privileges. Within the narrator's socio-cultural environment, she can make her own decisions, live alone and enjoy her privacy; however, her position of power does not make her feel any better about old age, and she views it as the onset of loneliness and emotional and 'sexual disqualification'.⁵⁶ As a menopausal woman, she feels 'abject', having lost her reproductive power and on the way to losing her sexual attractiveness.

Conscious of an uncertain and precarious future, she retreats into the little town of Suq al-Gharb, where she has ample time to withdraw by way of memory and reminiscence into a more stable and meaningful past represented by the living as well as the deceased members of her family. Still she cherishes her strategic house in the mountain that overlooks the city, allowing her to reflect on her life in the city, especially the changes that have affected the city and have defaced the sites of her childhood and youth. The post-war era proclaims her political disillusionment as well as the onset of old age.

The narrator asserts that old Beirut has lost its identity owing to the fifteen-year war and a destabilising and chaotic modernisation. After the war, the city is invaded by globalisation and by giant chains that have banished the old intimate cafés, and other locales and ways of life. Her neighbour in Beirut, the old pigeon man who was heard talking to his precious pigeons, has gone, together with the two cinchona and jasmine trees that he had watered and loved. Like the mother in *No Knives in This City's Kitchens*, she laments the gradual disappearance of the city. She regrets the vanishing of the old street vendors with their pickles, turnips, kidney beans, sweetened apples and iced lemonade, all of which were attacked by swarming flies that the vendors tried to chase away.

As a middle-aged woman, she becomes aware of the ephemerality of existence and focuses on the repetitiveness of her life: she returns home every evening to her old dog, her cigarette packet, her bottle of wine, her thirsty and drying plants, and old Egyptian films of the 1940s. At the same time, and as an educated woman, she makes use of all the modern equipment surrounding her which gives her better access to information. The remote control, the satellite dish, the mobile phone, the internet and the computer reveal that change is inevitable. Like the old city that is tainted by the modern, the narrator's middle-age experience is intricately linked to modernity. For instance, if Jihan, the narrator's friend, relapses into an a unadulterated traditional Sunni Beiruti identity, she does not give up drinking, but instead of doing it in public she drinks indoors to avoid the gossip of nosy neighbours. The past/present, tradition/modernity binarisms are disrupted, and the friends remain in a liminal space, oscillating between the two worlds.[57]

The narrator complains that her boyfriend Nidal, who is in his late fifties, has abandoned her for women in their twenties, while she, as an older woman, does not have similar chances. She is left with her lifelong female friends Jihan and Raw'a, mindful of the fact that the three of them have changed, have lost their earlier bloom and, in their present situation, live monotonous and uneventful lives. Female camaraderie sustains them but does not replace their need for men. After the defeat of their earlier progressive ideas and dreams of Arab unity, pan-Arabism and revolutionary fervour, they feel redundant and out of touch with the new world. The early 1970s were a time when 'one life was not enough, one man was not enough, and one orgasm per night was not enough',[58] but growing old, and having abandoned her earlier revered goals, she feels a strong sense of futility, marginality and ineffectiveness.

At fifty, the narrator's friend Jihan retires into an old house, itself a trope of the past that she had inherited from her parents, a place with a camellia tree and a decrepit water fountain. The house itself is decked with mirrors, Turkish side-lamps and photographs of her ancestors. Like the narrator herself, Jihan becomes addicted to Egyptian films of the 1940s and the old songs of Umm Kulthum, 'the old furniture' as she refers to them.[59] Jihan's revolutionary ideals are replaced by a sectarian identity enforced by community values and traditions. She abandons her old liberal, nationalistic, pan-Arab spirit, and adopts a factional and xenophobic identity.[60]

The three friends' trajectory to the past is their way of dealing not only with political disillusionment and a series of losses at the personal level, but also with the unanticipated signs of ageing. The narrator suffers from hot flushes and fears that her body is beginning to lose its youthfulness. Feeling abandoned and alone, she comes round to the idea that the ultimate fate of women is marriage and motherhood. She has sleepless nights on account of her present situation and realises that her failure to have a child and family explains the cul-de-sac she has reached. At a younger age she was repelled by the sight of children, but now she watches wistfully the children carrying flowers for their mothers on Mother's Day, and dreams of having a child that she will spoil and pamper. She recalls how a friend advised her to have a child by any man, but she had been busy pursuing her ambitions, work, freedoms, and had chosen men who were unwilling to start a family.

She sees the advantages of a traditional marriage and way of life by simply observing her own mother, whose husband is a role model for her. Despite her parents' traditional arranged marriage, love remained strong even after death. Her mother treasures her father's old possessions, his socks, aftershave, underwear and shiny shoes, and she is content to live for her children and does not have the manifold and complex problems faced by her daughter. Unlike the ageing narrator, a by-product of modernisation and nationalist thinking, her mother has achieved satisfaction with her own life while her daughter has to contend with a solitary and disappointing existence. Her lifelong rebellion against tradition places her on the threshold of biological decline and marginalisation.

Feeling hampered by a threatening and consuming old age, the narrator finds refuge in recollections and memories of the past and of her three deceased elderly spinster aunts and her ageing uncle. Her three veiled aunts lived a cloistered and asexual life within the sanctuary of the family. They are defined by the narrator as sidelined, absent, anachronistic, ineffectual and mere onlookers on events. Being unmarried, they had a stunted, lonely old age. The narrator's eldest aunt, blue-eyed Fatima, is depicted as a dried-up, hard, bitter, frustrated and neurotic spinster, harbouring a tendency for control. Her younger sister, Khan Zada, is depicted as an angel in the house. Like the stereotypical elderly woman, she is resigned, selfless, caring, austere, religious, subdued and voiceless. She uses no perfume or any other embellishment, and smells of soap. During her last days she had cancerous cysts in her breast but endured patiently, being sustained by a strong religious fervour. She rarely spoke about herself or articulated any desires, remaining enigmatic and effaced.

The narrator's roguish uncle Usama spent his life chasing women and prostitutes and his sister Fatima never forgave this lecherous 'devil' who chose a dissolute path that would damage the family's reputation. Fatima ordered her brother to leave after he returned home utterly intoxicated. Her 'righteous anger',[61] to use the words of Ruth E. Ray, consisted of lack of tolerance for his 'evil' ways. She reminded him that there were no 'alcoholics' in this pious house, but he never repented. Even as an old man he continued to sell bogus alcohol, but he was a kind-hearted and accommodating person who became all the more compassionate in his old age.

His feminine qualities surfaced when he was allowed to return home because of his age. He helped the narrator's mother in the kitchen, and she loved him. However, Usama suffered from dementia towards the end; he opened the pressure cooker to see what the narrator's mother was cooking, but it exploded and his face was burnt, while the vegetables hit the kitchen ceiling. His case deteriorated rapidly, and one day he went out in his shirt, tie, jacket and shoes, but without his trousers. When he died, his funeral was in accordance with the status of an old and traditional family. The narrator's mother took care of all the details of the funeral, the ritual of washing the body, sprinkling *zamzam* water and ensuring that the shroud was of the best quality, in addition to the inherited traditional 'Turkish cloth' that marks the status of the family and its purity of origin and nobility.[62] What is telling here is that in contrast to the nonconformist life the uncle led, he is given an honourable funeral that is fit for the upright and virtuous, while his sisters slip away silently and unobtrusively. In life and death her aunts remain effaced, voiceless and negated, very much like Umm Hasan and Safiya in *The Long Way Back*.

At her age, the narrator engages in unsystematic reminiscences and self-analysis by shifting between past and present and interrupting the linear flow of the narrative. She focuses not only on her political disillusionment, but also on her depleting body, which is losing resilience and sexual appeal. She notes the marks of ageing inscribed on her body – the wrinkles like crow's feet around her eyes, her filling buttocks and paunch, her flabby arms and legs and her sagging boobs – all signs of decline and erasure. Such 'hypervisibility' of ageing signs paradoxically leads to the 'invisibility' of the older female body[63] and the narrator's withdrawal from public life. Internalising socio-culturally prescribed ideals of body shape and appearance, the narrator yearns for the body of her youth and decides to restore it through anti-wrinkle creams, Botox, nutrition, dieting and exercise. The narrative is saturated with an ideology of youth that 'wizens the middle years' and 'amounts to envying oneself when young', regretting loss, and fearing death.[64]

As a result, her body becomes a 'project', a new brand of body upkeep, shaped by internalised cultural norms and global medical discourses pertaining to ageing and anti-ageing in her attempt to enhance her physical attractiveness and retain her youthful look and social value. Giddens's 'reflexive project' denotes self-monitoring, self-regulation and self-questioning, which are central to the preservation of a youthful figure. This is an act which is directly linked to a modern sensibility where the body becomes 'both subject and object, both project and projected upon' in 'a culture of narcissism'.[65] The three friends worry about their health and monitor their bodies for any signs of illness or decline. The narrator observes that she is visiting the toilet repeatedly and wonders whether she is drinking too much water or whether she has diabetes. To preserve her youthfulness, she maintains her body by pursuing numerous healthy lifestyles. She acts on her body by eating healthy food and performing her daily rituals before going to bed, such as applying creams to ward off wrinkles that have begun to attack her ferociously.

In performing agelessness, she ends up denying old age and becoming complicit with the general ageism within society that relegates age to an absent other. Biggs maintains that 'Masquerade draws on the idea that identity is performative: put on . . . in a particular context and for a specific audience, even if the audience exists in the inner world of the self'.[66] These techniques that mask the physical signs of ageing reveal the power of the cultural narrative and the 'seductiveness of agelessness' and a youthful appearance.[67] Being told that she does not look her age is taken as compliment. At fifty, she believes that she is still beautiful since that is what everyone says. She evaluates herself through her visibility to the outside viewer and through the performance of beauty and denial of age in order to circumvent any social denigration of her body that would drive her to an invisible corner.

Despite her attempts to come to terms with this new phase of life, she continues to feel sexually and socially redundant. She studies her schedule for the following day: work, lunch with her mother and siblings at the usual militarily precise time, an outing with Jihan. She is particularly excited about learning more about her friend's latest affair with 'this handsome man with grey hair',[68] who would get her out of the groove of seclusion. His grey hair heightens this middle-aged man's sex appeal, while it is a mark of diminished value when it comes to women, giving her even more reason to perform agelessness by all means available in order to restore her youthful attractiveness.

Unsexing the Female Body

'A Woman of Fifty' is a narrative that centres on a menopausal woman's sexuality and the right to her body within a social context that views sexuality at her age as grotesque and repugnant. The narrator is an educated woman whose career as a journalist is prospering, but whose success is interrupted by disturbing menopausal flashes that determine the onset of ageing. At fifty, and being confined within a social structure that entraps female sexuality within rigid patterns of differentiation and inequality, she feels psychologically and socially vulnerable.

Haunted by the ghost of ageing, which would marginalise and decrease her social value, the narrator looks in the mirror and congratulates herself on her youthful and firm body.

Like Nahleh, she is interpellated in the discourse that woman's value is based entirely on her corporeality, and that to retain her attractiveness she needs to simulate youth as the sole model of beauty. As the global world becomes increasingly obsessed with the pursuit of youthfulness through the dissemination and privileging of images of young bodies, the horror of corporeal ageing intensifies. Like many women of her generation, the narrator internalises the culture's denial of and aversion to ageing. As a result, she continues to care for her body with aromatic soap, lavender and lemon and looks at herself with great satisfaction. She finds her body still shapely, symmetrical and robust, and prides herself on having the body of a thirty-year-old. In a confessional mode, the female narrator focuses on menopause and its bearing on herself in a society that sees her as old and sexually irrelevant. She pursues a tall and handsome writer in his fifties who had won many literary prizes and is known to have a great interest in women's literature and admiration for women who break taboos, and she succeeds in making him pay attention to her.

Having retained a youthful figure, she intends to draw the writer's admiring glances and turn his head when he looks at her proportional and taut figure, which is equal to that of a woman of thirty. Obsessed by her youthful body, she believes that she could defeat him with her bodily endowments. In accordance with the expectations of a male-controlled society, she views her desirability and value in strictly corporeal terms. She believes that she has the right to love and be loved, especially since an active sexuality is sufficient proof that she has not lost all her weapons, although she is still overcome with a dread of ageing and the accompanying marginalisation and disparagement.

Because her sexuality depends on men, she is flattered when the writer tells her that he had never had such an orgasm with another woman, although she herself did not have one. But her hopes are soon dashed when he travels without bothering to inform her, as if by sleeping with her 'he had done her a favour'.[69] She feels offended and humiliated and believes that this is a sign of his determination to insult her dignity and femininity. In her anger, she admits that she had heard him refer to menopausal women disdainfully, but she had remained silent and did not protest against the insult attached to older women. But later she blames herself for complicity in her own oppression, and attributes her behaviour to insecurity and lack of self-confidence. However, her silence reveals her shame at the ageing female body and her realisation that her value as a woman comes exclusively from the male observer.

This is a man who brags about his sexual prowess, and of having had relations with four women at a time for more than three years. Such a chauvinistic attitude hides his own unconscious fear of a castrating old age, reassuring himself that he is still young and potent. Like 'a swelling peacock',[70] he brags about his adventures and infidelities and of possessing recalcitrant and penetrating intellectual and sexual abilities that cannot be satiated solely by one woman. His language is fraught with such words such as 'penetration', which reveal the strong connectivity between masculine virility and male intellectual endeavours described by Gilbert and Gubar as the 'metaphorical penis'.[71]

Although the narrator knows that his behaviour is scornful and derisive, she is still willing to have an affair with him, the permissive atmosphere of Beirut allowing them to have casual affairs and sexual relations outside marriage. Insensitive to the fact that he is having sex with a fifty-year-old woman, he has the insolence to tell her that his present mistress, now in her fifties, is in the process of invalidation. The narrator is shocked by the hypocrisy, insensitivity and double standards of a man who pursues her, but who has no scruples about degrading and de-sexualising his girlfriend in the presence of a woman who happens to be of the same age. He tells her that his present girlfriend is pitiable, with her fading, wrinkly lips and sagging neck, and that she has become a sexual neuter and should retire into invisibility. His girlfriend is seen as a corporeal being who is to blame for committing 'a heresy against [her] . . . own nature'.[72]

When the narrator asks him why he is having a relationship with her, a woman (like his girlfriend) in her fifties, he responds disparagingly that it all depends upon the 'moistness' of her vagina. Since his girlfriend is linked with corporeality and reproductive functions, her present sterile body and 'vaginal atrophy'[73] rules her out. In other words, a woman her age is biologically determined, and needs to consign herself to 'menopausal senescence'[74] and extricate herself from the feminine and from sexuality itself.

The narrator wonders how a man who claims to support the literary output of courageous women despises and humiliates women in their fifties, places them in a biological mould and denies them their femininity. Looking at him, she observes that not 'only women age'[75] but that he too is ageing; he has paunch, a saggy neck and wrinkles around his eyes, but since he is divested of corporeality, such marks do not brand him as sexually illegible, but rather make him all the more attractive.

After divorcing her husband, the narrator moves with her son into her father's home, where the father expects appropriate behaviour on her part, insisting that her son is worth all the men in the world. Her father's aim is to erase her femininity, demonise sexuality after fifty and turn her exclusively into a devoted mother who values modesty and sexual austerity. He wants her to age gracefully and retire into an idle and degenerating old age.

After being abandoned by the writer, she decides to 'retire sexually'[76] and withstand the worst of double marginality, ageism and sexism, although she is only fifty. Since menopause is considered the principal sign of ageing for women, the product of biology as well as cultural values attached to the female body, she blames herself for 'pathetically' and 'grotesquely' trying to please men.[77] Feeling sidelined at fifty, and facing 'the loss of prestige, status, visibility and value'[78] accorded to younger women, she decides to go through a process of self-scrutiny in order to cope with menopause, which announces the crossing of the threshold to the other side in a society that views menopause as a 'dysfunction'[79] and as an inevitable decline.

Since her sexuality depends upon the predominant cultural norms, she decides to retire from the world of men and asserts indignantly that no man is now able to warm her heart more than vodka. Viewing age and youth in binary opposition rather than in progressive stages, she asserts bitterly that she has 'spat them [men] out and vomited them and now they are outside me'.[80]

By a forced withdrawal from the world of men and a leap into somatic irrelevance, she finds refuge in female camaraderie, sisterhood and 'proclaimed transcendence of sexual needs'.[81] She decides with a group of women to start a woman's association through the assistance of Fabiolla, who owns a woman's boutique and who has connections with women from various social and religious backgrounds.

As women in a communal setting they reminisce about youth, marriage and motherhood, seeking to achieve what Holstein calls 'narrative repair'[82] of their ageing identities in brief fragmentary anecdotes that can be described as confessional but also 'generative and restorative',[83] enabling them to come to a better understanding of themselves, their life course and their sense of self. Now, they are determined to 'skin peel and rind themselves layer by layer' until they get to the truth 'buried under one thousand hijabs and one'.[84] Menopause has enabled them to move from 'reproductive' to 'reflective' concerns[85] and indulge in an attempt to change society and the 'calcified'[86] social patterns. In line with traditional norms about female ageing, they project themselves as possessing the maturity and wisdom that will no longer allow them to be deceived by men or by their own selves. Fifty is the age of 'self-reconciliation and the inauguration of a new beginning',[87] and a genuinely authentic life without men. They maintain that now they are free and will no longer accept the earlier 'prefabricated personality', which is worn the way they wear their 'shirt[s]'. They admit that they were 'made into women, our personality was cut out for us in accordance with scales and measures and special moral standards'.[88]

Feeling 'invisible, as the attention of a masculinised and youth-obsessed society ebbs away',[89] they share their stories and refuse to be silent, compliant and nurturing elderly women like the grandmother in *Mothballs*, and insist on resisting 'sexageism'[90] by taking ownership of their lives and challenging the prevalent culturally validated discourses on women. To borrow the words of Frida Kerner Furman, these women see themselves from the '"internalized male gaze"' and the '"internalized gaze of youth"'.[91] Since the age of fifty has de-sexed them and placed them outside the world of younger women, they compensate by indulging in an attempt to change society, especially the prevailing norms and traditions.[92]

They disapprove of old women who end up spending their time playing cards to kill time or playing the role of docile grandmothers who knit for their grandchildren and help their daughters and daughters-in-law with the children, and feel grateful when the new-born baby is given their names. These educated and modern women present themselves in opposition to traditional women, giving a different cadence to the earlier discourses about female ageing by refusing to be subsumed by orthodox images of older women. As new women, they engage in self-scrutiny and reflexivity, and believe that they have a mission for future generations, which is to shun the mistakes they had made in their lives when it comes to their relations with men. They see themselves as newly self-confident women who are determined to leave a trace behind them by disrupting normative constructions of older women and looking for meaning in their lives outside the domestic space.

For Fabiolla, one of this group of women, fifty is the age where a woman does not have to deceive herself any longer, and has to live for herself; it is the age of truth and 'truth is always harsh and painful'.[93] Fabiolla has finally de-sexualised herself, and asserts that having 'castrated' herself she is finally 'at peace'[94] with herself, and freed from the hegemonic world of men. She no longer needs to violate herself and her body or to offer up her femininity for the pleasure of men.

Another woman, Wafaa, relates that she had a loveless marriage and felt humiliation, enslavement and subjugation, but she went on looking after her children and following the rules of society. She only reacts a quarter of a century later as a disappointed woman facing menopause, affirming the connectivity between women's oppression and the devaluation of menopausal women, and between sexism and ageism. Ibtihal was a famous actress who prostituted herself by sleeping with the director and producer in order to get a leading role in a film. She became addicted to alcohol and medication, visited psychiatrists and had cosmetic surgery. Now she is no longer afraid to speak freely about herself. She no longer feels despair and panic when she discovers new wrinkles or when she gains a few kilos. She asserts that she has managed 'to exorcize a devil inside her'[95] through confession, which is the best way to shed the old self. Futun is an anaesthetist who fears spinsterhood. She grows up with the idea that she is physically unattractive. Having a good job, she spends a great amount of money to compensate for her lack. She buys expensive watches, jewellery and underwear and has several facelifting operations to improve her looks, feeling ashamed of her ageing appearance and the stigma of spinsterhood.

The fragmentary stories these women tell present a surface view of each woman without delving into their inner subjectivity. They maintain that they hope to achieve agency through commitment to female solidarity, and 're-engagement' by immersing themselves in a struggle for women's and human rights, cultural activity, self-reflexivity and 'resistance to middle ageism'.[96] However, it is not clear how they intend to go about this, especially since social values about menopausal women are still 'hammered' into their minds 'like nails'.[97] They mention lectures and seminars that are restricted to raising awareness about the plight of women in a patriarchal order. In these gatherings, they find their voices, tell their stories for the first time and feel a strong sense of autonomy and liberation within the precincts of the group. They see the age of fifty as their rite of passage into a sexless but more insightful and cognisant life. Ironically, the narrator thinks of inviting the writer to one of these sessions, revealing that she is unable to disentangle herself from the world of men. She continues to feel trapped in an ageing body, seeing it as 'a foreign species',[98] and a sort of 'identity stripping'.[99] While these women continue to rage against men and a patriarchal society, they betray a sense of defeat and an unconscious 'rejection of the age-altered body'[100] despite futile attempts at rational explanations and justifications.

The narrator asserts that while a man is important in a woman's life, what is more important is to do without him to emancipate herself from desire. She admits that like millions of other women she dreaded ageing, especially after her period stopped, viewing it as a turning point in her life and a preamble to decline. In line with social norms, she felt that she was on the verge of being transformed into an asexual and sterile being, in contrast to men, who are able to have children even at 'the edge of his grave'.[101] This sense of urgency and frustration drives the women to launch scathing attacks on men and hold them responsible for women's problems, and their withdrawal turns out to be an escape rather than a confrontation.

In spite of these women's defiance, a large portion of what they say is generally preachy and melodramatic, revealing a lurking sense of pointlessness despite their supposed 'relief' from the shackles of a patriarchal society. A great deal of what they say about the age of fifty represents their way of cheering themselves up and surrendering to their fate. Unknowingly, they are complicit with male values about menopause and try unsuccessfully to convince themselves that fifty is the age of making peace with oneself. Ironically, by retreating into invisibility and placing themselves outside the trail of desire, they are in effect capitulating to values imposed by patriarchy regarding the marginalisation of older women. Their awakening comes at a time when they cannot capitalise on it or turn it into useful account or practical results.

Conclusion

This chapter has examined female subjects forced to confront sudden and unexpected signs of ageing on their bodies. Unlike fictional works on women within traditional societies, this chapter has focused on educated career women aged between forty-five and their late sixties who are growing old in the city, allowing them personal autonomy, social interaction and spatial movement. Their modern style of living, whereby they dress according to fashion and employ cosmetic creams and procedures as well as physical exercise and diet, implies that, in line with a creeping consumer culture, they view their bodies as signifiers of age. They are drawn into a global culture of consumption, body maintenance and self-styled upkeep, aiming to retain an eroticised youthful female body. They represent a new image of older individuals 'dressing youthfully, having sex, dieting . . . and so forth'.[102] However, a consumer culture, coupled with the anachronistic pull of social and religious discourses, de-genders and de-sexualises them.

The narrator of 'An Abandoned Winter' attaches the value of the female body to its youthfulness,[103] causing ideologically determined inadequacy and disappointment, having internalised her subsidiary role as an ageing woman. Being in her late forties, she is terrified by the mirror image reflected back at her in the image of her own mother, who is in a state of biological decline.[104] Other women, like Nahleh in *The Inheritance*, take hasty measures against decline through a process of cosmetic maintenance in order to fight the signs of ageing and find a husband who would protect them from the stigma of spinsterhood. Despite a long career as a schoolteacher, Nahleh knows that as a jobless spinster she will end up a servant in her father's and brothers' homes. The protagonist of Lina Kreidiyyeh's *Khan Zada*, who had been a political activist in the 1970s and 1980s and who has had a rich sexual life, suddenly finds herself ageing and suffering from an existential and psychological crisis that causes vulnerability and capitulation to an impending futility. Her initial reaction to the menopause is to recapture a youthful body through cosmetics, Botox, as well as exercise and diet. However, coming to the grim realisation that her body is in a 'state of irreversible' physical decline[105] she experiences a never-ending isolation, especially in her inability to attract men in a patriarchal society that views older women's bodies as an aberration. She begins to see the advantage of traditional thinking where, like her own mother, one is surrounded by family, children, and religious compensation, that provide internal strength and contentment.

Similarly, in 'A Woman of Fifty' the narrator's body becomes paramount when she recognises that her value depends on the male observer who privileges youthfulness and views the cessation of menstruation as the gateway to a world of decline. Since society is more permissive of sexual activity in older men than in older women, the narrator decides to capitulate and eschew sexuality, and instead of adopting the traditional nurturing role she decides to engage in awareness campaigns aimed at patriarchal bias against younger women, who must learn from the experience of older women and avoid submitting to men. She decides once again to take control of herself, befriending other women her age and establishing a kind of female camaraderie. As modern professional women, they refuse to be silent, invisible, compliant and selflessly accessible for others. They avoid the fate of women who define femininity in accordance with patriarchal discourses that reduce women to their crude corporeality. Nonetheless, the text reveals that their efforts to resist sexageism remain in the realm of the theoretical rather than the factual.

Notes

1. Silver, 'Gendered Identities in Old Age', p. 383.
2. Woodward, 'The Mirror Stage of Old Age', p. 67.
3. Rubenstein, 'Feminism, Eros, and the Coming of Age', p. 9.
4. Ray, 'Toward the Croning of Feminist Gerontology', p. 118.
5. De Beauvoir, 'Introduction', *The Second Sex*, p. 6.
6. Sontag, 'The Double Standard of Ageing', p. 31.
7. Kristeva, *Powers of Horror*.
8. Giddens, *Modernity and Self-Identity*, p. 105.

9. Hayek, p. 19.
10. Gullette, *Declining to Decline*, p. 106.
11. See Coupland, *Discourse, the Body and Identity*, p. 4.
12. Ibid., p. 4.
13. Andrews, 'The Seductiveness of Agelessness', p. 302.
14. See Judith Butler, *Gender Trouble*, pp. xv–xvi.
15. 'Abandoned Winter', p. 20. All translations are mine.
16. Ibid., p. 25.
17. Ibid., p. 26.
18. Woodward, 'The Mirror Stage of Old Age', p. 104.
19. Gullette, *Declining to Decline*, p. 169.
20. Rich, *Of Woman Born*, p. 235.
21. 'Abandoned Winter', p. 54.
22. Ibid., p. 25.
23. Ibid., p. 53.
24. Woodward, 'Inventing Generational Models', p. 158.
25. Segal, *Out of Time*, p. 22.
26. *Inheritance*, p. 52.
27. Ibid., p. 92.
28. Ibid., p. 50.
29. Ibid., p. 51.
30. Ibid., p. 92.
31. Ibid., p. 93.
32. Zita, 'Heresy in the Female Body', p. 98.
33. King, *Discourses of Ageing in Fiction and Feminism*, p. xvii.
34. *Inheritance*, p. 50.
35. Powell, *Social Theory and Aging*, p. 56.
36. Zita, 'Heresy in the Female Body', p. 98.
37. Hepworth, 'Ageing Bodies: Aged by Culture', p. 104.
38. Slevin, 'The Embodied Experiences of Old Lesbians', p. 249.
39. *Inheritance*, p. 74.
40. Ibid., p. 72.
41. Ibid., p. 90.
42. Sontag, p. 31.
43. *Inheritance*, p. 80.
44. Ibid., p. 77.
45. Ibid., p. 119.

46. In 'The Disposition to Obsessional Neurosis' (1913), Freud refers to women who 'have lost their genital function' as undergoing 'a peculiar alteration' and becoming 'quarrelsome, vexatious and overbearing, petty and stingy', and as transformed from 'the charming girl' to the 'old dragon', SE 12:3, 17–26, 323–4.
47. *Inheritance*, p. 72.
48. Zita, 'Heresy in the Female Body', p. 98.
49. Ibid., p. 120.
50. *Inheritance*, p. 159.
51. Ibid., p. 170.
52. Ibid., p. 146.
53. Ibid.
54. Ibid., p. 165
55. Ibid., p. 169.
56. Sontag, 'The Double Standard of Aging', p. 32.
57. Aghacy, *Writing Beirut*, p. 52.
58. *Khan Zada*, pp. 121–2. All translations are mine.
59. Ibid., p. 7.
60. Aghacy, *Writing Beirut*, pp. 48–51.
61. Ray, 'Toward the Croning of Feminist Gerontology', pp. 110, 114.
62. *Khan Zada*, p. 81.
63. Bouson, *Shame and the Aging Woman*, p. 41.
64. Gullette, *Declining to Decline*, p. 6.
65. Lasch, *The Culture of Narcissism*.
66. Biggs, 'Age, Gender, Narratives and Masquerades', p. 46.
67. Andrews, 'The Seductiveness of Agelessness', pp. 301–18.
68. *Inheritance*, p. 126.
69. Ibid., p. 26.
70. Ibid., p. 5.
71. Gilbert and Gubar, p. 7.
72. Zita, 'Heresy in the Female Body', p. 98.
73. Ibid., p. 111.
74. Zita, 'Heresy in the Female Body', p. 98.
75. Gullette, *Declining to decline*, p. 105.
76. Walz, 'Crones, Dirty Old Men, Sexy Seniors', p. 109.
77. Greer, *The Change: Women, Ageing and Menopause*, pp. 2–4, 433–5.
78. Zita, 'Heresy in the Female Body', p. 102.

79. Ibid., p. 99.
80. 'A Woman of Fifty', p. 28. All translations are mine.
81. Segal, 'Forever Young: Medusa's Curse and the Discourses of Ageing', p. 52.
82. Holstein, 'On Being an Aging Woman', p. 331.
83. Woodward, 'Telling Stories', p. 151.
84. 'A Woman of Fifty', p. 105.
85. Woodward, 'Introduction' in *Figuring Age*, p. xiv.
86. 'A Woman of Fifty', p. 165.
87. Ibid., p. 94.
88. Ibid., p. 127.
89. Biggs, 'Age, Gender, Narratives and Masquerades', p. 49.
90. Bouson, *Shame and the Aging Woman*, p. 3.
91. Quoted in Ibid., p. 16.
92. 'A Woman of Fifty' p. 165.
93. Ibid., p. 28.
94. Ibid., p. 92.
95. Ibid., p. 123.
96. Gullette, *Declining to Decline*, p. 110.
97. 'A Woman of Fifty', p. 131.
98. De Beauvoir, *The Coming of Age*, p. 283.
99. Gullette, *Aged by Culture*, p. 130.
100. Bouson, *Shame and the Aging Woman*, p. 10.
101. 'Woman of Fifty', p. 10.
102. Oberg, 'Images versus Experience of the Aging Body', p. 103.
103. Hepworth and Featherstone, 'The Male Menopause', p. 283.
104. As Gullette, puts it, 'Fear of fifty intensifies fear of ninety', *Declining to Decline*, p. 94.
105. Hepworth and Featherstone, 'The Male Menopause', p. 283.

4

Senile Masculinity: The Male Body in Crisis

While the ageing women in Chapter 1 efface their bodies in accordance with social and religious values, the novels in this chapter, like the works written by menopausal women in the earlier chapter, feature elderly men very much aware of their bodies and their sexuality. These novels shed light on the male experience of ageing through the body, reinforced by social constructionist views that determine the representation of ageing masculinities in Arab societies, bearing in mind that the biological seems to take precedence when it comes to rural societies depicted in 'The Lovers of Bayya' and *Borrowed Time*. As for the more urbanised character in al-Daif's novel, the narrator tends to rely on social constructions that give agency to older men, but is continually destabilised by the biological changes in his body.

The old men in the Tunisian writer al-Habib al-Salimy's 'The Lovers of Bayya' ('*Ushshaq Bayya*, 2002) are seen by the authorial narrator, who represents the average view of the ageing body, as misshapen grotesques which reveal that men, like women, are 'not exempt from the influence of age',[1] and are fully implicated in the ageing process. These are frail old men reduced to their ageing bodies and depicting physical decline. As they live in a remote Tunisian village, their daily meetings under the olive tree are homosocial gatherings where they wash and clean their bodies, gossip and joke, and express desire for a young widow named Bayya. They are interrupted now and then by funeral processions passing by on their way to the cemetery. The latter topos represents the old men's awareness and fear of death and their attempt to familiarise themselves with it.

The Lebanese writer Hasan Daoud's *Borrowed Time* (2008) (*Ayyam Za'ida*, 1990) portrays the gradual decline of an old man who refuses to capitulate to decline and death without a bitter fight with his children.

Because of his stubborn resistance to decline he is ignored by his family and is left to clean his own room, which remains dirty. His relegation to housework tasks reflect his gradual feminisation, the squalor of his own existence, and his humiliating exposure and defeat under the youthful gaze of younger men and women.

The Lebanese writer Rashid al-Daif's novel 'O.K. Goodbye' (*O.K. ma' al-Salama*, 2008) depicts the relationship between a prominent writer in his sixties and a younger woman. The narrator anchors his masculinity in his incisive intellectuality and sexual potency, but he is soon abandoned by the woman for a younger man whose age is 'more appropriate'.[2] This rejection leads to hypochondriacal complaints, impotency, bouts of depression, and the realisation by the narrator that he is on the verge of decline and extinction.

Survival Games

'The Lovers of Bayya' features four decrepit working-class old men over seventy who live in an impoverished rural Tunisian village, most probably after the First World War. Since the time and place are not specified the novel takes on a more generalised perspective to encompass ageing in Arab/Islamic society. The younger authorial narrator constructs ageing in keeping with cultural views of horror and disgust with the obscene body to reinforce an essentialist view of ageing that perceives the ageing men as a monolithic category dispossessed of any singularity. He presents four men who can hardly be recognised as distinct individuals. In a half-comic tone, the narrator introduces a narrative where seriousness and laughter coexist, and where the old men retreat to Zaytunat al-Kalb (The Dog's Olive Tree), a derisive term implying diminishment and scorn, where they create their own rules of action away from controlling social mores in a lower-class rustic Islamic framework existing in the first half of the twentieth century.

The younger authorial narrator combines description, direct speech, commentary and irony in his presentation of the old men who represent Muslim social and religious values that dictate old men's behaviour. He presents the old men as comic and grotesque figures of physical decline, passing whatever time is left for them in petty talk, sexual fantasy, scatological jokes, and enervated pranks that conceal a lurking anxiety about approaching death. The emphasis is on the manner in which they cope with age and how they brush aside nearing death by fixing their attention on a young woman, although they know that carnal desire does not belong to them.

After their afternoon nap, they meet at Zaytunat al-Kalb, which is adjacent to the 'path of hearses'[3] where funeral processions head towards the cemetery. This proximity to the burial ground helps to make death less outlandish and unnerving. The four of them suffer from ailments. Mahmoud has tuberculosis and coughs all the time, while the others are afflicted with a long line of diseases whose names they do not even know.

In their homosocial gathering, they hurl insults at one another whenever they feel intimidated and express their desire for Bayya, a young widow. Al-Birni responds to al-Makki's disparaging remarks on the former's watch by telling him that the watch, which he has inherited from his father, is more valuable than 'all that your father and grandfather and great grandfather possessed all their lives'.[4] The reference to al-Makki's ancestors underscores the central role the family plays in Arab society. Al-Birni insists that such watches, made in Germany, are 'like flint' and last forever.[5] Like the others, he is bedazzled by the feats of Germany in the First World War (the Arabs supported the Germans against the Allies) and believes that anything that is rock-solid can only be made in Germany. He tells them about the hands of the watch that shine at night with a green light like the 'Prophet's horse',[6] and refers to its uniform ticking that sends him to sleep and reminds him of his wife's breathing at night before it turned into snoring. He adjusts it every morning with the early morning news, and the watch maintains its accuracy, 'not a minute more or less'.[7]

Al-Birni is proud of his old watch kept safely in his pocket, and when he cleans it he passes his fingers slowly and tenderly over its surface as if he were cuddling one of his grandchildren. The watch represents the old man's anxiety about time, but also his pride that, unlike his other friends, he has the privilege of owning a watch. When al-Birni brags about his watch, al-Tayyib responds facetiously that this is a watch that belongs to 'time immemorial'.[8] It is tacky, antiquated and dispensable, especially since the four of them normally rely on the shadow of the olive tree on the sand to determine the time of day, particularly prayer time, and have no need of al-Birni's watch.

In addition to his watch, al-Birni boasts of having memorised the Qur'an and travelled all over the country, meeting sheikhs and scholars on his way to trade cattle. Owing to such contacts, he is considered knowledgeable about the Qur'an. Accordingly, al-Makki, who is illiterate, has queries about the Day of Judgement that he wants al-Birni to address, and other key questions that only scholars and sheikhs can answer. As a result, al-Birni is cornered, and feels obliged to give accurate answers. Asked whether the fire of Hell is the same fire we light or cook with, he tells al-Makki that the 'infidels have the torture of hell and fire ... fire with flame. God has prepared chains, handcuffs, and a massive fire as high as the mountain which is enough to burn all infidels, "the Jews and the Christians", and all evil-doers.'[9] The use of hyperbole by the author is a deliberate tactic of exaggeration to expose al-Birni's ignorance, but also to give a derisory effect by mocking and infantilising the old man, and presenting all four men as gullible, unpolished, trivial and erratic.

Such an exchange between them is no more than a repetitive game that both al-Tayyib and al-Birni play and that gives them pleasure. To pass whatever time is left for them, they chat, and like Beckett's Vladimir and Estragon in *Waiting for Godot* play games, laugh and scoff at each other in order to achieve 'ontological security'[10] in a world that no longer gives them reassurance. The absurdity of their situation is underscored in the games they play to pass the time before the final encounter with death. Al-Tayyib does not feel insulted when al-Birni calls him 'blind', since such affronts and slurs are part of the game, that has its own rules as a pastime and a coping strategy. In this space of withdrawal, they dissociate themselves from society and immerse themselves in games, recollections and reminiscences that provide them with an ontological shield. The scoffing is accompanied by mockery and light swearing, for the game can take shape and become a source of enjoyment. Jesting, amusement, laughter and hilarity are diversions, which keep them going, for they are no heroes, but thieves, lecherous old men and clownish figures who invite laughter, and who mutate into grotesque victims of destiny.

In the absence of outside viewers, they feel their protruding ribs and tummies as if they wanted to make sure that their bodies can still endure their real and imagined illnesses. They clean their teeth and ears with whatever sticks they find; they cut their nails, treat their warts and blisters, and pour hot sand on their sores after cleaning them of pus and rancid blood. They also cut their hair and shave their beards, check their sexual organs, and feel the sagging flesh. The grotesque disintegration of their bodies gives rise to black comedy, with the elderly men acting like children, parading their flagging bodies, and underscoring the younger authorial narrator's horror and disgust with the obscene ageing male body portending death, but also his inner sense of the meaninglessness of human existence. By focusing on the corporeality of the old men's decaying bodies in a deliberately ambiguous place and time in Tunis, the novel reveals the narrator's complicity with an ageing discourse that links cultural attitudes of horror and disgust with the ageing male physique.

Al-Makki's son, with whom he had lost contact, returns unexpectedly from Germany and gives his father many gifts: a woollen cloak, a cane, a brass pitcher for ablutions, a rosary that shines with green light at night and a promise to sponsor a trip to al-Hajj. Since he views himself as superior and more privileged than the others, al-Birni is envious and starts belittling al-Makki's son's gifts. He tells his friend that all the gifts his son gave him are not *halal* (sanctified) because he bought them with the money of infidels (meaning Germans), and the pilgrimage to al-Hajj, which requires 'mountains of money', also comes from the infidel's money. Besides, al-Makki does not even know where people go to perform the ritual of hajj, and just refers to it as 'the land of the hajj'.[11]

In addition to this piece of news, the old men learn from Bayya's brother that his sister is now confined to the home, fearing men because Mahmoud seduced her and was about to rape her right under the open sky. When he helped her to hold the jar that was about to fall off the donkey's back, she felt him leaning towards her in an unexpected manner, but she did not think about it as it never occurred to her that a man of his age and status could even think of these things. But he groped her, removed her clothes and jumped over her. It was very fast, especially since she was not wearing pants. The narrator tells us that like all women her age who had started wearing them only recently, she had not grown used to them. Nevertheless, she gathered all her strength and pushed him away.

Al-Birni is curious to know what Mahmoud actually did with Bayya, and Mahmoud obliges by telling him that his hand fell unconsciously on one of her breasts, which felt 'smooth, soft, and tender like a plum',[12] and al-Birni thinks disappointedly of his wife's sagging breasts 'like a piece of skin' or 'an empty canteen'.[13] Al-Birni feels depressed at the state they have come to when he looks at Mahmoud's saggy organ that looks like 'hot dough'.[14] Captivated by the nubile young, represented by Bayya, the old men bemoan their age and impotence. They admit that they harbour strong desires for the young woman, which revive their youthful selves and longings. Admitting desire without sexual fulfilment is their way of reconciling erogenous youth and asexual agedness in a culture that frowns upon libidinous senescence and expects spiritual abstinence.

Despite al-Birni's own sexual desire for the young woman, male bonding has priority over any female even if she is young and desirable. Al-Birni decides to defend Mahmoud against Bayya's charges despite the loopholes in Mahmoud's story. He is sure the 'bitch'[15] surrendered to Mahmoud after only a slight struggle. Convinced of the '*kayd*' (cunning) of women, he feels sorry for this greying old man and cannot bear to see him disgraced just for a 'urine spot',[16] as he refers to Bayya. In fact, masculinity is about power relations that must absolve Mahmoud and reduce the young woman to a stinky blotch.

In their homosocial space under Zaytunat al-Kalb, they give rein to their libidinal fantasies and feel free to say and do anything. The use of salacious and uncouth language is in keeping with their generally crude and rudimentary brand of life, where at least two of them were thieves in their youth. The carnivalesque behaviour of these pleasure-loving old men who remain youthful in spirit can be seen in the uninhibited exposure of their bodies, their carnal desires, their indulgences, excesses and dissenting lecherousness, which mark them as agents of misrule. Nevertheless, they remain bound by the social and religious discourse that sexuality belongs solely to the young, which brings home to them their impotence and frustration, but creates defiance at the same time.

When Bayya marries al-Makki's son and goes abroad with him, they continue to fantasise about her. Al-Tayyib imagines her coming out of the bath with her soft straight hair – that had been washed with perfumed soap – falling supple and shiny like velvet on her shoulders, and looking like a wealthy woman in her new clothes, robes, stockings, shoes and even pants, in line with Western women's clothing styles. However, when al-Birni goes further, to describe what he would do with her, the others tell him that he should be ashamed of himself. The incongruity between social mores and individual desires explains their erratic and contradictory behaviour.

The comedy comes to a head when, despite Bayya's unsavoury encounter with Mahmoud, she still upholds the honour and respect due to age and decides to seek the assistance of the four old men who are supposed to be wise in the ways of the world and firmly rooted in true religion and godly reverence. She seeks advice about her husband's mistreatment of her and offers gifts for each piece of advice. She promises to send each one of them a rosary and a pitcher for ablution, and on learning that the Turks are Muslims she promises them a prayer carpet made in Turkey. She tells them that her husband was a burglar who stole radios, clocks and other electronic equipment. Convinced that stealing is *haram*, she concludes that the Germans are the 'true' Muslims because they have mercy and have given her more than enough to cover all her needs, while her husband stopped buying her clothes, prevented her from going out to visit friends or even opening the window, and beat her with the 'German's heavy, thick and coarse boots'.[17]

Knowing that he desperately needs Bayya's gifts, his rosary being old and his prayer carpet so shabby that he uses it solely to protect his forehead from the cold ground, al-Birni decides to help. On the basis of his religious belief in the inferiority of women, he maintains that the husband has the right to teach and discipline his wife and to be even more severe with widows and divorcees. Still, a wise man should not listen to everything a woman says because women are weak and feeble-minded, and if he wants to beat her, no one will deny him that, but it should not be on her head, eyes and knees because that may lead to death. The novel's derisive tone trivialises the supposed wisdom of the old and places them firmly within the confines of traditional discourses that give men total control over women's lives.

When al-Makki's son marries Bayya, the old men only attend the signing of the marriage contract, read *al-Fatiha*, drink loads of tea and return to their spot. They do not attend the wedding, since it is improper for men their age to be part of entertainment and youthful pleasures. At Zaytunat al-Kalb (the dog's olive tree in Arabic) with its echoes of triviality, rejection, and abandonment, they squat around the tree trunk, a trope of masculine virility in stark contrast to the old men all wrapped up in clothes which cover the head and body, making them 'look like huge crows'.[18] The whole area is empty: no woman drawing water from the well, no funeral processions, not even 'rambling animals or stray dogs',[19] which augments their ostracism and their sense of futility and ineffectiveness.

While young people celebrate life, the old men feel derelict, as if they were suddenly cast off into the mouth of death. Awaiting the wedding breakfast, they try to lighten the atmosphere and allay their fears by joking and jesting. But when Mahmoud goes into a fit of coughing and falls on the ground spitting three drops of blood, the mood changes and they start looking anxiously around them, without casting an eye on Mahmoud because of their horror and fear of death. Mahmoud looks at the hole in the olive tree and thinks of the tomb's hollow cavity, fearing that he may wake up after being buried. Al-Tayyib has a nightmarish vision of being buried in the scorpion-infested pit, although Mahmoud reassures him that he had never seen a scorpion in the hollow, only ants and beetles.

Mahmoud becomes more frail and skinny and less able to bear the cold or fight his illness. He feels that his end is coming and that 'the devil is ready to grab his soul'.[20] He has visions of his wife Khadija visiting him and imagines being placed naked and well-washed on a cold piece of wood. Knowing that 'the dead exude bad odours and need to be clean before they go up to God and the angels',[21] he envisages al-Birni supervising the whole operation. Mahmoud discovers that he is no longer able to recall an incident in its details, and that his memories come back to him in a disconnected and fragmented manner. He knows that his friends are very ill too. Al-Birni, who always makes sure to remain sturdy like steel, is suffering from what is referred to as botch or cancer, the same illness that killed his sister before she reached the age of thirty. Although they suffer from many diseases unknown to them, al-Makki and al-Tayyib have not set foot in a hospital for many years because they are scared of the doctors' needles. These are old men in poor health and without medical care, awaiting the inevitable. Unable to resist an unavoidable death, Mahmoud feels that having his friends by his side would allay his fears of facing death alone and give him peace of mind.

When Mahmoud dies, his friends want to know if he had suffered, and when they learn that he had not, they feel reassured that death is going to be easy. Al-Tayyib wonders if Mahmoud knows that he is dead since he has heard that the dead wake up and want to get out, but when they hit their heads against the ceiling of the grave they realise that they are dead. The other two old men become silent and self-absorbed. Al-Birni watches with trepidation the passing of time as he fixes on his watch. When they get up to do ablution and exclaim 'God is great',[22] only the empty space and mute desolation around them reverberates, underscoring the dark side of the ageing process that ends in closure.

Resisting Otherness

When Daoud's *Borrowed Time* came out in 1990, the author, who wrote about an old man with amazing insight, had not yet reached old age. When I commented on his deep familiarity with the quotidian details of an old man's life, his answer was that it was a portrait of his own grandfather who has touched his life. The novel powerfully evokes the experience of old age and dying within a particular local context that constructs ageing in accordance with deeply engrained social and religious principles. It is a vivid portrayal by the narrator, an old man over eighty, who describes his life after retirement and exposes how he is treated by his family when he gives up his work in Beirut in the early 1960s and returns to his village, which is considered the ideal rural setting for old-age disengagement, retirement and well-being.

In an illiterate rural society, age is calculated in terms of the time of year and in relation to significant incidents such as wars, the harvesting season, snowfall, deaths in the village and other occurrences. Accordingly, neither the narrator nor his family know the narrator's exact age, especially since he was registered long after his birth. He tells us that his ID card indicates that he is 94, but he knows that he is three years younger because his father had raised his age in order to get him 'out of military service'.[23] His children, on the other hand, claim that he is three years older than indicated on his ID card, and of the same generation as his fellow villagers, Abu Ali Yousef and Hajj Ali Farhat, but the narrator knows this is untrue since 'they were off on their first trip to Palestine when I was not old enough to be alone with the cows'.[24]

Assuming that he has reached old age, his children decide that he must retire to avoid reproach from relatives and other families in the village, for allowing an old man to work in Beirut, a sign that ageing is not solely determined biologically, but also socially. It was he who established the thriving bakery in Bab Idris, but by making him return to a static life in the village, which is generally spent indoors, his sons force him into a domestic, feminine space that excludes him from the more familiar masculine world of work. The impingement of youth on age marginalises the old man, places him in a position of demotion and exile and transforms him, eventually, into a humiliating dependency.

Because his identity as a man and head of the family has depended upon his dominance, authority, success, economic control, and physical fitness and vigour, the oppressive insistence on the resolute fixity of chronological age robs him of his masculinity and selfhood. He asserts that lately he has stopped arguing with his sons about his age, since they

> take a month and turn it into a year. Between one visit and the next someone will add a year to my life ... For some of my grandchildren I am ninety-five and for others I am ninety-seven. They're in a hurry for me to reach a 100.[25]

As a result, he gives up defending his real age because it 'requires a tenacity and stubbornness I no longer possess'.[26] This tendency to increase his age reminds him of a neighbour, Abu Muhammad Nassim, who died before he reached ninety although his family 'added years to his age over time, and when they found him dead on the terrace they added seven more right then and there, proclaiming him 107 years old'.[27]

As a formidable bastion of authority, the old man realises that he is gradually losing his grip on the family and is suffering from bouts of amnesia. After settling in the village, he tells us that he couldn't recall many things that happened in his life and could not even remember what the bakery looked like from inside. His sudden forgetfulness attests to the damaging effect of disengagement and movement to the village on the old man. Nonetheless, he is determined to resist and to show them his true mettle.[28] Rather than projecting himself as a kindly, patient, doting and passive old man, he initiates action against them, and sets about it aggressively and determinedly, insisting on defining his life not as a stage separated from, but as a continuation of, the life course.

After losing his wife, he finds no one to cook for him because his son's wife had stopped caring for him. In protest against her neglect, he confronts his family by commenting on their moral obligations: 'it isn't right for me to be left alone with no one to cook for me when I turn 100'.[29] Their reaction is to avoid him, but they continue to have mixed feelings of fear and aversion towards him. They try to take no notice of him when they pass by his window, but he shouts at any member of his family who happens to be on the stairs for ignoring him.

Barred from work, he is spatially confined to his room and estranged from his family, being 'othered' and regarded as part of the category 'old' which is separate from earlier life stages. Wobbly and unstable, he goes about doing the housework himself, filling the water jug and washing his plate and clothes on the *mastaba*. He sweeps up the dust, the dried leaves and scraps of bread into a pile of refuse behind the door, the way his wife, Hajja Khadija, used to do, and spends his time unsuccessfully cleaning the house, which remains dirty. Unable to clean the filth drying on the floor of the toilet, he starts urinating on the concrete below the *mastaba*, further complicating his relationship with his family and drawing them away from his nauseating smell and the mess he is making all over the place. This disparagement of ageing and the terrible state of disarray in and around the house is their way of obliterating his history and eventually wiping it out completely by selling the house after his death since, in their view, the old man and the house are no more than residual relics.

For him at 94, his body becomes paramount, making him more conscious of the signs of ageing on his small build, stooped back and shrunken belly. The re-territorialisation of the old man within the bounds of the domestic space and the repetitiveness of life within it downgrades him and denies him the power and control he has enjoyed all his life. The space in which he moves shrinks, and he ends up, like his late wife, shuffling between the kitchen, the *mastaba* and the bedroom. His withdrawal from the masculine world of action, his idleness and unproductivity and his forced engagement in housework underline his effeminisation, and loss of effectiveness and control.

He was in his seventies when he began to notice that he could no longer execute deeds that he took for granted in his youth, but he continues to challenge discourses of decline normally attached to old men using his physical strength to perform feats that require youthful robustness and vigour. He goes down the well at age 70, and when he reaches the pit he suddenly feels drained and suffocated. Feeling utter panic, he shakes the rope around his waist, and when he is finally lifted out he is half-naked and unable to catch his breath because of sudden heart trouble. The farcical scene in the well destabilises his machismo, youthful arrogance ordinarily seen as unbecoming at his age, while his sudden feebleness and dependency feminise and humiliate him.

Although he begins to lose his earlier youthful vigour, he remains a ruthless and despotic man. He treats his ailing first wife brutally and takes a second wife, Khadija. He recalls that when the sick woman stood in front of the windowpane staring at him and his new wife as they were having lunch, he would scream at her and order her to 'cover up her tumor' with its 'fine blue veins . . . like those on a cow's stomach'.[30] He goes as far as mocking his first wife's religious faith and claiming that she was slow in everything she did, including in prayers. Watching her pray, he would 'step in front of her and wave, whereupon she adopted a demeanour of piety and contemplation, as if she were enjoying the meaning of the words in the verses that I knew she didn't understand'.[31] When it comes to his prayers, he describes the 'booming sound of my prayers' that 'would frighten her, as if my only purpose in reciting a prayer or verse was to transmit panic and alarm into her heart'.[32] Since infirmity and defencelessness is an index to castration and feminisation, he brushes off such degradation 'by shouting out loud'[33] as a sign of his abiding masculinity.

Rather than demonstrating piety, temperance and mercy, prayers are his way of petrifying and controlling his wife. He is a recalcitrant old man whose two wives have no choice but to behave with proper submission. Being trapped between what Ann Robertson refers to as 'a social ethic of independence, and a service ethic which constructs [him] as dependent on the other'[34] instigates hostility and anger. His fierce aggression is his way of compensating for the loss of masculine power within his family, letting off all his anger and wrath on his ageing first wife, whose gender and age make her doubly disadvantaged and vulnerable. He is also abusive to his first wife's older sister, whom he would push 'to the terrace and to the cow shed' and scream at whenever he spotted 'her standing hunchbacked in the middle of the house'.[35] When she does not respond, he assumes that she is demented and cannot understand his 'scolding and shouting', though he had noticed that when her sister talked to her it looked as though 'she were addressing a rational, sane woman'.[36] Her dread of him makes her speechless, although she is unreserved and communicative with her own sister.

He did not treat his second wife any better, where he would drive her into his room to sweep, 'and she'd go about swatting the floor lightly with the broom'.[37] He always raised his voice when he addressed her, and she dreaded it until the day she died. As a village woman, and under her husband's pressure, she becomes selfless almost to the point of erasure. The old man has the upper hand and the women around him are flattened characters, no more than appendages and voiceless automata devoid of any inner life.

Having absolute control over his wives, he spends his remaining days trying to reinstate his authority over the rest of the family. Although he makes intermittent references to past successes at work, he is not the man to bask in nostalgic memory; he wants to carry on as he has always done. His aim is to control the present the way he did the past. Far from being the doting old man, he is critical of his children and of their attitude towards him. He refers sullenly to his daughter Bahija, who tries to gain control by standing 'tall like a man'.[38] He notes that as she grows older her new make-up makes her look less feminine and more abrasive. Her visits to him are brief, consisting of asking after his health, putting the food she had cooked for him in the pantry, and opening the window to air the room.

Likewise, his other children make short visits and busy themselves arranging his room and tidying up his medicines and numerous other things, leaving no time for talk or any form of communication. They do not listen to his needs, but attend to what they assume an old man his age requires. He also has negative feelings about his daughter Nayefa, who has appropriated the house he had bought in Beirut and expelled all his other children. He asserts ironically that the fabric she used for her clothes was utilised to cover the sofas and that the 'skinny legs of the sofa, seen from below, even looked like her bony legs'.[39]

Watching an old neighbour and hearing her jabber in the darkness of her room, the old man maintains that old age is harder on women than on men ('how quickly their bodies change and waste away, how their lips narrow and tighten, and their eyes fade'[40]), indicating that the value of women is solely related to their physicality. Whenever he is challenged by a woman, he retaliates without hesitation. He curses his daughter-in-law and talks about 'her imbecilic family in Nabatiyah . . . the color of her dull-witted face, her large teeth, her slack, open mouth, and her constant hateful inquisitorial stare'.[41]

His children are amused when a friend maintains that the old man is 'sleeping alone',[42] and is in need of a wife. They are tickled to think that the old man fantasises about having a libido, and believe that his only way of relieving 'his feeble desires'[43] is through empty talk. Their hilarity springs from their conviction that his humiliating sexual dysfunction has no remedy. When he starts moaning with pain, his son lectures to him about his need to get over his fear of death, but avoids any eye contact under the pressure of filial piety that demands awe, respect, obedience and subservience to the authority of elders. But now, since his value has decreased, they greet him when he comes to visit them but resume their talk with one another, ignoring him completely. They also patronise him and take his complaints less seriously, denoting a disconnect within his family owing to the urbanisation of his children, who spend most of their time in Beirut, and the old man's dependence on them physically and financially.

When he screams with pain from his illness, he is gutted when his daughter-in-law ignores him and resumes her chatting with the neighbours who gathered round him hoping that it was the end. But he disappoints her and comes back from the doctor's visit 'walking up the dusty trail from the car to the house unaided, carrying my medicines'.[44] He feels elated to have won this round against her, and in order to intensify her rage he brags that 'Azraa'eel, the angel of Death, cannot touch me'.[45]

Far from being the tight-knit family his children like to project, the extended family has fissures within it. The old man is no indulgent grandfather, but rather a man who views his grandchildren as annoying, loud and messy, and his male children as not men enough, while their wives are wily and ignorant. When the old man watches his son bent over sweeping his father's dirty room instead of making his wife do the job, he gets 'the feeling that they have expelled both of us [his son and himself]'.[46] He envisages his son's wife simultaneously 'cleaning and taming [her husband's] moods'[47] in the same way she cleans and controls the house. The old man's vicious treatment of his own wives discloses a deep-rooted dread of women and of being at their mercy, especially since he is aware that as an old man he has to compete with women and with the hegemony of the young over the old.

Unlike the sulky and disagreeable narrator, his old Beiruti friend Sheikh Abdul Latif likes to sit at home with his family, his neighbours and his water pipe, but the narrator sees him as soft, unmanly, and smiling like a woman. Such differences between rural and urban men subvert dominant stereotypes of ageing. Through the intersection of social setting, class, gender and economic factors, multiple masculinities are produced that challenge the prevailing model. As the narrator shrewdly puts it, 'Those who do not live as we live, do not die as we die'.[48] He protests that his children are sidelining him and depriving him of his earlier activities:

> I didn't stop going out to my lands because of fatigue, but rather because they kept telling me it wasn't fitting for me to work at my age. I was over eighty then, although both my legs were still strong. I killed the tortoise that had scared my son's son in the terraces. I pounded it with a stone until its back was pulverized and the blood appeared deep red . . . I could still lift stones so high that my shirt nearly split at the armpit.[49]

His aggressive behaviour in old age is in effect a continuum that goes back to his youth and adulthood and his entire life. Simultaneously, it is his way of countering marginalisation, disempowerment and social exclusion.

His children deprive him of his old male company in the bakery and give him only brief reports about a distant relative or two who come by. They want him to befriend Muhammad Habib, another old man in the village – 'My son imagines the proximity of our ages alone is enough for us to walk about our town like old buddies' – and reacts sardonically: 'They want Muhammad Habib and me to go out and play.'[50] The old man protests against infantilising him, controlling his life, and choosing his friends and companions. When asked by his grandson why he has not shaved his beard, he complains that his children neglect him and do not take him to Nabatiyah for a shave, and when they come to see him, they spend their time blaming and scolding him.

When he is overcome by illness, he asserts that his son stands among his visitors and relates to them the embarrassing details of his father's illness the night before, without checking to see if his old father is conscious or whether he can hear what he is saying. As a result he deduces that his children have turned him into an inoperative and discarded article, 'a broken-down machine',[51] as the old man refers to it. For his sons, he is a comatose body stretched on the bed, his remaining life not worth living.

Because his children's voices keep 'coming down to me until midnight' and prevent him from going to sleep, the narrator retaliates by waking up early and 'turn[ing]the radio up as far as it can go to get them up and out of their beds and pillows'.⁵² When his son Qassem complains about the loud Qur'anic recitation at daybreak, the old man's reaction is that it was 'God speaking and they needed to listen to *Him*',⁵³ but his son gives him a knowing look as the old man is 'no pious hermit'.⁵⁴ He has fallen behind when it comes to religious devotion, and admits that he stopped 'praying two or three years ago. As for fasting in Ramadan, I have never been able to make it through the entire month. Because of boredom, not hunger. I could never stand to just sit around waiting for something or someone.'⁵⁵ His sons know that he has also hung a verse from the Qur'an on the wall of the old room to cover up the hole where weapons are stashed. The old man defies the rules of conduct and any stoic principles of tolerance and restraint normally associated with old men.

Since his sense of personal identity has depended upon supremacy and control, age has shaken the very foundations of his masculinity. His belligerence, normally unbecoming in an old man, is his way of insisting on his difference and on his will to resist. He admits that 'I do turn the radio on high to wake them up . . . This is all that is left of my influence on the household. I turn up the radio full blast to test my authority; every time I turn it up I wait for someone to yell at me.'⁵⁶ Far from being passive and peace-loving, he is determined to regain lost territory. Despite his age, he accepts no subservience and retaliates by defying his family and making them 'fidget in their beds'.⁵⁷ He adopts a mischievous, infantile attitude, played out in comic colours, to emphasise his non-compliance with any social values and expectations that conspire to remove him from the epicentre.

The doctor they usually send for does not take him seriously either. He examines him hastily, asks about his sleeping habits and talks to him as if he were talking to a child. Although the old man is in deep old age, he is an imposing figure who has no wish to be intimidated. Knowing that his children believe that he is full of guile, he sets about inventing new tricks to confuse them. When the old man asks his sons to summon Sayyid Mahdi, they acquiesce immediately, thinking that it signals that he is finally surrendering to death. But the old man does not tell the sheikh that he saw his '"grandfather in a dream"' and is now ready to die as his sons had assumed, but rather tells him that he ' "want[s] them [his children] to obey me, Sayyid Mahdi" '.[58]

His situation becomes more precarious as his health deteriorates. He is reduced to a mere body when he is exposed to the corrosive gaze of younger women who are assigned to nurse him and who associate old age with corporeal disintegration. He endures the indignities of a humiliating exposure when they take charge of his naked body, which they see as a trope of deterioration, diminished strength and repulsive physical decay. His body is a critical site for the re-inscription of gender roles in old age where the young encroach upon the old and appropriate their power. In the eyes of the young women, he is a grotesque, hideous old man associated with body substances and waste such as urine, saliva, excrement and other discharges. Under their care, his body is reduced to a 'docile' feminised physique normally viewed as 'fluid, leaky, swampy, soft, compared with the hard, defined, contained bodies of men',[59] and his power is dismantled by age and gender that assign him the position of 'other'.

He loses his ability to make decisions about his body, and is barred by his frailty from retaining his earlier unchallenged authority. He is full of anger and disappointment that his sons have assigned two revolting women to nurse him and make fun of him. In a society that prioritises a youthful physique, the old man becomes a victim of ageism and its intersection with gender. He is exposed to ridicule by the two women when they start pretending to be 'brides hard-to-get'[60] on their wedding night. He views them as obscene and disgusting as they begin searching 'for my genitals among the filth', a situation which presages childhood dependence and incontinence. Since sexuality and age do not go together, the women comment sarcastically that 'it', that is, his sexual organ, ' "has disappeared" '.[61] For the women, he is the stark image of morbid anatomy and decrepitude which triggers aversion to the ageing male-sexed body: ' "Have you become cleaner now than before?" one of them asked me . . . while the other squished the rose into her nose, so that she wouldn't have to inhale my stench." '[62] His present 'docile' body is meant to produce compliance and defeat under the gaze of youth. The final scenes are articulated through ironic layers that shift from mockery to farce, showing what it means to live into deep old age and what happens when the body takes centre stage.

The farcical and repugnant intersect in an incongruous agglomeration of the comic and the grotesque. Body defilement and contamination evoke dread and revulsion, and confirm the dependence, the subordination of age and the hegemony of adulthood over age. Realising that the women are in effect preparing him for death, he is ready to resist invalidation by telling his sons that the two women have ' "washed me the way they wash a corpse. And they put me back in my bed still dirty." '[63] In the eyes of his family, he has become the spitting image of the bizarre, the macabre and the morbid. He comes face to face with the facticity of death, and despite the fact that he had not thought about it in any serious manner, he admits that he is not afraid of death. What terrifies him most is the grave itself: 'What I mean is the fear of what dead folks live with, in their graves, of the djinns and the angels that are hovering over them.'[64]

As he grows old, his horizons shrink and he begins to feel closer to the end. His deteriorating health, and the fading of earlier achievements, roles, dreams and ideals, cause him a strong sense of lowered self-esteem. Yet, he protests fiercely and incessantly, and even at the edge of extinction his agitation, restlessness and rage do not abate.

The Castrating Modern

Unlike 'The Lovers of Bayya', Rashid al-Daif's semi-autobiographical novel titled 'O.K. Goodbye' focuses on an urban educated man who comes face to face with senescence and the inevitability of death. The unnamed first-person narrator is a man in his sixties (the same age as al-Daif when he wrote the novel) who recounts a personal story that centres on his confrontation with his ageing self. At 65, and with brief and sporadic allusions to past events that disrupt the chronology of the life review, he meets a younger woman. The narrator has a great deal in common with the author, both of whom are in their sixties, and both are intellectuals, writers and university professors. As a result, the self-reflexive narrative blurs the line between the narrator and the author and between fiction and autobiography, with the ageing narrator as the central focus of a narrative preoccupied with ageing. The unnamed narrator also represents many older men his age who embark on relationships with younger women.

The narrator's story is punctuated with lurking fears about his mother's senile dementia, which causes her to forget and to urinate in her pants. Being only sixteen years younger than his mother and suffering from minor memory lapses, he feels utter dread of cognitive impairment, and his possible susceptibility to its arbitrary depredations. The narrator's sister carries the burden of caring for his mother (a job normally associated with women), while he pursues a younger woman. His relationship with a young woman in her thirties named Hama increases his anxiety about ageing, but he remains reassured since he is in general good health. Still, he monitors his body fastidiously, and ensures that it is in keeping with socio-cultural norms and prescribed ideologies about male potency and relevance in old age, although deep down, he yearns for a body 'in its youthful habitus'.[65]

The tone throughout the text is nonchalantly sardonic, especially in the narrator's pretended naiveté and the verbal detachment he assumes to cover up his fear of ageing and of death. The darker tenors of the ageing process are fused with the comic to mask his hidden anxieties and uncertainties. In order to assure himself that he is credible and compatible with Hama, he tells us that he urinates without any problems and asserts ironically that his heart beats so regularly that 'Switzerland should be proud'[66] of the regularity of his heartbeats. As for his hair, although it fell out many years before, baldness is not a shame, although hair is of course better. Besides, 'no one can do anything about the blue sky',[67] and therefore he does not make a big issue of it.

The narrator maintains that Hama has returned to Lebanon after spending twenty-five years abroad shuttling between Europe and New York, where she worked in 'the world of banks and money'.[68] Having spent her childhood and youth in Western countries, Hama has a different perception of male–female relations, and the narrator embraces the new and appreciates a woman's individual choice irrespective of family and kinship pressures. He tells us that he views himself as a rational being, possessing a neutral temperament and measured feelings, but it takes youth to ignite the passion of an older man. This time, his new love 'had the impact of an explosive TNT bomb'.[69]

The narrator meets Hama at a lecture he gave at the American University of Beirut, and he tells us that she was mesmerised by his words. He claims that she listened to him 'with all her body' and his words had a strong erotic impact as they 'absorbed her being'.[70] His success in seducing her with his intellectual muscles and aphrodisiac words inflates his narcissistic ego and hones his masculinity, especially since he had not thought of himself as belonging to a gendered category. He asserts that she 'assured me that after reading my book and meeting me in person afterwards, I looked identical with the image she had envisaged of me: complexion, eyes, face and even feet. Even my voice coincided with what she had imagined it to be.'[71]

Through ironic understatement and derisive humour, the narrator scoffs at his own folly and his own denial of senescence. Having tasted the magic potion that would give him a taste of youth, he is so euphoric that he almost loses his balance. The double-entendre reinforces the humour aimed at his insecurities and bewilderment. The facetious mockery of the narrator's adolescent behaviour accentuates the derisive irony that pervades the text. He admits that these were feelings he had never experienced with any other woman since he had never trusted women, including his own mother, and he almost agreed with his father when he once told him: ' "Sleep with your wife in accordance with the number of children you want to have and not one time more. Prostitutes are more humane and compassionate." '[72]

From the start, the narrator is overwhelmed by the hegemony of the English language, and especially by his students, who are 'satisfied with their knowledge of English and are indifferent to any other language',[73] including Arabic. However, after meeting Hama, he becomes more convinced of the need to learn a language that represents the values of a competitive, commercialised and youthful global world order. Otherwise, he will be discarded as obsolete knowledge and expendable debris. Undaunted, he hires an English teacher since at his age he cannot join a class where boys 'hear me spelling words, stumbling, and making mistakes, and also discovering that I am forgetful and hard of hearing'.[74] Having internalised the common stereotypical views about ageing, he does not want to end up as the laughing-stock of the class. Learning a new language is torture to him, but he persists and increases the number of sessions from three days a week to five. He cannot imagine being downgraded, and discarded as antiquated knowledge, and intends to be a potent constituent of the new world.

However, in learning the language, he finds himself forgetting what he has learnt. He tells us that he learnt the phrase 'sore throat',[75] but he was unable to use it because his sore throat had healed. But when he needed the word again it was impossible to recall it. Furthermore, he tries desperately to avoid attributing his loss of hearing to the uninvited guest of age, and blames it on the horrors of the Lebanese civil war, addiction to smoking for many years, and the sleeping tablets and tranquillisers he had taken.

To cover up his humiliation at failing to give Hama an orgasm, he puts up a façade of wisdom and dignity by lecturing about the need for a woman to feel safe and secure with the man to respond to him sexually. To borrow the words of Hearn, Rashid wants to project himself 'as a maker of power . . . even when power is lacking'.[76] Knowing that sex has not worked well with them, he assures her that it will not be too late before 'it is regulated and adjusted'.[77] Ironically, the narrator's stale ideas and his adherence to culturally prescribed gender roles fall flat on a woman like Hama. When she tells him that she normally takes time to orgasm, he takes a purposely informed attitude, asserting that man is more bestial while woman is more spiritual and more bashful, especially in 'our' part of the world, but her response is agreement 'without enthusiasm'.[78] Viewing man as the polar opposite of woman, the narrator ignores the contingent and complex multiplicity of gender relations, and his own convoluted relationship with Hama. As if doubtful about the impact of his words on her, he adds ironically: 'yes, I was the one who explained to her, and I was the one who reassured her! After all she is the weak sex and I am the strong man, the wise and experienced sheikh of the tribe.'[79] This reveals the incongruities at the core of a misogynistic male who is no longer certain of his autonomy and his performance in accordance with social mores, and who begins to see that gender relations are more fluid than he had expected, and that the rigid patterning that he had thought invincible is beginning to fall apart.

In the novel, sexual potency is treated as a motif of despair. Since the narrator links masculinity with sexual performance, he wants to restore erectile potency, central to male empowerment, which is normally 'represented as active, strong, urgent and penis-driven'.[80] He thinks of Viagra as an outlet or 'antidote', as Gullette refers to it,[81] but it was still a new release and very few people had ventured to try it. Gradually he begins to recognise that the impetuous desires of youth have become increasingly unrealisable, causing forebodings about ageing, and deep worries about mortality. He knows that Hama is aware of the excessive effort he makes, his exhaustion and paralysis, and the saliva that falls irrepressibly from his mouth whenever he has sex with her. The irony and sarcasm in the novel are aimed at his denial of ageing, the mutations in his body, his indignation at his fluctuating erectile capacities, and the general decline of his sexual performance. This reveals that he views masculinity as 'a *doing* rather than a *being*'[82] and that his main problem with ageing is, as John Stoltenberg puts it, his obsession with 'penile tumescence'.[83]

To top it all, he observes that Hama's interests are different from his own. While she does not like to stay at home and prefers to go out to restaurants and nightclubs and to own cell phones and luxurious cars, he would rather remain indoors, particularly since he cannot afford to go out. He also feels wary about going to the beach with her and exposing his ageing body. He does not want her to be revolted by the signs of ageing on the surface of his body, since youth must be seen in primarily visual terms, while the ageing body must be concealed. He does not want her to see the dense hair on his body and his revolting big mole, especially since the doctor had advised him not to expose it to the sun. The doctor also advised him to be moderate in his sexual relationships, as they would have dire effects on his prostate gland. Behind the humour lie acute feelings of alienation, isolation, and a strong sense that youth and age are irreconcilable, that ageing is closely aligned with the body, and that he is basically an 'embodied social agent'.[84]

Standing on the line between the old and the new world, he experiences the harsh pull of history and change, and he comes to the bitter realisation that his potency is abating and that sexuality is the domain of the young, causing him frustration and 'narcissistic trauma over his waning and unpredictable sexual performance'.[85] To compensate, he thinks of telling Hama that he loves her, but he knows it is not easy for a man in his sixties 'to say it like a young man'.[86] He begins to understand what it means to be outside the norm of youthful sexuality. As Edward H. Thompson puts it, 'in most discourses one can be masculine and one can be old, but not both'.[87]

Since he has internalised socio-cultural values about physical ageing and decline, his condition deteriorates. His sister tells him that a relation with an insatiable youthful woman who would not be content with one man will lead to loss of honour and dignity. She complains that while she is taking care of their mother, he is 'drowned' up to his ears in his affairs with young women, which is unbecoming at his age. She accuses him of violating the norms of propriety through his juvenile behaviour, and that in order to avoid social humiliation, he needs to put an end to sexual indulgences and behave as an old man ought to.

Since he is unable to use Viagra, he tries to recuperate his sexual prowess by securing a stock of pornographic films to be used as aphrodisiacs at the right moment, although he feels ashamed of himself. He watches a pornographic film before Hama arrives, since he believes that sustained 'sexual functionality and potency' is the only way to resist ageing,[88] but when she suggests that they take their time, his enthusiasm wanes and he loses his erection. His strategy to mend fences between them is undercut by Hama's desire to take her time, which puts him on the defensive. Despite his desire to control Hama, he ends up occupying a subordinate position in relation to a woman who appears to be winning the battle of youth against age.

Hama dumps him when she finds a man of her 'generation' whose age is more 'appropriate',[89] and the narrator's devastation is complete, particularly since his model of manliness is the younger man. By preferring a younger man, Hama succeeds in dismantling the narrator's masculinity. He never thought that he would ever experience 'such deep effusive and strong passion', but now he feels crushed and humiliated and harks back to his father's words: 'the ugliest quality in a human being is his need of a woman especially his sexual need because it makes him lose his honour, and dignity'.[90] The shattering humiliation that he experiences is linked with his deeply ingrained belief that old age is solely about processes dominated by a 'decline ideology'.[91] Rejecting *waqar* as a form of resignation from all desires, notably corporeal desire, transforms the body into the central signifier of old age, and renders his relationship with Hama even more complicated.

The narrator's affair with Hama ends lamentably when she leaves him eaten up by jealousy and desire for revenge, and with feelings of inferiority and wounded pride that smell of rankness and decay. He wonders how she had the heart to deal so irresponsibly with an old man, and views it as 'an assassination attempt'.[92] Like the male poet in the *Jahiliyya* who wept over deserted encampments (*al-buka' 'ala l-atlal*), the narrator weeps over lost youth (*al-buka' 'ala l-shabab*) and energy which are vital to his identity as a man. He is devastated, as he still has her love-letter in which she maintains that she is ready to have his child: ' "I dream of a child by you, who inherits your piercing eyes." '[93]

In considering his relation with Hama as 'a ray of light from eternity',[94] he builds castles in the air, making use of clichéd and exaggerated praise, and signalling irony at his own expense. Yet, when he surrenders to his fate, his body becomes visibly marked by age. He suffers from irregular heartbeats and has to take 'concor', which costs him 14 dollars a month. All this means more expenses as his salary is low and is decreasing with inflation. Since he has no insurance, he is forced to withdraw $2,000 from what he had saved for his old age to pay for his health problems, which have suddenly erupted after her departure. In addition to palpitations, he has urination irregularities and needs to visit the bathroom recurrently day and night, and suffers from a swelling in the prostate gland.

Consequently, he decides to retaliate by raising legal proceedings against her for inflicting a variety of damages to his health, including palpitations, amnesia and irregularities in his prostate gland. He imagines himself at a court of law asking the judge to give him justice, a man in his sixties who has lost the dream and has only one hope, which is to withdraw from this life silently and with dignity and with a minimum of pain and surprises. He seriously considers raising a case against her, but his attorney tells him that an affair between an old man and a young woman will cause a scandal, instigating shame and disgrace for the man.

This is a grimly humorous representation of the angsts of living for a man who feels that he is now on the brink of an abyss of vacuity, and existential malaise. It is what Hepworth and Featherstone refer to as the 'male menopause' where 'ageing into old age is perceived as problematic and in which the relationships between men and women are undergoing significant changes'.[95] His anger is transformed into deep grief, dejection, and an uncanny sense of the mysteriousness and the inevitability of the mortal condition. He admits that he is having memory lapses, which speak to his inner fears of dementia, especially since his mother is suffering from it. He recalls other incidents of forgetfulness: he left his apartment forgetting the keys in the door; he turned the gas key on and went out to return to the pungent smell of gas all over the place; he forgets people's names, especially when he is tired, and wonders how he is going to learn English.

He also complains about struggling to hear what his English teacher is saying. Pulling at both his ears and closing his eyes so as to be able to hear, he wonders whether his teacher is trying to stop herself bursting into laughter at such a sight. At his age, he realises that he needs to contend with the unforeseen prevalence of his corporeal body. When his friend Hassan dies of a heart attack, he is discouraged and sees the futility of all his efforts: 'Nothing will help Hassan now: whether he ate or drank or learned English at sixty.'[96]

His relation with Hama was his way of resisting senescence by restoring youthfulness. However, his desire for youthful vigour and potency betrays an inherent misogyny, where the woman herself is a scapegoat for his own problems with ageing. His affair with a young woman also betrays an uncanny dread of age and death and a tragic awareness of the close link between Eros and Thanatos, where death and desire are absurdly, but intricately, connected. While the narrator represents the old being trampled upon by the forces of youth and global modernity, al-Daif's ironic style reveals not closure but what Edward Said refers to as 'intransigence, difficulty, and unresolved contradiction'.[97]

Conclusion

In the earlier novels that focus on traditional values, men are depicted as figures of respect and veneration, like al-Sayyid in *Sugar Street* and the patriarch in *The Long Way Back*, who find refuge in religious faith and indulge in reminiscences of a blissful past. The texts in this chapter have examined a diverse group of older men who contradict and even subvert dominant stereotypes of manhood through the presentation of manhood as a problem. These men find refuge not in doting fatherhood or grand fatherhood, but in male homosocial relations and in 'trespassing generational boundaries'[98] by pursuing younger women, as seen in 'O.K. Goodbye' and 'The Lovers of Bayya'. 'The Lovers of Bayya' exposes images of frail old men who are no longer certain of their autonomy and sexual performance. Since the authorial narrator is a younger Tunisian man, these old men are exposed to the humiliating gaze of the narrator, who presents them as carnivalistic figures of mockery and hilarity. Other male characters also suffer humiliating exposure and defeat under the youthful male and female gaze.

Although Arab society cast men as figures of authority that should be revered, their manifestation in fiction is much more complex and fraught with ambiguity, especially in the denigrating portrayals of the ageing male body. Unlike traditional female characters who generally avoid allusions to sexuality, men's works are fraught with libido and complaints about sexual potency, cognitive decline and physical impairment. Through the lens of age, male writers raise concerns about diminished sexuality, physical attraction, the ability to attract younger women, and medical barriers to a potent sexuality. In a world of shifting values, they come to the realisation that the ethic that ruled the world is quickly vanishing and that older men are becoming more aligned with women. To borrow the words of Gullette, 'the medical/commercial forces that have been bringing women their public menopause are on the verge of bringing men their public climacteric'.[99] The narrator suffers from the 'borrowed'[100] male menopause, which is 'associated with a kind of midlife crisis, which in itself is less *of* a hormonal change than a change *in* life mostly related to work, status, cultural expectations, sexuality, and bodily imagery'.[101] Accordingly, older men, like women, are becoming more self-conscious about ageing, as seen in Rashid al-Daif's 'O.K. Goodbye', and about their vulnerability and feelings of obsolescence.

The differences among the old men in the novels subvert dominant stereotypes of ageing and reveal multiple masculinities in accordance with positionality, social setting, class, gender and economic factors, endorsing the fact that masculine identity in old age, as at any other life stage, is not secure but unstable and mobile. Despite the idiosyncrasies of each character, there remains some overlap among the representations. While these men insist on retaining a confident masculine identity through domestic and sexual control, the humour generated by the narratives conceals dreary lurking expectations of loss and sorrow that accompany the wearisome process of ageing.

Notes

1. Wyatt-Brown and Rossen, *Aging and Gender in Literature*, p. 1.
2. 'O.K. Goodbye', p. 56. All translations are mine.
3. 'The Lovers of Bayya', p. 14. All translations are mine.
4. Ibid., p. 7.
5. Ibid., p. 10.
6. Ibid., p. 11.
7. Ibid.
8. Ibid., p. 8.
9. Ibid., p. 23.

10. See Giddens, *Modernity and Self-Identity*, pp. 43–56.
11. *The Lovers of Bayya*, p. 72.
12. Ibid., p. 47.
13. Ibid., p. 48.
14. Ibid., p. 50.
15. Ibid., p. 51.
16. Ibid., p. 44.
17. Ibid., p. 182.
18. Ibid., p. 86.
19. Ibid.
20. Ibid., p. 88.
21. Ibid.
22. Ibid., p. 229.
23. *Borrowed Time*, p. 9.
24. Ibid., p. 9.
25. Ibid., p. 12.
26. Ibid., p. 11.
27. Ibid., p. 12.
28. Twigg makes a distinction between age resistance and age denial in 'The Body, Gender, and Age: Feminist Insights in Social Gerontology', p. 63.
29. *Borrowed Time*, p. 12.
30. Ibid., p. 14.
31. Ibid., p. 100.
32. Ibid., p. 106.
33. Ibid., p. 44.
34. Quoted in Cruikshank, *Learning To Be Old*, p. 17.
35. *Borrowed Time*, p. 48.
36. Ibid., p. 49.
37. Ibid., p. 18.
38. Ibid., p. 16.
39. Ibid., p. 56.
40. Ibid., p. 49.
41. Ibid., p. 75.
42. Ibid., p. 72.
43. Ibid., p. 73.
44. Ibid., p. 25.
45. Ibid., p. 24.

46. Ibid., p. 51.
47. Ibid., p. 71.
48. Ibid., p. 14.
49. Ibid., p. 89.
50. Ibid., p. 86.
51. Ibid., p. 97.
52. Ibid., p. 103.
53. Ibid., p. 101.
54. Ibid., p. 100.
55. Ibid., p. 99.
56. Ibid., p. 101.
57. Ibid.
58. Ibid., p. 133.
59. Twigg, 'The Body, Gender, and Age: Feminist Insights in Social Gerontology', p. 68.
60. *Borrowed Time*, p. 159.
61. Ibid., p. 160.
62. Ibid., p. 165.
63. Ibid.
64. Ibid., p. 96.
65. Featherstone and Wernick, *Imags of Aging*, p. 251.
66. 'O.K. Goodbye', p. 13.
67. Ibid., p. 14.
68. Ibid., p. 15.
69. Ibid.
70. Ibid., p. 19.
71. Ibid.
72. Ibid., p. 22.
73. Ibid., p. 16.
74. Ibid., p. 93.
75. Ibid., p. 150.
76. Hearn, 'Imaging the Aging of Men in Images of Aging', p. 102.
77. 'O.K. Goodbye', p. 41.
78. Ibid., p. 41.
79. Ibid., p. 42.
80. Quoted in Calasanti and Slevin, *Age Matters*, 142. See also Potts et al., 'The Downside of Viagra: Women's Experiences and Concerns', pp. 697–719.

81. Gullette, *Declining to Decline*, p. 147.
82. Spector-Mersel, 'Never-Aging Stories: Western Hegemonic Masculinity Scripts', p. 69.
83. Quoted in Gullette, *Declining to Decline*, p. 147.
84. Nettleton and Watson, 'Introduction', p. 9.
85. Segal, *Out of Time*, p. 78.
86. 'O.K. Goodbye', p. 45.
87. Thompson, 'Guest Editorial', pp. 1–4.
88. Marshall and Katz, 'Forever Functional', p. 45.
89. 'O.K. Goodbye', p. 22.
90. Ibid., p. 20.
91. Gullette, *Declining to Decline*, p. 122. See also pp. 132–5.
92. 'O.K. Goodbye', p. 51.
93. Ibid., p. 52.
94. Ibid., p. 111.
95. 'The Male Menopause' in The *Body in Everyday Life*, p. 287.
96. Ibid., p. 140.
97. Said, *On Late Style*, p. 7.
98. De Falco, *Uncanny Subjects*, p. 130.
99. Gullette, *Declining to Decline*, p. 116.
100. Quoted in Hepworth and Featherstone, 'The Male Menopause' in *The Body in Everyday Life*, p. 292.
101. Marshall and Katz, 'From Androgyny to Androgens', p. 84.

5

Yarns of Later Life: Transgressive Strategies

This chapter centres on ageing men and women who are confident enough to write about their ageing experiences as well as their personal lives, subverting traditional autobiography, which focuses exclusively on public achievement. The works affirm the importance of autobiographical writing, which tells of aspects of their lives that have been hitherto in the dark. Age is presented not as an experience that focuses on public achievement correlated in sequential order, but rather as an idiosyncratic and unstable phase that fluctuates between past and present, revealing that the later years are 'no longer the clearly defined or scripted period of life they once seemed'.[1]

The Palestinian/Lebanese writer Nazik Yared's semi-autobiographical novel *Improvisations on a Missing String* (1997) (*Taqassim 'la watarin Da'i'*, 1992) demonstrates the extent to which childhood and youth experiences could have a lasting effect on the individual's subsequent psychological and social development. The past infiltrates the present and exists only as it is remembered, created and re-created in its interaction with the present. For the narrator, this latter period is one of introspection, anxiety, and fears of possible illness and decline, as well as flight into the affairs of the present, particularly her work at school, where she finds succour with her students/children. Despite her sense of the fleetingness of life, especially after two operations, Saada is unwilling to disengage from life.

In the Palestinian writer Randa Khalidy's semi-autobiographical novel titled 'An Unheroic Autobiography' (*Sira Ghayr Butuliyya*, 2016), the narrator decides to abandon her earlier silence and speak her mind after being under the lifelong control of her husband and all he has represented. By writing her personal story, she liberates age from the constraints of stoicism and capitulation, and expresses her defiance against a life of neglect and erasure. Her narrative vacillates between past and present to give her a better understanding of the past and of her present situation. By so doing, she unveils the unique, idiosyncratic and unknowable aspect of her personality.

The third novel by the Lebanese writer Abbas Baydun, titled 'The Album of Defeat' (*Album al-Khasara*, 2012), depicts the repetitive daily life of a man in his sixties who feels that he is beginning to suffer from dementia and views his companion, his daughter's old cat, as an uncanny double that mirrors decline and death. In his present condition, he has no interest in nostalgic reminiscence and expresses impatience with memory, and his discourse is digressive, repetitive and touched by senile confusion that disrupts the progressiveness and causality of linear plotting, revealing the unpredictable experiential daily life of an old man.

Self-reflexive Reminiscences

The narrative centre of consciousness in Yared's semi-autobiographical novel *Improvisations on a Missing String* is the ageing female narrator Saada (Yared was 64 when she published the novel), who is lying in a hospital bed suffering from cancer. In contrast to her frail body on the bed, her pallid 'haggard' face and the 'blue veins so puffy and swollen',[2] her mind is active, announcing her internal journey into the self, which she undertakes by dwelling simultaneously on the present and the past. Unlike the narrator of 'A Woman of Fifty', who focuses on present action, Saada conjures up the past as a source of reflection and self-evaluation.

Living in close proximity with death (surgery, pain, insomnia, and fear of death), and conscious of her intense embodiment, she escapes the tyranny of a body suffering from cancer, through anecdotes and reminiscences that resurrect the past and enable her to reflect upon herself and make peace with the past, each recollection adding new significance and meaning. Her brief and fragmentary anecdotes of the past are reassessed through her present perspective in such a way that past and present intermingle and '"everything happens at once"'.[3] By recourse to her retrospective narrative, that covers her life in Jerusalem, Egypt and Lebanon, she tries to make sense of the past in light of her present situatedness in her hospital bed, making her story all the more poignant. Saada's story consists of anecdotes about her personal history, reflections on her present health problems, and speculations about a future of ageing, sickness and aloneness.

In her attempt to sum up her life 'as a whole, as if it were a coherent narrative',[4] she encounters gaps in her narration. The interplay between past and present disrupts linearity and interrogates a stable identity, replacing it with multiple versions of the self, or 'hybrid' selves in a 'state of perpetual transformation', as Valerie Anishchenkova refers to it.[5] This is a self in constant changeability, 'always in the process of coming together and of dispersing'.[6] In other words, these reminiscences reveal the self as fluid, amorphous and linked to social, political, economic and historical factors. Such instability dispels the idea of an authentic self, replacing it with more malleable versions of the self. In the face of looming death, she tries to make peace with diverse versions of herself, revealing 'the difficulty [of] plotting a life as a single, coherent narrative'.[7] Her reminiscences of the past are disjointed, focusing on incidents pieced together with the narrator as the sole link to these occurrences. These personal stories are historical, but also contingent upon her present situation and frame of mind, where clock time gives way to 'human time'[8] since it is measured by feelings that intersect with memories of the past and her present situatedness.

The intimate voice of the narrator is destabilised by the strange sick woman on the bed, who appears to have nothing in common with the 'I' that she has known all her life. The objectification of the bedridden woman by the 'I' narrator creates a sense of self-alienation, with the narrator disowning the woman that she sees herself becoming. The narrator shifts between first and third person, producing a narrative in which the first-person narrator often views her aged self as a distinct character. She refers to her sick self in the third person, a self metonymically linked with the hospital as a trope of disease, passivity, dependence and annihilation.

The narrator's sense of alienation from herself and her fear of death is manifested in her focus on the hospital room and on a print of Van Gogh's *Irises in a Jug*. The painting catches her eye, particularly 'the irises with the broken stems, their heads bowed down over the wooden table', revealing her ability to see relations between art and life and her identification with the artist's 'defeated spirit' and his failure 'to obliterate the certainty of death'.[9]

Lying in bed in hospital, Saada recalls her mother's philanthropic mission in the neighbourhood in Palestine, which consisted of assistance to the poor. For instance, she recalls how her mother helped the wife of an alcoholic to find a job, sent their children to school, and bought them school uniforms and books. She visited the poor and needy, but remained detached, standing apart from them and solidifying boundaries between the two classes. Saada maintains that she was prevented by her mother from befriending a girl whose father was a laundryman on the basis that 'we make friends from our own class, but the others we pity and help'.[10]

Saada is aware of her mother's double standards, but is unable to extricate herself from a woman who remains the pivotal point in her life. In fact, she herself has acquired her mother's snobbery and overweening attitude to the less privileged. When a woman abandoned by her husband falls ill, the narrator's mother calls on her, accompanied by Saada. The narrator describes a woman sleeping on a mattress without sheets, and covered with a torn blanket. She observes three filthy children playing with an aluminium plate and a spoon on a mat littered with rice and bits of mouldy bread. She tells us that her mother gives the children the chocolate she had bought them, and sits down on the sick woman's bed, talking to her with a great deal of sympathy. As for Saada herself, she tells us that she stands 'by the door disgusted, afraid of getting my clothes dirty if I sat on the only chair in the room'.[11] Even at this early age, Saada is class-conscious, moulded by her class, and unable to escape the marks left on her by her mother. When the 1948 Arab–Israeli war broke out, large numbers of the Palestinian population were displaced. Saada, who was a student in Cairo at the time, tells us that she was stunned to learn that her own sister Suha was in a refugee camp in Cairo and was horrified to think 'my sister Suha, beautiful Suha, alone among strangers, villagers, ruffians maybe?'.[12]

In her room in hospital, she realises that her bond with her family is much stronger than she had envisaged, and that her adoration of her mother started at an early age. She recalls how she watched her mother as she was preparing to go out:

> she would turn around in front of the mirror, checking her dress, straightening the line of her stockings, and putting back a strand of hair that had fallen out of place. She would sit down to apply eyeliner, put on rouge,

lipstick . . . when the fragrance of Parfum des Anges, her favorite perfume, tickled my nostrils, I felt that I was the happiest child.[13]

Her mother's and sister's beauty – their green eyes, slim figures, upturned noses – fills her with jealousy and resentment. It makes her deeply aware of her own lack, which leaves a strong impact on her choices in life, resulting in spinsterhood.

In actual fact, her relationship with her mother is fraught with contradictions, with love and hate that vacillate over the years. The narrator is devastated when she overhears her mother's friend commenting on Saada's looks: '"If only she [Saada] looked more like you, or her sister even!"' What makes it worse for Saada is that her mother had already considered a solution to Saada's problem: '"she's intelligent. She can keep studying; enter some profession so she won't need a husband to provide for her."'[14] Being an urban upper-middle-class Christian woman, Saada's mother believes that her daughter ought to fend for herself through education and a job, and not end up a servant to her brothers or father inside the home, as in the case of Nahleh in *The Inheritance*. Since a woman is defined by her beauty and the ability to draw the admiring male (and female) gaze, Saada's appearance does not fit into prevalent cultural discourses of female beauty. As a result, she is masculinised and dispossessed of her sexuality and femininity. Through 'better education' and her mother's modern 'perception of women's role', Saada confronts the stigma of spinsterhood.[15]

The impact of this incident has a lasting effect on Saada, isolating her from her family. In her room in Jerusalem, she stands

> before the mirror, examining my reflection: medium height, slightly plump; sleek black hair gathered in two braids; olive complexion; small, dark, sparkling eyes; a small, snubby nose; an average-sized mouth with full lips . . . So I was ugly. Sitt Wadad thought I was ugly. Mama thought I was ugly. I scrutinized the image reflected in the mirror: my ugly face; my short fat, ugly body.[16]

Her narrative voice is angry, bitter, and loathing.

Yet, such discourses about female beauty in occupied Palestine were inextricably bound up with colonial values and power, and Saada soon comes face to face with her alterity. When she is sent by her mother to the house of Mrs Setney to pick up a book, Mrs Setney's cold 'steely blue eyes'[17] stared at her condescendingly; she shuts the door in the girl's face and keeps her waiting outside. Saada concludes that the British woman thinks she is a thief, and her immediate reaction is that she is treated in this manner because she does not possess the colonial standard of beauty. She is considered 'ugly, dark-skinned, because I wasn't blonde like her, like my [German] friend Kristel?'[18]

Realising that her country is under British rule, she becomes aware of her subordinate position, and to compensate for her sense of inferiority she tries to imitate and adopt the values of the coloniser and his model of beauty. Anishchenkova describes Saada's physiological difference as an 'abnormality' and maintains that cancer has given her what she had always wanted: 'The disease makes [her body] slim and gives the dark skin the desperately desired whiteness.'[19] Such an interpretation runs contrary to Saada's real problem, which can be described as cultural ambivalence as Homi Bhabha refers to it. As a colonised subject, Saada internalises the coloniser's values, education system and models of beauty, that denigrate the culture of subjugated people. This leads to a negative self-image and disparagement of one's own culture and values. The trauma of cultural displacement that she endures in her homeland is referred to by Bhabha as 'unhomeliness',[20] which causes her a sense of geographical and psychological alienation, and frames her as 'subaltern', a woman who experiences double colonisation under the twofold subjugation of colonialist and patriarchal ideologies.

The British pedagogic project in Palestine propagated colonial, cultural and educational values. Saada's mother wanted her to study medicine, but even her mother does not know that schooling under colonial rule teaches British rather than Arab history, and bars girls from subjects such as biology to stop them from going into professions such as the medical profession or other professions monopolised by men. Saada's sense of degradation and ambivalence impel her to transgress the colonial discourse by studying Arabic literature at the university, her subaltern resistance to this cultural colonisation, in order to restore the dignity of her nation.

In her attempt to understand her family's behaviour, Saada allows her sister a voice and ownership in her own autobiography, feeling an obligation to give her sister space to express her own point of view.²¹ If Saada feels disparaged and abandoned by her family, Suha has similar feelings towards her sister. The latter, who is accorded a voice in Saada's autobiography, views the young Saada as 'So arrogant! How I hated her! Our teachers – it never occurred to any of them that comparing me with Saada only increased my contempt, loathing, and resentment.'²² On her side, Saada attributes her family's lack of interest in her studies in Egypt to their jealousy and sense of inferiority. Feeling that the world sees her as 'other', she is always alone with her books away from the company of her family and friends. Education is her sole weapon against her feelings of inferiority in a society that has doubly de-sexualised and de-feminised her.

As an older woman, Saada is critical of her 'chameleon' self that changes in accordance with external circumstances, provoking a disorienting unsteadiness and creating mutability rather than stability. Her autobiography is an amalgam of the selves that she had been, that have generated 'complex layerings of identity'.²³ Saada combines multiple selves: Palestinian, Egyptian, Lebanese. In Egypt, she speaks with an Egyptian accent that cannot be distinguished from the accent of any local, and her Egyptian experience gives her a sense of belonging that she had never felt in her native land.

Taking part in a demonstration in Cairo, she sees all 'the physical and cultural differences between me and them [the Egyptians]' disappear. She sees herself submerged 'in that awe-inspiring and tumultuous sea'²⁴ of protesters. When she hears of the four students who were killed, she weeps: 'I didn't know who they were, nor to which college they belonged, but I never felt they were any different from me.'²⁵ Her estrangement is transformed to a sense of belonging where 'differences' become 'similarities'.²⁶ She discovers that she feels at home in Egypt and a stranger in her own family. She maintains that at home, she felt inferior to her mother and sister, who regarded her as fat and dark-skinned, but in Egypt no one disapproved of darkness or obesity.

Her multiple voices and identities are her way of coping with a sense of lack, ostracism and 'unhomeliness': as an angry young woman whose outer appearance does not match up with ideals of beauty; a confidant and proud student in Egypt; an unmarried teacher devoted to her career; and a middle-aged woman confronting cancer and death. Unlike that of her sister Suha, who is 'a rock, a rock firmly rooted in [her Palestinian] ground',²⁷

Saada's identity is unstable, and she yearns for her sister's sense of stability and belongingness.

However, years later Saada is ready to acknowledge that it was her own pride that drove her away from her sister. Her negative attitude to her sister, mother and other members of her family begin to change when she realises that she misunderstood their behaviour because of her stubborn self-centredness and anger with herself at looking different. For her part, her sister recalls how Saada helped her father rain blows on Suha because of her low grades at school, which made her lie to her father and tell him that she had lost her school report card. However, for Suha, all this is now forgotten and she feels 'a wave of compassion surge in her heart'.[28] She recalls 'the skeletal form' of her mother slumped on the bed, 'her cheek bones and nose protruding from under the transparent, yellowish skin' with one glimmer of life coming out of 'her green eyes which seemed so much larger because she was so thin . . . Cancer had eaten into her bones, leaving nothing but an empty shell.'[29] Watching over her sister in the hospital, Suha wonders whether Saada is going to suffer her mother's fate, and a shudder runs through her frame.

As a middle-aged woman, Saada comes to the conclusion that belonging is not about 'wearing a dress and then putting on another a month or a year later',[30] nor is it about changing one's accent in accordance with external circumstances. Family roots are deeper than she had assumed, and she realises that she is tied to her family by an indissoluble bond. Life-review helps her to come to a better understanding of her family and herself, to bring closure to her lifelong anxieties through narrative therapy. Even in Muslim Egypt, where she feels a strong sense of belonging, she continues to go to church each Sunday, revealing a deeper link with her family and her Christian identity, 'which showed me my [religious] faith was only another facet of the strong bond that tied me to them'.[31]

When an old lover visits her in hospital after a lapse of twenty-two years, she comes to the realisation that he abandoned her not because of her looks, but because of her religion; his wife is a Muslim like himself. With her clarity of vision as an experienced middle-aged woman, she is able to see the religious barriers that separate them and realises that differences in life are diverse and do not rotate solely around one's physical appearance. Ali Saber, a man she loved twenty-two years before, sends her flowers and visits her with his wife in hospital. She receives them without manifesting any trepidation about her changing looks or her ageing appearance after the lapse of time. Saada has succeeded in promoting her intellectual and professional life, while de-sexualising herself and sidelining her corporeality, although her body continues to plague her in her present illness. Although she sees her body as a site of abjection, disease and decay, she is not about to hide it from her former lover or express any feelings of shame about her appearance.

As an older woman suffering from cancer, she becomes emotionally dependent on her family. When her sister tells her that she needs to eat in order to gain strength, she prefers to sleep: 'I just need sleep. Didn't Mama say when Nadia was born that sleep was more important to a child than eating?'[32] Feeling like a child reveals her vulnerability and dependency. Now she is unable to escape the trap of her corporeality, her body turning into a potential site of infirmity and decrepitude. When she learns that her sister Suha and her family are emigrating to Canada away from the civil war raging in Lebanon, she feels hollow and alienated:

> There would be no more spending the weekend with Suha, no more calling her every evening to tell her about what had happened that day, to listen to her news. There would be no Suha to show the new dress she had bought, to tell when she got a raise . . . They would go away, and behind them would be left an emptiness of time and space as an eternal reminder of their presence . . . and absence.[33]

Sitting on the balcony gazing at the sea at sunset, she becomes aware of approaching finitude and decline as she watches the receding waves on the shore:

> Glimmering on its surface here and there, flecks of white edged closer and closer. As they moved across the surface of the sea, they turned into ripples – wide, wide ripples which gathered momentum as they came nearer, rising and rolling, their crests crowned with glittering silver before crashing onto the shore in a creamy foam . . . their force spent, leaving on the sand their wet footprints.[34]

The Lebanese war erodes family support and separates families, leaving the older members alone and defenceless. The demise of the extended family is accelerated by the war, and the sudden changes that occur force the younger members to build a future outside the country and away from the family. Now that her sister and her family are thousands of miles away, Saada will be alone and has to cope with another relapse and endure another operation by herself. Constrained by illness, she sees the precariousness of life and the lonely fate awaiting her.

She comes to the realisation that her past choices were disappointing. She discovers that at her age, she has no single friend to tell her fears to or to comfort her. She has acquaintances, colleagues, but not a single friend. She recalls people's opinion of her as conceited and arrogant, and now she is paying the price for her superior attitude and knowing airs, and she discovers that agency in old age is rooted in family, community and social relations, and envisages a lonely old age. She declares her love for children and admits that teaching has always been a form of compensation: 'I love teaching because I love children . . . My students are my children.'[35] Education was only a second choice that erased her femininity, denoting the 'incompatibility between education and the proper development of womanhood'.[36]

Having erased her body and sexuality, and having no friends to lean upon, she anticipates a forsaken and ailing old age. If she is self-critical and conciliatory, she is also cynical and bitter. She questions her achievements as a teacher and sees the failure of her choices and the futility of being a *'successful teacher'* and wondering *'compared to whom?'* Now, all that she is left with are her students with their 'dull and mediocre' assignments: 'What great comfort and consolation!'[37] She feels the futility and emptiness of life in a war-torn Lebanon and wonders whether nationalism and Arabic literature have any value in a ferocious place where militancy is the dominant mood, and where people's very existence has become precarious.

Harbouring a strongly cynical attitude about her choices, she suddenly discovers that her former students still love her and value the education she has given them. One of her students, who is studying medicine, happens to be at the hospital when she had her second operation and asks another friend to look after her. Another student is there when she wakes from anaesthetic, although she mistakenly thinks it is Suha. She feels proud of her achievements as a teacher who is loved and respected by her students. After the operation, the doctor informs her that no cancerous cells were found in her lungs. Feeling relieved, she forgets her earlier despondency and can hardly wait to go home and back to her students. She is unwilling to disengage from life because of growing old, and more importantly, she is determined to carry out her own sense of 'age identity'[38] by 'deconstructing age ideology and constructing optimal resistance to its narratives',[39] although she is aware of the limitations of ageing. Accordingly, she goes back to her school and immerses herself in work, though at the back of her mind she sees a future of ageing, sickness and aloneness. Her story does not end in closure, but in a determination to abandon bewilderment and uncertainty and return to her daily routine despite lurking fears about the possible recurrence of her disease.

From Margin to Centre

The female narrator in Khalidy's 'An Unheroic Autobiography' (*Sira Ghayr Butuliyya*, 2016) is the central consciousness of this autobiographical novel written when the author was 80. The story is addressed to a special reader who is in a position to understand her situation and empathise with her. Addressing such a narratee, she is at liberty to focus on herself without inhibitions. At eighty, she does not feel obliged to please any one and is ready to speak her mind and uncover her thoughts and feelings. Unlike traditional male autobiography that derives identity from personal achievements, hers is described as an 'unheroic' journey that has erased her and stifled her voice. The reason she gives for publicising intimate details of her personal life is her wish to resuscitate and heal herself before it is too late. Instead of atrophy and decay associated with old age, she manifests a vibrant spirit and an indefatigable desire to write herself through a first-person narrative where her life is seen through the lens of subjectivity and personal experience, and where she projects herself as a forceful 'biographical being' and not just a 'biological' being or a 'social construction'.[40] While she embraces an active late life, she remains conscious of imminent possibilities of frailty, illness, forgetfulness, disability, dependency, and the inevitable 'condition of human transience'.[41]

Her autobiography focuses predominantly on her present life as an octogenarian widow, her relationship with her husband and other fragmented occurrences in her life, especially those related to her childhood in Jerusalem. The dialogue between past and present selves also makes it possible for her to come to terms with the various thorny issues that have plagued her marital life. The interplay of past and present challenges linear notions of time and chronology common to traditional narratives, and replaces them with a sense of synchrony where past and present interpenetrate.

Her story is punctuated with digressions and memory lapses that disrupt linearity and chronology, challenge established cultural and social norms, and convey a sense of freedom in old age that makes her indifferent to what people might say about her, as well as providing her with an increased sense of self-worth and power rather than deterioration and decline. Hers is a journey backwards and forwards in time undertaken in her 'everyday time-travelling'.[42] As an elderly woman living alone in Damascus, she is constantly interrupted by the past, affirming a more fluid notion of the life course where time is conceived as cyclical rather than linear.

The narrator fluctuates between past and present to the extent that, at times, past and present occur simultaneously, as when she recalls her husband's past remarks about her 'bourgeois' attitude, such as her keeping track of and celebrating birthdays of loved ones. Her struggle with Hassan, her husband, persists even after his death. She continues to talk to him as if he were alive by addressing the photograph on her desk, revealing the porous boundary between the living and the dead. She is conscious that the reader, like her husband, might view the practice of commemorating birthdays as a hateful bourgeois practice that comes from the West and as totally unrelated to Arab culture, but now she voices her opinion and asserts that she finds no problem with birthdays: 'Let it be. I am not the only one. Besides, holding birthdays for the ones we love and even celebrating one's birthday [her eightieth] alone as I am about to do does not hurt anyone.'[43]

Through a self-reflexive process, she attempts to understand her equivocal relation with her husband, and her attitude to him is one of fluctuating endorsement and rejection. For instance, she blames herself for naively searching for romantic love in her marriage and sees her husband's attitude as more honest and genuine. She admits that she is the by-product of Hollywood and Egyptian films of the 1950s and 1960s which portray 'legendary paradises'[44] and romantic love. But her husband never pretended to be romantic and believed that her feelings were trivial and impractical.

After her husband's death, and being tired of her earlier 'Bedouin'[45] diplomatic life as an ambassador's wife, she decides to live in a small apartment in Damascus and maintain no communication with the ghosts of the past, her earlier friends and acquaintances. Now, she has an apartment of her own in Damascus and is happy to be alone and sedentary after a long life of travelling and mobility. Rather than taking place in a vacuum, the narrator's ageing experience intersects with social, cultural and demographic dynamics that shape her personality and make her distinctly different from other women her age. Her social class and education determine her lifestyle in old age, and enable her as an old woman to live alone, be independent, and enjoy spatial mobility, intellectual buoyancy and heightened alertness and energy. She eats when hungry and is not bound by anyone, and does not need any commitments or social engagements. At this age she is careful about what she eats, and avoids watermelon, which causes gastronomic problems and is in itself nothing but 'water and sugar in red colour'.[46] She no longer worries about her weight after spending many years depriving herself of the pleasures of food in order to preserve her 'shapeliness'.[47]

Now she has 'a room of [her] own',[48] and avoids all commitments and engagements. Despite her strong sense of individual control, she is aware that she is no longer able to cut her toenails as she cannot reach them anymore. It is clear that she is also aware of prospects of infirmity and dependency in old age, especially since she is 80. Looking more closely at her husband's photograph on her desk, she suddenly realises that she no longer needs anybody's permission to disclose feelings and thoughts that have haunted her with a strong sense of urgency and persistence. She maintains that she does not need to consult with him any longer and does not want to. As an octogenarian, she feels free to do what she likes, without a husband who has controlled her life, decisions and mind. She no longer relies on his approval regarding her self-worth or conforms to societal demands and assumptions regarding her actions and thoughts, conscious of the widening gap between her 'private sense of self-in-time, and the stripped and distorted version of age identity' that is imposed on her.[49] She focuses on aspects of her life that have been trivialised and effaced in an effort to resuscitate a self which is swamped in oblivion.

In her reminiscences, she explodes stereotypes of the older woman and challenges dominant discourses of old age. Through her autobiography, she achieves agency by challenging the patriarchal and social values that have silenced and marginalised her. She talks of her sexuality and of potentially compromising incidents in her relationship with her deceased husband. Her journey from past to present challenges notions of weakness in old age by demonstrating a 'newly self-knowledgeable, self-confident, and individual' person.[50] She admits that she fell in love with Hassan [her husband] because both of them realised that the chemistry between them was strong and that their sexual attraction could not be underestimated. Despite her sexual inhibitions fostered by the nuns at school where she studied, and her awareness of the 'estrangement between myself and my body',[51] she discovers on her wedding night hitherto hidden 'abilities'[52] that she thought she did not possess. She admits that many a time she had imagined herself in his arms, but she never expected 'the softness and understanding'[53] that he displayed on their first night together.

As a younger woman, she dreamed of playing an active role in the Palestinian struggle and Arab women's rights. When her husband is serving the Syrian Ministry of Foreign Affairs in New York, she decides to return to Damascus and commit herself to her 'Palestinian-ness', join the resistance, have military training, wear a military uniform, stay up late at night, and take to smoking, because ironically, the 'struggle does not work without smoking'.[54] She tells us that during the period of military training, she contented herself with eating chickpeas and falafel, which caused her skin to become coarse.

She worked with a Palestinian fighter named Abu al-Fidaa, and since she viewed him as a Guevara figure she allowed 'herself to fall in love with him'.[55] Heedless of the consequences, she invited him to dinner at her place. When she put the food on the table he pounced upon it and began eating voraciously, filling his mouth with huge morsels, totally oblivious to her presence and indifferent to whether she was eating or not. When he finished 'munching and swallowing',[56] he sat next to her and put his arm around her: 'How dare he treat me as if I were a sexual object . . . a hungry man finishing his dinner and now it is dessert time.'[57] This mocking tone trivialises her role in the resistance as well as her insipid ideals about the resistance, and resistance fighters. At eighty, she sees the ludicrousness and frivolity of her brand of nationalism and mocks her 'adolescent' behaviour.[58]

Furthermore, she has no scruples about divulging her infidelities when her husband was stationed for two years in New York while she remained in

Damascus teaching English Literature at the university. When she discovers that her colleague at work was in love with her, she blames herself and attributes his conduct to her coquettish personality and injudicious behaviour. As a result, when she gives him a watch on his birthday, he is shocked and embarrassed, and ventures to kiss her on the mouth in front of everyone in the restaurant.

Living with her husband in an unnamed European country, she spends long hours looking in the mirror, scrutinising new wrinkles, and wondering whether Hassan is attracted any longer to her face, body, hair, or even the touch of her skin. In an attempt to seduce him, she buys a lavish piece of lingerie 'which fascinated me, stirred my instincts, and made me nostalgic to the past, to my frozen femininity, my desires and the passionate nights that I have not tasted for many long months'.[59] However, he does not even notice her sexy night garment, which makes her feel shame and humiliation: 'There I am offering myself to you begging you to love me, but you turn your face as if you have not seen me.'[60]

Even though her story can be potentially scandalous in a patriarchal society, it is also empowering in that it enables her to challenge the social expectation that, as an old woman, she must remain invisible, submissive and attendant to the needs of others. Hers is a defiant idiosyncratic brand of ageing navigated by an autobiographical journey that challenges normative views of ageing for women and transgresses the boundaries of the 'sacrosanct space' of the family, as Souad Joseph refers to it.[61] At eighty, and living alone in Damascus since the death of her husband twenty years before, she is no bitter frustrated old woman. She is active and independent, 'declining to decline',[62] challenging the rules attributed to the behaviour of old women in the Arab world, 'undisciplining' normative constructions of ageing and subverting 'dominant truth-making practices'.[63]

Unlike the two old women in *The Long Way Back*, who are imprisoned within the inner space and are at the mercy of the father/patriarch and the younger women in the family, the narrator is at liberty to do what she wants. She writes her reminiscences without any external pressure, especially since she comes from a privileged family and holds a Ph.D. Her autonomous individuality as a woman is the result of the intersection of gender, class and geography, which give her the physical, mental and financial resources to grow even at this late stage and pursue successful ageing. At present, she is unwavering about freeing a self, long held captive by the rigid rules imposed by her husband.

At eighty, she turns the latter part of her life into a distinct period of ripeness, self-appraisal and psychological growth. In her old age, she challenges normative constructions of old women in her society through a discourse of resistance expressed through her reminiscences and the kind of life she lives in the present. Her *reifungsroman*, or 'novel of ripening',[64] is her 'resistance discourse'[65] and declaration of agency through artistic consciousness. It is an attempt to restore a bruised self, to reintegrate neglected aspects of herself in order to recover her voice, and to achieve autonomy and authenticity by reclaiming the masculine assertive side of her personality. Conscious of her own temporality, she sees her autobiography as her way of perpetuating her life beyond the grave, seeking immortality, entering history, and leaving a trace of herself to posterity.

Admitting that she has forgotten her favourite granddaughter's birthday, she is all the more determined to keep track of all her children's and grandchildren's birthdays in her elegant leather copybook, which she consults daily, fearing possible forgetfulness or dementia since her 'memory cannot hold all these dates'.[66] She recalls how her deceased brother described their mother's forgetfulness:

> If we assume that memory is like a wardrobe where we put all our clothes, we will discover that the wardrobe will fill with time so that we need to cram them in. As we add new clothes, the wardrobe can no longer take them in so the new garments fall off. The same with memory which retains the old recollections, making it very difficult to preserve more recent reminiscences.[67]

In her notebook, she records the items she needs to buy: a birthday card for her son, vitamins, cotton and shampoo, stockings, nylon tights, pure honey, biscuits for the cat, the newspaper *al-Hayat*, and flowers on her way back home. These items reveal her desire to maintain a brand of healthy ageing, retain her old habits, take care of her pets and keep abreast of political developments in the area without forgetting the flowers that she buys regularly as a sign of her aesthetic predisposition.

In her narrative, she bridges the gap between the living and the dead by making use of multiple traces such as archival photographs, family albums, postcards, letters, geographical sites, historical allusions and dreams. In her sitting-room, she keeps photographs of loved ones both alive and deceased, and the walls where she hangs them are her 'museum of photographs'.[68] Among her collection of photographs are the ones that belong to her deceased husband, Hassan, whose photograph also appears on her desk, where he wears 'a light brown suit' and sits 'on a swing on the farm staring at the camera'.[69] This photograph sums up her husband's character; he looks 'reproaching, and contemplative, as if he underestimated the photographer's skill, or with his long diplomatic training remains cautious about advancing any opinion [to the photographer]'.[70]

Being possessed of spatial freedom, mobility and personal independence, she decides to visit an old friend who is suffering from dementia and has been installed by his family (living in London) in the *Dar al-Saʿada* [Home of Happiness] shelter in Damascus. She enters the place, which houses so many of her earlier acquaintances. Since her aim is not to encroach upon ghosts of the past, she covers her face in order not to be recognised by other residents of the refuge. She chooses this friend in particular because she feels sorry for an abandoned old man. Knowing that he liked to play Scrabble, she decides to have a few games with him, but she suddenly observes that he is wearing a nightgown without his pants on, making his sexual organ clearly visible. Feeling panicky, she decides to leave as she did not want anyone to have ideas, particularly since any association with sex in old age, or 'geriatric sex' as Gullette refers to it,[71] is culturally inconceivable, especially in a traditional Damascene society where such an incident would make her the laughing stock of Syrian society. This scene of comic 'exposure' transgresses the system and challenges gender hierarchies where the old man is positioned in a subordinate situation in relation to the old woman.

The view that sanctions old men's sexuality is deconstructed by the narrator's own brother, who decides to forget masculinity when he turns sixty; he no longer feels the need to compete with other men and he maintains facetiously that he no longer constitutes any danger to the other sex. Referring to his sexual organ, he declares jokingly, 'I shot him. Now he has eternally rested allowing others to rest too.'[72] The narrator's sense of humour pervades the work, underpinning a strong rebellious spirit that does not abandon her throughout her life. What really distresses her is the fact that the sense of humour or coquetry that was part of her relationship with Hassan vanishes over the course of their marriage. Regretfully, they find themselves wrapped up in rigid officialdom as if they had become truly serious about their 'diplomatic roles'[73] when in the early days of their marriage; they used to make fun of it. Her sense of humour never abandons her, especially when she jibes at the diplomatic circle that her husband belonged to, and comments upon their lack of wit and imagination. She tells him sarcastically: 'You know, Hassan, I do not recall that anyone flirted with me or tried to seduce me in our long diplomatic life.'[74]

After a long, bitter experience, she voices her comments on Syrian society, which is marred with gossip and a warped understanding of religion. When the errand boy refers to her as *hajji* (pilgrim), she reacts, 'May you go on a lame camel to the hajj',[75] to stop him from bestowing the noble title of hajj on everyone, deservedly or undeservedly. At eighty she defies a society that believes that dogs are 'impure' in Islam, rages against their ignorance of Islam, and feels sorry that they will never understand the true meaning of a dog's 'truthfulness, loyalty and devotion',[76] which ironically her husband did not possess. Despite the fact that 'The Garden of Tishrin' bans dogs from entering, she removes the notice every time she takes her dog there and mentions that her dog's barking once saved her, her cat and the house from fire.

From the start, she has her critical views of Arab societies, especially of Syrian society, having lived there for a large portion of her life. Conscious that old women are more susceptible to 'the stigma attached to age'[77] than men, she tells us that she has read that old women have a distinct smell like the smell of 'rotten onion'[78] and that their urine has a very bad and revolting smell. She wonders if it is not enough to add more worries to women's problems when they have to endure tyranny in Arab/Islamic societies. However, mindful of the cultural internalisation of these views, she decides to air the apartment daily and make sure that no putrefied food is left to spoil the general odour of the house. Nevertheless, she admits that as a younger woman she bathed daily, but that today she fears for her lungs from the cold, especially since she is trying to economise on electricity and not turn the thermostat on every day. Another concern is denying the old woman the looks of admiration which had followed her for many years. In her view, this is 'a conspiracy to exclude the old, especially women, from society',[79] and she is determined to affirm in old age full personhood in a society that sanctions diminishment and obliteration.

At her age, she remains active and helps the errand boy regain his job after being beaten and spat on by his master. She also rescues a little girl whose 'thick black hair reaches the middle of her back'[80] from the lap of a perverted shopkeeper who appeared not to have even noticed the old woman (the narrator) who was buying some items from the shop as he was busily trying to molest the child. She recalls how she herself was molested by a man who worked for her father and is all the more determined to take action; her strong resolve is an integral part of her active interaction with the community around her. She is not the serene, invisible, compliant grandmother, but rather a woman who reclaims her assertive, forceful self that she had struggled to revive unsuccessfully throughout her married life.

The narrator's feelings for Hassan remain ambivalent – a man whom she loved and hated. Despite the fact that she holds a doctorate and serves as a professor at Damascus University, she is obliged to give up her career to be an ambassador's wife and cater to her husband's needs. She still keeps his first letter to her written some fifty years before, which she describes as the letter of a businessman addressing his employee from a distance. She maintains that his communication with her consisted of a series of instructions: '"tell the ministry to stop sending the newspapers and magazines to the house."'[81] In addition to the first letter, she looks feverishly for a card that he sent her fifty years earlier where he expresses his love for her: '"My Darling, this picture summarizes my feelings for you. You are my first and last refuge."'[82] She remembers Hassan at the airport looking aristocratic and handsome and wearing a striped black suit, a white shirt and a tie, and admits that she cannot forget the red silk handkerchief hanging from his pocket, and the smell of 'the expensive male perfume whose thrilling scent'[83] still haunts her even now at her age.

Her mixed feelings towards him are reflected in a dream that she still remembers with trepidation:

> Sitting in a chair on the farm, I looked to the left and saw Hassan walking towards me soaking wet. He was wearing the shirt of his wine coloured pyjamas and very naked in his second half. He looked like a drowned man

who had succeeded in getting out of the water. He walked towards me . . . sat in my lap and relaxed. I touched his forehead and became convinced that he is dead and cold.[84]

She wakes up shaking, but never tells him about the dream. The dream is a trope of her conflicted feelings for him, represented by desire, marked by his nakedness; her mothering role, as revealed in his sitting on her lap; and his death, representing her fear of losing him as well as her desire to rid herself of him. Such contradictory feelings reveal her inability to fathom or understand a man full of incongruities, although his 'love' letter reveals his dependence on her in times of sudden vulnerability.

She maintains that Hassan's official career is the love of his life, to the extent that it has become 'an official co-wife'.[85] Whenever she complains about his lack of feeling, his reaction is one of mockery and derision, wondering whether she wants him 'to knock at the door with a red rose between my teeth'.[86] Hassan is a man she could not gauge being cold, detached and cynical. She tells the reader that he was reclusive and depressive, and had an aversion to impassioned feelings; he was secretive, reticent and private like the Sphinx, and owing to his reserve and emotional stinginess she is unable to understand his icy coldness because in her own family people are not ashamed to express their feelings. For example, when Hassan hits his head against a porcelain statue, he bleeds profusely. She panics and bursts out crying, but he remains calm and silent as if he were waiting for the actress [his wife] to finish her role on the stage and disappear behind the curtain. The allusion to Shakespeare's famous soliloquy in *Macbeth* points to her educational background and aligns her husband's fate with the tragic fate of Macbeth. When she staggers and bruises her lip he does not even notice, and her reaction is 'Hassan does not see me'.[87] Unlike her husband, the narrator was raised in a liberal family where the mother was a renowned women's rights activist (Anbara Salam Khalidy)[88] and where there was no discrimination between male and female children.

According to the narrator, Hassan has a convoluted personality that inclines towards dejection and gloom, and he is unsteady and temperamental. She tried to avoid clashing with him, but he always pushes her to lose control and use swear-words to defend herself, especially when she fails to get any reaction from him, or when he silences her with a cynical comment. The narrator admits that she was the one who started the arguments because she 'needed to attack the one who simplified my femininity and totally ignored me as a woman'.[89] Her present insurgent voice is consistent with her earlier habits, fits of anger and protests against her marginalisation. Such anger and frustration coincide with a rebellious narrative that gives her agency after a long period of marginalisation and ineffectiveness.

Thinking that Damascene people approved of her, she tries to accommodate them, but they do not reciprocate the respect she has always held for them. Moving from a liberal background in Lebanon to conservative Damascus, she tries to avoid confrontations, but now she is no longer willing to compromise and is determined not to change her habits to please such rigid people. As an old woman, she no longer accepts playing a secondary role to anyone and will defend herself and speak her mind.

She tells us that despite her education and intelligence, she ends up a sidekick to her husband, and admits that her role in the diplomatic corps was simply 'cosmetic'.[90] Living in a closed society, she knows that she will be the target of gossip if she leaves her husband alone in Europe and returns to her academic job in Damascus. To justify to herself her willingness to leave her academic job and serve her husband, she decides to allude to her domestic work not as a duty, but as her 'touch of love'[91] for Hassan and her children. However, he takes her for granted and insists on relegating her to a mere housewife, the butt of his humour and sarcasm. For instance, he pokes fun at her melodramatic sentimentality by wondering whether she had added a 'touch of love' to the spaghetti sauce or had 'honoured' his navy suit that needed cleaning with a 'touch of love'. His tendentious jokes reveal the violence behind his cynical remarks. When in New York, she tells him that she is unable to cope with the children and the home and that she misses her family and friends and wants to return to Syria, and he responds sarcastically: 'What did you expect in New York, my love . . . a palace in the outskirts of Manhattan or a British Nanny for the children?'[92] His cynical comment is aimed at her class and her bourgeois attitude. This lack of appreciation makes her feel bitter, scorned and demeaned, and her memoirs are her attempt to reclaim her integrity and individuality by writing back to the 'coloniser', her husband.

While she remains critical and sees the drawbacks of the Syrian Ministry of Foreign Affairs, she maintains that for Hassan the ministry 'was above reproach', and any criticism was a form of 'heresy'.[93] His devotion was such that he dedicated all his intellectual, physical and moral abilities to it. Whenever they returned home from a dinner or diplomatic party, he would lecture her on any injudicious behaviour, and what she should do or not do. He makes it clear that she should not laugh in a loud voice, giggle, or have a cigarette in one hand and a glass of alcohol in the other. As far as she is concerned, Hassan did not see in diplomacy anything that is funny or entertaining; it was a solemn undertaking, with its own rules and rituals, and its own protocol that do not allow the exchange of honest views, whether personal or political.

She admits that her role as the wife of a diplomat contradicts her spontaneous and open personality, which she admits is incompatible with her husband's rigidity. He makes it clear to her that she must clip her wings, stifle her enthusiasm and refrain from expressing any personal opinion or engage in any political argument. She soon discovers that all the serious work falls within his field of specialisation, while she takes care of all that is trivial and irrelevant. She asserts that now that they have reached a high diplomatic position, 'we are considered pioneers of this regime and are grounded in it. We are now part of a society that spends its time attending parties, dinners and cocktails, a social group whose insipid and petty news covers social magazines and newspapers'.[94] Being swamped in such a society, she maintains that she began to use diplomatic/political terminology in her daily life. When her relationship with her husband deteriorates, she tells us that she had no choice but to 'declare war' on him and 'lay mines along the length of the borders between them'.[95] She also describes the cold relationship between Hassan and her mother as a 'diplomatic estrangement'.[96]

Despite her submersion in her husband's diplomatic world, she is critical of the Foreign Ministry, which is indifferent to the diplomat's family and deals with it in a slapdash, apathetic and inhuman manner. They do not take into consideration the interrupted education of children, or whether the wife has a job in Syria or not, dealing with them in a chaotic and inhuman manner. As a result, she tells us that the Foreign Ministry has failed to win her allegiance since it is in the service of a government that does not take the situation of those who serve it into consideration. Furthermore, the Government does not take the salaries of its employees into consideration, causing them to ignore their duties and focus on taking care of themselves by indulging in prohibited businesses and transactions.

Putting her husband's needs first, she ended up mothering him, a privilege that he took for granted and considered one of his 'earned rights'.[97] Even now at the age of eighty, she reproaches him for coming to her solely when his self-confidence is shaken, or when he is depressed. Sacrifice and self-denial were her way of dealing with him, while he continued to act like a spoilt child. At eighty, she becomes conscious of her role in spoiling him: 'No one had asked me to act like a slave'[98] or accept being a doormat to him. She admits that she chose this role of her own free will.

When he asks her to help him deal with a woman who was stalking him and threatening to expose him, the narrator responds immediately because she wants to prove to him that she loves him and that she is a devoted wife and mother, and quite capable of facing problems. She wanted him to admire and respect her, and to compare her behaviour with the impudence of that strange woman who is threatening his position, but who turns out to be his mistress. The narrator learns that the woman is pregnant and that she is threatening to kill herself and to tell the Ministry, the other 'bogey'[99] which is everything in her husband's life. The narrator wonders why she should help a man who has humiliated her for so long, but she stands by him.

Fearing an impending scandal related to the pregnant mistress, they return home, settle on a farm outside Damascus and live an ostracised life away from the outside world. This stage of their life on the farm remains shrouded in mystery. After her husband's death, the narrator asserts that she visits his grave intermittently although he had never asked her to, being an unbeliever. However, the scars have not healed, and despite her indignation her resentment against his mistress remains tragically strong:

> Suppose I went to visit him and saw an old woman dressed in black weeping and wailing? . . . Will I attack her and prevent her from coming near a grave that belongs to me? . . . Let that woman die of rage; she will not find him no matter how she tries. I have hidden him among the rose and jasmine trees in a grave without name totally forgotten where she can never find it.[100]

Despite the fact that she achieves self-autonomy after her husband's death, her emotional attachment to him is steadfast and unwavering. Having been unable to possess him in life, she ensures that he belongs exclusively to her in death.

Constructing an Uncanny Double

The first-person narrator in Lebanese writer Baydun's *Album al-Khasana* ('The Album of Defeat') (Beirut: Dar al-Saqi, 2012) is a man in his sixties (Baydun was 67 when he published the novel) whose eponymous name is Abbas Baydun. He works in a small department in a news agency and spends the remaining time at home taking care of his daughter's old cat Nino. The increasing numbers of elderly people who live alone in Beirut reveal that the traditional family institution is gradually loosening. The narrator's two children, who are traditionally supposed to care for their father, are outside the country, and the ties between them are slackening. Unlike the traditional father/grandfather figure in the earlier novels, Abbas lives in urban Beirut where the power of the elderly parent within the family is diminishing.

The narrator's relationship with the reader is casual and unsystematic, mirroring the kind of life he leads from day to day; his style is digressive and he does not hesitate to refer to the practicalities of narrating his story. A great deal of the novel is self-reflexive, which is his way of trying to understand how the process of ageing affects him. He focuses on the physiological problems that accompany old age. For instance, he asserts jokingly that old age, like an uninvited guest, showed up suddenly and that, owing to the deterioration of his hearing over the years, he did not hear the sound of its steps. Immersed in monitoring his ageing body, he fears that 'bone calcification', which had started some thirty years before[101] with the gelatine around his bones eroding, has slowed down the pace of his life. He also fears that the open-heart surgery that he underwent some time before has made his heart more vulnerable and more likely to 'assassinate me in my sleep'.[102] He admits that he wakes up terrified that his tear glands and his saliva have dried out; he does not rule out the possibility that he might wake up one day without a liver. Fearing that his body is turning against him, he is struck with haunting corporeal obsessions that presage a disturbing decline.

His sole companion at home is his daughter's old cat Nino (which is 13) and which represents the narrator's own way of reifying the abstract concept of senescence in order to come to terms with it. Being an intellectual, he ruminates on the meaning of ageing and monitors his physical deterioration by looking at the elderly feline double and identifying with it. Although he does not like cats, he takes care of Nino since he wants to project to his children, who live in France and who have become westernised, a positive image of himself as an agreeable old man. He also wants to communicate to them, who appear to be more concerned about the cat than their own father, that they have also abandoned their old father and that it was not only the cat that 'lacked love'.[103] The father's declining role within the family has eroded traditional filial obligations, and the narrator has been accorded by his children a second-rate status in relation to the cat.

Referring to himself and the cat, the narrator asserts that as 'an aging couple'[104] their relation with the inner space is not the same. Nino lives in every corner of the house, while the narrator is limited to his bed, the sofa, the table and the desk. Nino is all over the place; Abbas spots him 'in the wardrobe, on the computer desk, the CD box, the sofa, the bathtub, or sitting proudly over my clothes'[105] as if his intention were to dislodge the old man and take his place. The cat marks the whole place with his leftovers as though, like the narrator, he 'doubts his control over the place'.[106] Nino sleeps peaceably on the narrator's bed, while the latter struggles with insomnia.

For Abbas, insomnia is as an exhausting nightly operation which ends in 'the ugly sight of my messy bed',[107] and with the animal staring at him. This makes him feel worse, particularly since he does not like animals, but he keeps this secret from his children fearing that it will make him old-fashioned and obsolete in their eyes. When his daughter comes to visit he severs the 'aging pact'[108] with Nino and stops feeding him. His daughter takes the cat to the vet and is told that he suffers from a non-malignant cancer, which if removed will recur within a few months. The second time the cat is taken to a vet the narrator recommends a cheaper one, considering the amount of money his daughter had spent the time before, but the new veterinary doctor turns out to be inexperienced, causing Nino to return home with a curious 'swelling'.[109]

After the departure of his daughter, Nino goes back to his old habit of moving aimlessly around the house, but this time the narrator prevents him from entering his room for fear of leaving his annoying hair behind.

When the animal stops eating he contemplates putting him to sleep, but he is surprised to discover that his identification with the cat is very strong. He assumes that if he kills the cat God will kill him too: 'in the age we are both in, we could fight over the sofa and the bed; I might feel disgusted with him . . . I could kick him with my foot, but I cannot kill him.'[110] What also bothers him is that he cannot understand what the cat wants and realises that he can only give him food, but when he stops eating, there is nothing else the narrator can do. Having had a bad cough like 'an electric saw'[111] for three days, Abbas fears that it is a premonition presaging death. On his side, Nino is stunned 'by my barking',[112] and almost stops mewing. Referring to his cough as 'barking', the narrator aligns himself with Nino. Despite his rough manner with the cat, he discovers that he has developed a feeling of empathy with the animal that the latter reciprocates.

In addition to allusions to ageing and death, the narrative also incorporates references to the narrator's potency and sexuality. He mentions that Ikram, an old flame, is in town after an absence of thirty years and wonders whether they will meet 'like two old wrecks'.[113] He recalls how thirty years before she would not leave him, before ruining his relationship with a woman he was planning to marry. Ikram had married a forty-year-old man at age 14, but he divorces her after a few months. Rumours say that 'she was not a virgin' and that her husband was 'stunned to see her take off her clothes shamelessly in front of him, and wondered how the daughter of believers could act in this manner'.[114] Ikram is the one who had the most impact on him. Although she was veiled, she had no inhibitions about having sex with anyone she liked, and when she held parties she had no scruples about offering alcohol. He tells us that Ikram had sex with him only once, although she claimed that it was her most fulfilling experience. Ironically, she does not repeat it despite the fact that she is renowned for her promiscuity. However, she told Abbas that he is the only man her husband is jealous of. Such bizarre and nebulous stories about Ikram have the function not only of enhancing the narrator's masculinity at a time when he is falling behind, but also of raising questions about his own mental well-being and his reliability. For instance, he mentions parenthetically that he is 'in a relationship'[115] which has lasted twelve years, but we learn nothing about it. His relationship with his girlfriend is riddled with ellipses, and she remains invisible. The only creature that is seen around his house is Nino, his companion, and the living manifestation of his own fears of decline and extinction.

Tending towards digression, circularity and senile absent-mindedness, the narrator resists the progressiveness and causality of linear plotting and centres on the daily repetitiveness of an ageing man's life. Commenting upon his life story, he maintains that it is deficient in many ways, particularly since the manuscripts and photograph albums left by his father have been lost, and the two photographs of his uncle who had emigrated and of his father with his eye-glasses, his pocket watch and his tarbush, are gone. As a result, he is left with no memory of them. The narrator tells us that he acted like the 'executioner'[116] of his family when he left the family manuscripts and photographs unattended in a mildewed shack. As a result, and after losing the family photographs, he feels that he has lost his father and uncle since he had no other memories of them.

His autobiographical memories are fractured and disconnected, disrupting chronology for lack of concrete information and because of lapses in memory, which generates a rambling narrative. Conscious of his unreliability as a narrator, he refers to 'quasi-memories', imagined memories, emotional memories, health memories, political memories, family memories,[117] all of which are piecemeal and unverifiable. But he maintains that such deficiency should not be a problem when one is 65, especially since he no longer has any interest in the truth, and believes that with a little manipulation and falsification one can re-invent one's life in a dislocated autobiography. That is why he spends a great deal of time in metafictional speculations on the most fitting way to tell his story; however, his aim in writing his story is not so much to record the past but to deal with the present, and in doing that there can be no stylistic or thematic limitations. He asks, if 'we narrate to ourselves why not change the endings?',[118] and convert autobiography into fiction. In order to come to terms with the instability of old age, he comes up with an open-ended postmodern novel where words are jotted down and erased in line with the old man's impaired state of mind.

He admits his fear of Alzheimer's, the thought that 'nothing in the world sticks to us, that the world becomes a blank sheet of paper, that forgetfulness gets ahead of us to all things'.[119] He tells us that he has forgotten his French and that his acquaintances are decreasing since he has stopped recognising some of them, and that his own precious memories are fading. When he wakes up without dreams he is afraid that his 'unconscious is drying up'.[120] He forgets important and unimportant events haphazardly and senses that he is forgetting words and names, and his friends find him more composed, less chatty and less mobile. At home he spends long hours of silence watching the cat that has gone senile, leaving its litter everywhere.

The digressive style, prosaic and disconnected incidents and random reminiscences attest to a sense of degeneration and impairment. He recalls how he beat his son in the bathroom with a towel or pair of trousers, which was like a whipping, especially since his son was naked. The narrator knows that his son still remembers the incident and still begrudges his father's behaviour. Although the narrator intends to talk to his son (now in Paris) about it, the incident ends with intentions and no further references to it. Abbas recalls scrappy images from the past such as references to his activism in the Communist Party during the Lebanese war, and how a privileged young man joins the party and is eventually killed in Damour. Such references remain partially narratable, transitory and inconsequential, and the text hovers between autobiography, fiction and non-fiction.

His self-reflexive style is always about interrupting the narrative, revising, ruminating, reflecting, demystifying, and trying to understand his present situation. As an ageing man, he comes to the conclusion that to go by the rules simply means to stop living: to use a cane, to chew properly while eating, to follow a special diet, to drink coffee or tea without sugar, to eat the egg without the yoke, to walk an hour daily, and not to take off winter clothes prematurely. He wonders whether there are certain thoughts and desires suitable for an old man: 'Does this mean that you should not do anything you desire, and do everything by the rules?'[121] The narrative establishes links between the age of the author and the narrator, and the impact of authorial age on his style, which is self-referential, partial and fragmented. The novel pursues an anti-narrative approach 'to problematise the entire process of narration and interpretation'[122] in order to present a life of staleness and lack of achievement, and an equally banal senescence where the narrator spends dull, repetitive days in the company of a fellow geriatric, awaiting the final leap into the inevitable.

At 65 he still works in a news agency that follows cultural activities, which are on the increase, although the agency consists of older people who 'no longer believe that a person in his twenties can think and write a good novel or compose a musical piece'.[123] This tendency to trivialise the work of the younger generation widens the gap between age and youth and further isolates the narrator from the new world taking shape outside.

As the cat's health deteriorates, it is transformed into an eerie double, where the narrator's body becomes pre-eminent as he experiences himself as temporal and finite. The narrator maintains that human beings and cats lose their hair, their teeth, perhaps their hearing, and their sight. They age together and go off food together. When Nino stops eating, the narrator too is tired of food. The colour of the soup, and the sight of the fish in the pan, nauseate him, and he admits that eating alone is a sort of 'persecution' where bleak and gloomy thoughts interfere with the meal and make one lose one's appetite.[124] When the cat dies, he describes its death as a 'nightmarish prophecy'[125] proclaiming his own demise. The departure of his girlfriend, his daughter and Ikram reduces him to a grotesque void, which is inextricably bound up with obliviousness and dissolution.

Conclusion

This chapter has shown that the Arabic novel is beginning to witness fictional accounts written by ageing individuals about their own experiences of senescence, in which ageing women and men speak in their own voices. With the growing number of educated individuals and increasing longevity through medical advances, the numbers of ageing individuals who are conscious of ageing and the meanings attached to it have encouraged autobiographical and semi-autobiographical novels. Unlike traditional autobiography that focuses on public achievement, these are works that centre on subjectivity and conscious awareness of the physical and cognitive experience of ageing within social and political settings. These works are written by male and female individuals who live alone in urban settings, and have the courage to violate modesty and speak freely about their private lives. The narratives are idiosyncratic revelations that centre on these individuals' intent to challenge erasure, re-evaluate their lives, make new decisions, concentrate on their present quotidian life, speak out by 'narrativising their life course'[126] and reveal their capacity for growth, even at a late age. These ageing individuals write semi-autobiographical narratives according to their own experiences of ageing within specific contexts. The works are concerned with a revaluation of the past and the movement towards a future in close proximity with death.

'The Album of Defeat' by Baydun focuses on an ageing man whose daughter's ageing cat living with him becomes an uncanny double through which he monitors his gradual passage into death. Saada, in *Improvisations on a Missing Spring*, resists by ignoring the possibility of a recurrence of her illness, and defying her failing body by resuming her work at school. In 'An Unheroic Autobiography', the narrator discovers herself at eighty and seeks freedom by exploding stereotypes of the older woman and violating decorum through an uninhibited exposure of her private life. Rather than embracing their protagonists' lives 'as a whole, as if it were a coherent narrative',[127] these works abandon closure and immerse themselves in an open-ended process of reminiscence, which serves an 'adaptive function'.[128] The works expose the fluidity of identity, and 'the difficulty of plotting a life as a single, coherent narrative'.[129]

Notes

1. Twigg, *Fashion and Age*, p. 38.
2. *Improvisations on a Missing String*, p. 3.
3. King, *Discourses of Ageing in Fiction and Feminism*, p. 114.
4. Woodward, 'Telling Stories', p. 150.
5. Anishchenkova, *Autobiographical Identities in Contemporary Arabic Culture*, p. 4.
6. Sidonie and Watson, *Reading Autobiography*, p. 74.
7. De Falco, *Uncanny Subjects*, p. 18.
8. Randall and Kenyon, 'Time, Story, and Wisdom: Emerging Themes in Narrative Gerontology', pp. 333–46.
9. *Improvisations on a Missing String*, p. 17.
10. Ibid., p. 5.
11. Ibid.
12. Ibid., p. 35.
13. Ibid., p. 6.
14. Ibid., p. 7.
15. King, *Discourses of Ageing in Fiction and Feminism*, p. 17.
16. *Improvisations on a Missing String*, p. 7.

17. Ibid., p. 14.
18. Ibid.
19. Ibid., p. 100.
20. Bhabha, 'The World and the Home', pp. 141–53.
21. See Hanadi al-Samman's reference to 'mosaic autobiography' in *Anxiety of Erasure*, p. 65.
22. Ibid., p. 56.
23. Segal, *Out of Time*, pp. 4.
24. *Improvisations on a Missing String*, p. 25.
25. Ibid., p. 26.
26. Ibid., p. 25.
27. Ibid., p. 58.
28. Ibid., p. 57.
29. Ibid., p. 61.
30. Ibid., p. 30.
31. Ibid., p. 32.
32. Ibid., p. 58.
33. Ibid., p. 112.
34. Ibid., p. 106.
35. Ibid., p. 96.
36. King, *Discourses of Ageing in Fiction and Feminism*, p. 40.
37. *Improvisations on a Missing String*, p. 127.
38. Gullette, *Declining to Decline*, p. 206.
39. Ibid., p. 213.
40. Kanyon and Randall, 'Narrative Gerontology', p. 4.
41. Lamb, 'Permanent Personhood or Meaningful Decline', p. 42.
42. Segal, *Out of Time*, p. 4.
43. 'An Unheroic Journey', p. 9.   All translations are mine.
44. Ibid., p. 254.
45. Ibid., p. 47.
46. Ibid., p. 69.
47. Ibid., p. 155.
48. Ibid., p. 182.
49. Gullette, *Declining to Decline*, p. 217.
50. Waxman, *From the Hearth to the Open Road*, p. 17.
51. 'An Unheroic Journey', p. 130.
52. Ibid., p. 130.

53. Ibid.
54. Ibid., p. 186.
55. Ibid., p. 187.
56. Ibid., p. 188.
57. Ibid.
58. Ibid., p. 189.
59. Ibid., pp. 224–5.
60. Ibid., p. 228.
61. Joseph, *Intimate Selving in Arab Families*, p. 9.
62. Gullette, *Declining to Decline*.
63. Katz, *Disciplining Old Age*, p. 136.
64. Waxman, *From the Hearth to the Open Road*, p. 16.
65. Gullette, *Declining to Decline*, pp. 113, 216.
66. 'An Unheroic Journey', p. 9.
67. Ibid., p. 146.
68. Ibid., p. 13.
69. Ibid., p. 14.
70. Ibid.
71. Gullette, *Agewise*, p. 125.
72. 'An Unheroic Journey', p. 88.
73. Ibid., p. 235.
74. Ibid., p. 197.
75. Ibid., p. 10.
76. Ibid., p. 55.
77. Woodward, *Figuring Age*, p. xiii.
78. 'An Unheroic Journey', p. 110.
79. Ibid., p. 11.
80. Ibid., p. 156.
81. Ibid., p. 78.
82. Ibid., p. 85.
83. Ibid., p. 212.
84. Ibid., pp. 83–4.
85. Ibid., p. 78.
86. Ibid., p. 79.
87. Ibid., p. 282.
88. Anbara Salam (1897–1986), Lebanese feminist and author who contributed to the emancipation of women in the first half of the twentieth century and

wrote an autobiography titled 'A Tour of Memoirs between Lebanon and Palestine' (1978), translated by Tarif Khalidi as *Memoirs of an Early Arab Feminist* (2013).

89. 'An Unheroic Journey', p. 236.
90. Ibid., p. 210.
91. Ibid., p. 248.
92. Ibid., p. 195.
93. Ibid., p. 37.
94. Ibid., p. 43.
95. Ibid., p. 236.
96. Ibid., p. 169.
97. Ibid., p. 248.
98. Ibid., p. 51.
99. Ibid., p. 286.
100. Ibid., p. 300.
101. 'The Album of Defeat', p. 8. All translations are mine.
102. Ibid., p. 8.
103. Ibid., p. 137.
104. Ibid., p. 11.
105. Ibid., p. 12.
106. Ibid., p. 13.
107. Ibid., p. 14.
108. Ibid., p. 137.
109. Ibid., p. 19.
110. Ibid., p. 20.
111. Ibid., p. 21.
112. Ibid.
113. Ibid., p. 26.
114. Ibid., p. 25.
115. Ibid., p. 26.
116. Ibid., p. 56.
117. Ibid., p. 74.
118. Ibid.
119. Ibid., p. 38.
120. Ibid., p. 173.
121. Ibid., p. 35.
122. Scholes, 'Language, Narrative, and Anti-Narrative', p. 211.

123. 'The Album of Defeat', p. 36.
124. Ibid., p. 95.
125. Ibid., p. 253.
126. Gullette, *Declining to Decline*, 79.
127. Kathleen Woodward, 'Telling Stories', p. 150.
128. Revere and Tobin, 'Myth and Reality', p. 16.
129. De Falco, *Uncanny Subjects*, p. 18.

Conclusion

Bearing in mind the scarcity of intellectual work done on ageing in the Arab world, fiction is a valuable resource that infiltrates the recesses of the ageing process and portrays the experiential everyday lives of ageing individuals. The study has included an array of novels by different authors old and young, who represent ageing in the process of transformation and change, fluctuating between active and passive, urban and rural, and modern and traditional. The selected fictional works represent men and women in their senescence living in traditional and urban settings where changing historical, demographic, socio-economic and educational factors are altering individual lifestyles and gender relations, and producing varied constructions of agedness that challenge a single paradigm of ageing and contest traditional patterns associated with it. City life, for instance, offers more freedoms, more mobility, more diversified modes of living, and better access to information technology and other sources of knowledge, producing varying ageing individuals and ageing processes.

Through close consideration of fifteen fictional works, the study has conveyed the ambiguities and uncertainties of old age, which is not a rupture from other life stages, but a continuation of the life cycle. The study has shown that individuals are affected by ageing in diverse ways, revealing that there is no prototype of old age, and that the ageing process, like any other stage of life, is multi-layered, indeterminate, and shaped simultaneously by social, economic and political factors. The major tropes that represent each chapter are not tightly self-contained; rather, they are porous, converging into the general trajectory of the study that presents ageing as nuanced and in a continual process of becoming. While the novels are related by young and older narrators, works that centre on older characters who reflect on their own ageing identity are few, confirming that ageing is still dominated by biological, historical and social phenomena that confine the old within procrustean moulds, and perceive them as a homogeneous category that is supposed to withdraw from life and prepare for death.

The novels reveal that family support is high in traditional societies where the elderly are honoured and privileged within the family and where they enjoy filial and community care, having given the family a sense of history and identity. In line with the patriarchal bargain[1] that has shaped Arab traditional societies, both parents are given the care and respect due to them within the family. These works centre on traditional families that are committed to a hierarchical structure where the male, as in *The Long Way Back*, is the head of the household who retains his familial and economic position. In these narratives, old women take centre stage only after their husbands die, and their power rests predominantly in nurturing and caring roles sanctioned by society, such as the focus on religious and moral values. In such communities the body is disregarded in favour of the cultivation of the spirit, where personal needs or desires are non-existent. As a result, the narratives emphasise the public side of these women's lives while their private selves remain unknown. In *Mothballs*, more attention is given to the grandmother's actions than to her mid-life concerns about growing old. In line with social values, the elderly woman is supposed to be dignified, stoical and philosophical rather than angry, hostile and offensive,[2] although the grandmother in *The American Granddaughter* harbours strong feelings of rage, humiliation and resentment and dies feeling betrayed when her granddaughter taints their national integrity and purity when she sides with the Americans. In other words, the political situation in Iraq determines a particular form of involvement in the community, which is tied to national identity and the threat generated by the American invasion of Iraq. Rahma's death is the result not so much of existential angst but of the pressures of occupation and the threat to national identity.

The study has shown that transformations in the city increase old men's and women's sense of anxiety as they watch the scene of childhood and adulthood being incrementally destroyed in the same way as their own bodies deteriorate and decline. Many of these ageing individuals look back over their shoulder to a supposedly more holistic and revered past, which is considered superior to the present. Since the mutations taking place in their urban abode are synchronised with the alterations taking place within their own physique, the result is alienation and forced withdrawal.

Another cluster of narratives represent female characters that break the silence surrounding their sexuality, and speak openly about their embodied experiences, the impact of ageism on middle-aged women, and the insidious manner in which culture devalues them. The effect of ageing on these urban women is destabilising, leading to depression and fixation on signs of ageing on the surface of their bodies, where they experience ageing as a frightening process of 'othering'. They decide to resist a culture that invalidates menopausal women by using cosmetics and other techniques aimed at restoring an absent youthful appearance. Under the influence of globalisation, consumer culture, and discourses that stigmatise, deny ageing and encourage body maintenance and reconstruction, these women reject the inevitability and fixity of the ageing body, and insist on seeing the body as an ongoing project in the process of transformation.

With Western culture further infiltrating the Third World, men too, like women, suffer from the stigma of ageing and are affected by prejudice, illness, loneliness and anxiety, and the old regard for ageing men is gradually diminishing and further complicating the problem of senescence. According to Featherstone and Hepworth, in a fast-changing world '[traditional] male immunity to midlife ageing' is being eroded, 'bringing men psychologically closer to the situation that women are supposed to experience at midlife'.[3] The novels reveal that both men and women suffer from the hegemony of youth. As a result, dominant male stereotypes are subverted in works where older men, like women, are vulnerable to loss of power, humiliation, and the tyranny of globalisation and rapid change where the supremacy of adulthood is being entrenched.

The study also presents the emergence of works that begin to fill a gap where ageing people speak in their own voices and reflect on their present lives. These works manifest a potential for transformation and continued growth where new modes of narrative are being constructed, and where the experience of ageing is becoming more discernible. Some fictional accounts of senescence challenge the notions of weakness in old age by presenting 'newly self-knowledgeable, self-confident, and independent' individuals.[4]

The novels focus on urbanised, educated and more privileged individuals who transgress the traditional role assigned to them by focusing on the ageing process through self-questioning and self-reflexivity. These narratives are semi-autobiographical works by men and women and centre on active individuals who manifest awareness of their senescent experience and dwell upon it in the present, but also focus on the past and on aspects of their lives that have been erased.

Bearing in mind that this study is based on Western theories of ageing for lack of such works in the Arab world, the study has taken into account the specific social, historical and geographical factors that make ageing in the Arab/Islamic world different. Despite common biological factors, ageing individuals in the Arab region have concerns on a different scale from in the West. The general lack of stability, wars, colonisation and displacement, as well as the challenges of modernity, make the ageing process multifarious and more traumatic. For instance, wars diminish the value of ageing individuals, who in the midst of death and violence are swept aside and forgotten as they are seen as unimportant in comparison to young lives threatened by wars and death. Furthermore, while there are similarities among the various Arab countries related to tradition and religious values, each country has its own challenges: ageing in Lebanon is different from ageing in Egypt or Iraq.

Similarly, the upper classes in Egypt or Aleppo age differently from the poorer sectors of society and tend to have different problems and expectations, as in the case of al-Aswany's two elderly men or the mother in Khalifa's *No Knives in This City's Kitchens*. While the invasion of globalisation has generated similar problems to those in Western society such as loneliness, solitude, fear of death and obsession with youth and body maintenance, the unstable political situation makes ageing in the Arab world all the more problematic.

Given the historical and cultural context and the fluid social, demographic and political situation, one expects the ageing process in the Arab world to take different directions from in the West as local and regional challenges necessitate different reactions and different forms of survival. Bearing in mind the present silence regarding ageing in the MENA region, it is hoped that this monograph will pave the way for further investigation on ageing, especially since it involves a rapidly growing segment of Arab/Islamic society that will have to be contended with in the coming years.

Notes

1. Yount and Sibai, 'Demography of Aging in Arab Countries', p. 291.
2. As Woodward maintains in 'Against Wisdom', 'Anger in the old is outlawed', p. 63.
3. Featherstone and Hepworth, 'The Male Menopause', p. 161.
4. Waxman, *From the Hearth to the Open Road*, p. 17.

Bibliography

Works in Arabic Cited in the Text

al-Aṣwāny, Alā' (2003), *The Yacoubian Building*, trans. Humphrey Davies, Cairo: The American University in Cairo, 2004.

al-Daif, Rashid (1995), *Dear Mr. Kawabata*, trans. Paul Starkey, London: Quartet, 1999.

al-Daif, Rashid (2008), *O.K. Ma'al-Salāma*, Beirut: Riyād El-Rayyes li al-Kutub wa al-Nashr.

al-Ḥabīb, al-Sālimy (2002), *'Ushshāq Bayya*, Beirut: Dār al-Adab.

al-Ḥāyek (1994), *Portré li al-Nisyān: Short Stories*, Beirut: al-Markaz al-Thaqāfi al-'Arabi.

al-Ḥāyek (1994), *Shitā' Mahjūr*, Beirut: al-Markaz al-Thaqāfi al-'Arabi.

al-Ḥāyek (2002), *Bayrūt 2002*, Beirut: al-Markaz al-Thaqāfi al-'Arabi.

al-Takarli, Fuad (1980), *The Long Way Back*, trans. Catherine Cobham, Cairo: The American University in Cairo Press, 2001.

Baydūn, Abbās (2012), *Album al-Khasāra*, Beirut: Dār al-Sāqi.

Baydūn, Abbās (2014), a*l-Shāfiyāt*, Beirut: Dār al-Sāqi.

Bitār, Hayfa (2015), *Imra'a fi al-Khamsīn*, Beirut: Dār al-Sāqi.

Daoud, Hassan (1990), *Borrowed Time*, trans. Michael K. Scott, London: Telegram, 2008.

Faramān, Gha'ib To'ma (2015), *'Ālam al-Sayyid Ma'rūf*, Beirut: Mu'assassat al-Mada li al-I'lām wa al-Thaqāfa wa al-Funūn.

Inaam, Kachachi (2008), *The American Granddaughter*, trans. Nariman Youssef, Bloomsbury: Qatar Foundation Publishing, 2010.

Khālidy, Randa (2016), *Sīra Ghayr Butūliyya*, Beirut: Bīsān.

Khalīfa, Khālid (2013), *Lā Sakākīn fi Maṭābikh Hādhihi al-Madīna*, Beirut: Dār al-'Ādāb.

Khalifah, Sahar (1997), *The Inheritance*, trans. Aida Bamia, Cairo: The American University in Cairo Press, 2005.

Khoury, Elias (1986) *White Masks*, trans. Maia Tabet, Quercus: MacLehose, 2013.

Khoury, Elias (1989), *The Journey of Little Gandhi*, trans. Paula Haydar, Minneapolis: University of Minnesota Press, 1994.

Kreiydiyyeh, Līna (2010), *Khān Zāda*, Beirut: Dār al-Adāb.

Mahfouz, Naguib (1957), *Sugar Street*, trans. William Maynard Hutchins and Angele Botros Samaan, New York: Anchor Books, 1993.

Mamdouh, Alia (1986), *Mothballs: A Novel of Baghdad*, trans. Peter Theroux, New York: The Feminist Press, 2005.

Subūl, Taysīr (1968), *Anta Mundhu al-Yawm*, Beirut: Dār al-Nahār lī al-Nashr.

Usayrān, Layla (1998), *Ḥiwār Bila Kalimāt fī al-Ghaybūba*, Cairo: Markaz al-Ahrām li al-Tarjama wa al-Nashr.

Yared, Nazik Saba (1992), *Improvisations on a Missing String*, trans. Stuart A. Hancox, Fayetteville: University of Arkansas Press, 1997.

Works in Other Languages Cited in the Text

Abd al-Rahim, Sawsan, Kristine J. Ajrouch, Alicia Jammal and Toni C. Antonucci (2012), 'Survey Methods and Aging Research in an Arab Sociocultural Context – A Case Study from Beirut, Lebanon', *Journals of Gerontology Series B: Psychological Sciences*, 67(6), pp. 775–82.

Abd al-Rahim, Sawsan, Kristine J. Ajrouch, Alicia Jammal and Toni C. Antonucci (2015), 'Aging in Lebanon: Challenges and Opportunities', *The Gerontologist*, 55(4), 1 August, pp. 511–18.

Aghacy, Samira (1998), 'The Use of Autobiography in Rashid Dear Kawabata', in Robin Ostle, Ed de Moor and Stefan Wild (eds), *Writing the Self: Autobiographical Writing in Modern Arabic Literature*, London: al-Saqi, pp. 217–28.

Aghacy, Samira (2006), 'Contemporary Lebanese Fiction: Modernization without Modernity', *International Journal of Middle East Studies*, 38(4), pp. 561–80.

Aghacy, Samira (2009), *Masculine Identity in the Fiction of the Arab East since 1967*, Syracuse: Syracuse University Press.

Aghacy, Samira (2015), *Writing Beirut: Mappings of the City in the Modern Arabic Novel*, Edinburgh: Edinburgh University Press.

al-Hassan Golley, Nawar (2003), *Reading Arab Women's Autobiographies: Shahrazad Tells Her Story*, Austin: University of Texas Press.

al-Samman, Hanadi (2015), *Anxiety of Erasure: Trauma, Authorship, and the Diaspora in Arab Women's Writings*, New York: Syracuse University Press.

Andersen, Margret L. and Patricia H. Collins (eds) (2007), *Race, Class and Gender: An Anthology*, 6th edn, Belmont, CA: Wadsworth/Thomson Higher Education.
Andrews, Molly (1999), 'The Seductiveness of Agelessness', *Ageing and Society*, 19, pp. 301–18.
Andrews, Molly (2000), 'Ageful and Proud', *Ageing and Society*, 20, pp. 791–5.
Anishechenkova, Valerie (2014), *Autobiographical Identities in Contemporary Arabic Culture*, Edinburgh: Edinburgh University Press.
Arber, Sara and Jay Ginn (eds) (1995), *Connecting Gender and Ageing: A Sociological Approach*, Buckingham: Open University Press.
Barakat, Halim (1993), *The Arab World: Society, Culture, and State*, Berkeley: University of California Press.
Beck, Ulrich (1992), *Risk Society*, London: Sage.
Bhabha, Homi (1992), 'The World and the Home', *Social Text, Third World and Postcolonial Issues*, 31/32, pp. 141–53.
Biggs, Simon (2004), 'Age, Gender, Narratives and Masquerades', *Journal of Aging Studies*, 18, pp. 45–58.
Bilger, Audrey (1998), *Laughing Feminism: Subversive Comedy in Frances Burney, Maria Edgeworth, and Jane Austin*, Detroit: Wayne State University Press.
Boehm, Katharina, Anna Farkas and Anne-Julia Zwierlein (eds) (2014), *Interdisciplinary Perspectives on Aging in Nineteenth Century Culture*, New York and London: Routledge.
Bouhdiba, Abdelwahab (2004), *Sexuality in Islam*, trans. Alan Sheriden, London: Dar al-Saqi.
Bouson, Brooks J. (2016), *Shame and the Aging Woman: Confronting and Resisting Ageism in Contemporary Women's Writings*, London: Palgrave Macmillan.
Butler, Judith (1990), *Gender Trouble: Feminism and the Subversion of Identity*, London and New York: Routledge.
Bytheway, Bill (1995), *Ageism*, Milton Keynes: Oxford University Press.
Calasanti, Toni M. (2004), 'Feminist Gerontology and Old Men', *Journal of Gerontology: Social Sciences*, 59 B(6S), pp. 305–14.
Calasanti, Toni M. and Kathleen F. Slevin (eds) (2006), 'Introduction: Age Matters', in *Age Matters: Realigning Feminist Thinking*, New York and London: Routledge, pp. 1–17.
Calasanti, Toni M. and Kathleen F. Slevin (eds) (2006), *Age Matters: Realigning Feminist Thinking*, New York and London: Routledge.
Cavaliero, Glen (2000), *The Alchemy of Laughter: Comedy in English Fiction*, Basingstoke: Macmillan.

Chase, Karen (2009), *The Victorians and Old Age*, Oxford: Oxford University Press.
Chase, Karen (2014), '"Senile" Sexuality', in Katharina Boehm, Anna Farkas and Anne-Julia Zwierlein (eds), *Interdisciplinary Perspectives on Aging in Nineteenth Century Culture*, New York, London: Routledge, pp. 132–46.
Chivers, Sally (2003), *From Old Woman to Older Women: Contemporary Culture and Women's Narratives*, Columbus: Ohio State University Press.
Clark, John R. (1991), *The Modern Satiric Grotesque and its Traditions*, Lexington, KY: The University Press of Kentucky.
Cohen-Mor, Dalya (2013), *Fathers and Sons in the Arab Middle East*, New York: Palgrave Macmillan.
Cole, Thomas (1992), *The Journey of Life: A Cultural History of Aging in America*, Cambridge: Cambridge University Press.
Cole, Thomas, David Van Tassel and Robert Kastenbaum (1992), *Handbook of the Humanities and Aging*, New York: Springer.
Colletta, Lisa (2003), *Dark Humor and Social Satire in the Modern British Novel*, New York: Palgrave Macmillan.
Coupland, Justine and Richard Gwyn (2003), *Discourse, the Body and Identity*, London and New York: Palgrave Macmillan.
Cruikshank, Margaret (2003), 'Introduction', in *Learning To Be Old: Gender, Culture, Aging*, New York and Oxford: Rowman & Littlefield, pp. 1–7.
Cumming, Elaine and William E. Henry (1961), *Growing Old: The Process of Disengagement*, New York: Basic Books.
Deats, Sara M. and Lagretta T. Lenker (1999), *Aging and Identity: A Humanistic Perspective*, Westport, CT and London: Praeger.
De Beauvoir, Simone (1972), *The Coming of Age*, trans. Patrick O' Brian, New York: Putnam.
De Beauvoir, Simone (2009), *The Second Sex*, trans. Constance Borde and Sheila Malovany-Chevalier, New York: Alfred Knopf.
De Falco, Amelia (2010), *Uncanny Subjects: Age in Contemporary Narrative*, Columbus: Ohio State University Press.
Estes, Carol, Simon Biggs and Chris Phillipson (2003), *Social Theory, Social Policy and Ageing: A Critical Introduction*, Maidenhead: Open University Press.
Featherstone, Mike and Mike Hepworth (1985), 'The Male Menopause: Lifestyle and Sexuality', *Maturitas*, 7, pp. 235–46.
Featherstone, Mike and Mike Hepworth (1991), 'The Mask of Ageing and the Postmodern Life Course', in Mike Featherstone, Mike Hepworth and Bryan

S. Turner (eds), *The Body: Social Process and Cultural Theory*, London: Sage, pp. 371–89.

Featherstone, Mike and Andrew Wernick (eds) (1995), *Images of Aging: Cultural Representations of Later Life*, London: Routledge.

Fiedler, Leslie (1979), 'Eros and Thanatos: Old Age in Love', in David D. Van Tessel (ed.), *Aging, Death and the Completion of Being*, Philadelphia: University of Pennsylvania Press.

Fiedler, Leslie (1986), 'More Images of Eros and Old Age: The Damnation of Faust and the Fountain of Youth', in Kathleen Woodward and Murry M. Schwartz (eds), *Memory and Desire: Aging – Literature – Psychoanalysis*, Bloomington: Indiana University Press, pp. 37–50.

Freud, Sigmund (1913), 'The Disposition to Obsessional Neurosis', *SE*, 5(12), pp. 323–4.

Friedan, Betty (1993), *The Fountain of Age*, New York, London, Toronto and Sydney: Simon & Schuster.

Giddens, Anthony (1991), *Modernity and Self-Identity: Self and Society in the Late Modern Age*, Cambridge: Polity Press.

Gilbert, Sandra M. and Susan Gubar (1980), *The Madwoman in the Attic: The Woman Writer and the Nineteenth-Century Literary Imagination*, New Haven and London: Yale University Press.

Gilliard, Chris and Paul Higgs (2005), Aging and its Embodiment, in Miriam Fraser Gregeo and Monica (eds), *The Body: A Reader*, London and New York: Routledge.

Gravagne, Pamela H. (2013), *The Becoming of Age: Cinematic Visions of Mind, Body and Identity in Later Life*, Jefferson, NC: McFarland.

Greer, Germaine (1991), *The Change: Women, Ageing and the Menopause*, London: Hamish Hamilton.

Grosz, Elizabeth (1994), *Volatile Bodies*, Bloomington: Indiana University Press.

Gubrium, Jaber F. (2000), *Aging and Everyday Life*, Cambridge: Blackwell.

Gubrium, Jaber F. and James A. Holstein (eds) (2003), *Ways of Aging*, Malden, MA: Blackwell.

Gullette, Margaret M. (1997), *Declining to Decline: Cultural Combat and the Politics of the Midlife*, Charlottesville: University of Virginia Press.

Gullette, Margaret M. (2001), *Agewise: Fighting the New Ageism in America*, Chicago and London: University of Chicago Press.

Gullette, Margaret M. (2004), *Aged by Culture*, Chicago: University of Chicago Press.

Hamdar, Abir (2014), *The Female Suffering Body: Illness and Disability in Modern Arabic Literature*, Syracuse: Syracuse University Press.

Havighurst, Robert (1965), 'Successful Aging', *Gerontologist*, 1, pp. 8–13.

Hazan, Haim (1994), 'The Social Trap', in *Old Age: Constructions and Deconstructions*, Cambridge: Cambridge University Press, pp. 13–27.

Hearn, Jeff (1995), 'Imaging the Aging of Men in images of Aging: Cultural Representations of Later Life', in Mike Featherstone and Andrew Wernick (eds), *Images of Aging: Cultural Representations of Later Life*, London and New York: Routledge, pp. 97–115.

Hepworth, Mike and Mike Featherstone (1998), 'The Male Menopause: Lay Accounts and the Cultural Reconstruction of Midlife', in Sarah Nettleton and Jonathan Watson (eds), *The Body in Everyday Life*, London and New York: Routledge, pp. 276–301.

Hepworth, Mike (2000), *Stories of Ageing*, Buckingham: Open University Press.

Hepworth, Mike (2003), 'Ageing Bodies: Aged by Culture', in Justine Coupland and Richard Gwyn (eds), *Discourse, The Body, and Identity*, London and New York: Palgrave Macmillan, pp. 89–106.

Hillyer, Barbara (1988), 'The Embodiment of Old Women: Silences', *Frontiers: A Journal of Women Studies*, 19(1), pp. 48–60.

Hobbs, Alex (2016), *Aging Masculinity in the American Novel*, Lanham and Boulder: Rowman & Littlefield.

Holstein, Martha (2006), 'On Being an Aging Woman', in Toni M. Calasanti and Kathleen F. Slevin (eds), *Age Matters: Realigning Feminist Thinking*, New York and London: Routledge, pp. 313–34.

Holstein, Martha (2015), *Women in Late Life: Critical Perspectives on Gender and Age*, London: Rowman & Littlefield.

Johnson, Malcolm L. (ed.) (2005), 'The Social Construction of Old Age as a Problem', in *The Cambridge Handbook of Age and Ageing*, Cambridge: Cambridge University Press, pp. 563–72.

Joseph, Suad (1999), *Intimate Selving in Arab Families: Gender, Self, and Identity*, Syracuse: Syracuse University Press.

Kaminsky, Marc (1992), 'Introduction', in Barbara Myerhoff (ed.), *Remembered Lives: The Work of Ritual, Storytelling, and Growing Older*, Michigan: The University of Michigan Press, pp. 1–97.

Kanyon, Gary and William Randall (1999), 'Narrative Gerontology: An Overview', *Narrative Gerontology*, 4, pp. 3–18.

Katz, Stephen (1996), *Disciplining Old Age: The Formation of Gerontological Knowledge*, Charlottesville: University Press of Virginia.

Katz, Stephen (2002), 'Forever Functional: Sexual Fitness and the Ageing Male Body', *Body & Society*, 8(4), pp. 43–70.

Katz, Stephen (2005), *Cultural Aging Life Course, Life Styles, Senior Worlds*, Peterborough, ON: Broadview Press.

Khalidy, Anbara Salam (2013), *Memoirs of an Early Feminist: The Life and Activism of Anbara Salam Khalidi*, trans. Tarif Khalidy, London: Pluto Press.

Khalifah, Sahar (2005). *The Inheritance*, trans. Aida Bamia, Cairo: The American University in Cairo Press.

King, Jeannette (2013), *Discourses of Ageing in Fiction and Feminism: The Invisible Woman*, London: Palgrave Macmillan.

Kristeva, Julia (1982), *Powers of Horror: An Essay on Abjection*, New York: Columbia University Press.

Lamb, Sarah (2014), 'Permanent Personhood or Meaningful Decline? Toward a Critical Anthropology of Successful Aging', *Journal of Aging Studies*, 29, pp. 41–52.

Lasch, Christopher (1991), *The Culture of Narcissism*, New York: Norton.

Laz, Cheryl (2003), 'Age Embodied', *Journal of Aging Studies*, 17, pp. 503–19.

Le Gassick, Trevor (1988), 'The Faith of Islam in Modern Arabic Literature', *Religion and Literature*, 20(1), spring, pp. 97–109.

Marshall, Barbar L. and Stephen Katz (2002), 'Forever Functional: Sexual Fitness and the Aging Male Body', *Body and Society*, 8, pp. 43–70.

Marshall, Barbar L. and Stephen Katz (2006), 'From Androgyny to Androgens: Resexing the Aging Body', in Toni M. Calasanti and Kathleen F. Slevin (eds), *Age Matters: Realigning Feminist Thinking*, New York and London: Routledge, pp. 75–97.

Marshall, Barbar L. and Stephen Katz ((2012), 'The Embodied Life Course: Post-Ageism or the Renaturalization of Gender?', *Societies*, 2, pp. 222–34.

Matti, Moosa (1994), *The Early Novels of Naguib Mahfouz: Images of Modern Egypt*, Gainsville: University of Florida Press.

McMullin, Julie A. (1995), 'Theorizing Age and Gender Relations', in Sara Arber and Jay Ginn (eds), *Connecting Gender and Ageing: A Sociological Approach*, Buckingham: Open University Press, pp. 30–41.

Meadows, Robert and Kate Davidson (2006), 'Maintaining Manliness in Later Life: Hegemonic Masculinities and Emphasized Femininities', in Toni M. Calasanti and Kathleen F. Slevin (eds), *Age Matters: Realigning Feminist Thinking*, New York and London: Routledge, pp. 295–312.

Meyer, Stefan G. (2001), *The Experimental Arabic Novel: Postcolonial Literary Modernism in the Levant*, New York: State University of New York Press, pp. 39–40.
Millet, Kate (1977), *Sexual Politics*, London: Virago.
Moody, Harry R. (1988), 'Toward a Critical Gerontology: The Contribution of the Humanities to Theories of Aging', in James E. Birren and Vern L. Bengston (eds), *Emergent Theories of Aging*, New York: Springer, pp. 19–40.
Morgan, David (1992), *Discovering Men*, London: Routledge.
Morris, Pam (1977), 'Women's Writing: An Ambivalent Politics', in Alastair Renfrew and Andrew Roberts (eds), *Exploring Bakhtin*, Glasgow: Strathclyde University Press, pp. 57–74.
Myerhoff, Barbara and Jay Ruby (1992), 'A Crack in the Mirror: Reflexive Perspective in Anthropology', in Marc Kaminsky (ed.), *Remembered Lives: The Work of Ritual, and Growing Older*, pp. 307–40.
Nettleton, Sarah and Jonathan Watson (1998), *The Body in Everyday Life*. London: Routledge.
Oberg, Peter (2003), 'Images Versus Experience of the Aging Body', in Christopher A. Faircloth (ed.), *Aging Bodies: Images and Everyday Experience*, Walnut Creek, CA: AltaMira Press, pp. 103–39.
Olmsted, C. Jennifer (2005), 'Gender, Aging and the Evolving Arab Patriarchal Contract', *Feminist Economics*, 11(2), July, pp. 53–78.
Oro-Piqueras, Maricel (2011), *Ageing Corporealities in Contemporary English Fiction: Redefining Stereotypes*, Lap Lambert Academic Publishing.
Ostle, Robin, Ed de Moor and Stefan Wild (eds) (1998), *Writing the Self: Autobiographical Writing in Modern Arabic Literature*, London: al-Saqi Books.
Pearsall, Marilyn (ed.) (1997), *The Other Within Us: Feminist Explorations of Women and Aging*, Boulder: Westview Press.
Potts, Annie, Nicola Gavey, Victoria Grace and Tina Vares (2003), 'The Downside of Viagra: Women's Experiences and Concerns', *Sociology of Health and Illness*, 25(7), pp. 697–719.
Powell, Jason L. and Charles F. Longino (2001), 'Towards the Post Modernization of Aging: The Body and Social Theory', *Journal of Aging & Identity*, 6(4), pp. 20–34.
Powell, Jason L. (2006), *Social Theory and Aging*, Lanham: Rowman & Littlefield.
Randall, William L. and Gary M. Kenyon (2004), 'Time, Story, and Wisdom: Emerging Themes in Narrative Gerontology', *Canadian Journal on Aging/La Revue Canadienne du vieillissement*, 23(4), pp. 333–46.

Ray, Ruth E. (2004), 'Toward the Croning of Feminist Gerontology', *Journal of Aging Studies*, 18, pp. 109–21.
Revere, Virginia and Sheldon Tobin (1980–1), 'Myth and Reality: The Older Person's Relationship to his Past', *International Journal of Aging and Human Development*, 12(1), pp. 15–26.
Rich, Adrienne (1977), *Of Woman Born: Motherhood as Experience and Institution*, London: Virago.
Rich, Adrienne (1986), 'Notes Toward a Politics of Location', in *Blood, Bread, and Poetry: Selected Prose*, New York: Norton, pp. 210–31.
Rubenstein, Roberta (2001), 'Feminism, Eros and the Coming of Age', *Frontiers: A Journal of Women's Studies*, 22(2), pp. 1–19.
Russo, Mary (1995), *The Female Grotesque: Risk, Excess and Modernity*, New York: Routledge.
Russo, Mary (1999), 'Aging and the Scandal of Anachronism', in Kathleen Woodward (ed.), *Figuring Age: Women, Bodies, Generations*, Bloomington: Indiana University Press, pp. 20–33.
Said, Edward (2006), *On Late Style: Music and Literature Against the Grain*, New York: Pantheon.
Saleh, Tayyib (1969), *Season of Migration to the North*, trans. Denys Johnson-Davies, London: Heinemann.
Salter, Charles A. and Carlota D. Salter (1976), 'Attitudes Toward Aging and Behaviours Toward the Elderly Among Young People as a Function of Death Anxiety', *The Gerontologist*, 16(3), pp. 232–6.
Schaie, Warner K. and Andrew W. Achenbaum (1993), *Societal Impact on Aging: Historical Perspectives*, New York: Springer.
Scholes, Robert (1980), 'Language, Narrative, and Anti-Narrative', *Critical Inquiry*, 6(1), pp. 204–12.
Segal, Lynne (2007), 'Forever Young: Medusa's Curse and the Discourses of Ageing', *Women: A Cultural Review*, 19, pp. 41–56.
Segal, Lynne (2013), *Out of Time: The Pleasures and the Perils of Ageing*, London: Verso.
Sharabi, Hisham (1988), *Neopatriarchy: A Theory of Distorted Change in Arab Society*, New York: Oxford University Press.
Shuraydi, Hasan (2014), *The Raven and the Falcon: Youth Versus Old Age in Medieval Arabic Literature*, Leiden: Brill.
Sibai, Abla M. and Rouham Yamout (2012), 'Family-Based Old-Age Care in Arab Countries: Between Tradition and Modernity', in Hans Groth and Alfonso

Sousa-Poza (eds), *Population Dynamics in Muslim Countries*, Heidelberg: Springer, pp. 63–76.

Silver, Catherine B. (2003), 'Gendered Identities in Old Age: Toward (De)gendering?', *Journal of Aging Studies*, 17, pp. 379–97.

Slevin, Kathleen F. (2006), 'The Embodied Experiences of Old Lesbians' in Toni M. Calasanti and Kathleen F. Slevin (eds), *Age Matters: Realigning Feminist Thinking*, New York and London: Routledge.

Small, Helen (2014), 'The Double Standard of Aging: on Missing Stendhal in England', in Katherine Boehm, Anna Farkas and Anne-Julia Zwierlein (eds), *Interdisciplinary Perspectives on Aging in Nineteenth Century Culture*, New York and London: Routledge, pp. 210–31.

Smith, Sidonie and Julia Watson (1993), *Reading Autobiography: A Guide for Interpreting Life Narratives*, Minneapolis and London: University of Minnesota Press.

Sontag, Susan (1972), 'The Double Standard of Ageing', *Saturday Review of Literature*, 39, pp. 29–38.

Spector-Mersel, Gabriela (2006), 'Never-Aging Stories: Western Hegemonic Masculinity Scripts', *Journal of Gender Studies*, 15(1), pp. 67–82.

Thompson, Edward H. (2004), 'Guest Editorial', *Journal of Men's Studies* 13(1), pp. 1–4.

Turner, Bryan (1992), *Regulating Bodies: Essays in Medical Sociology*, London: Routledge.

Twigg, Julia (2004), 'The Body, Gender and Age: Feminist Insights in Social Gerontology', *Journal of Aging Studies*, 18, pp. 59–73.

Twigg, Julia (2013), *Fashion and Age: Dress, The Body and Later Life*, London, New Delhi, New York and Sydney: Bloomsbury.

Wada, Shuichi (1995), 'The Status and Image of the Elderly in Japan: Understanding the Paternalistic Ideology', in Mike Featherstone and Andrew Wernick (eds), *Images of Aging*, London and New York: Routledge, pp. 48–60.

Walz, Thomas (2002), 'Crones, Dirty Old Men, Sexy Seniors', *Journal of Aging and Identity*, June, pp. 99–112.

Waxman, Barbara Fey (1990), *From the Hearth to the Open Road: A Feminist Study of Aging in Contemporary Literature*, New York: Greenwood Press.

Woodward, Kathleen (1986), 'The Mirror Stager of Old Age' in Kathleen Woodward and Murray M. Schwartz (eds), *Memory and Desire: Aging—Literature—Psychoanalysis*, Bloomington: Indiana University Press, pp. 97–113.

Woodward, Kathleen (1991), *Ageing and its Discontents: Freud and Other Fictions*, Bloomington: Indiana University Press.
Woodward, Kathleen (1997), 'Telling Stories: Aging, Reminiscence, and the Life Review', *Journal of Aging and Identity*, 2(3), pp. 149–63.
Woodward, Kathleen (1999), 'Inventing Generational Models: Psychoanalysis, Feminism, Literature', in *Figuring Age: Women, Bodies, Generations*, Bloomington: Indiana University Press, pp. 149–68.
Woodward, Kathleen (1999), 'Introduction', in *Figuring Age: Women, Bodies, Generations*, Bloomington: Indiana University Press, pp. xi–xxix.
Woodward, Kathleen (2003), 'Against Wisdom', *Journal of Aging Studies*, 17, pp. 55–67.
Woodward, Kathleen (2006), 'Performing Age, Performing Gender', *NWSA Journal* 18(1), pp. 162–89.
Wyatt-Brown, Anne and Janice Rossen (eds) (1993), 'Introduction: Aging, Gender, and Creativity', in *Aging and Gender in Literature: Studies in Creativity*, Charlottesville: University Press of Virginia, pp. 1–15.
Young, William C. and Steney Shami (1997), 'Anthropological Approaches to the Arab Family: An Introduction', *Journal of Comparative Family Studies*, 28(2), p. 11.
Yount, Kathryn M. and Abla M. Sibai (2009), 'Demography of Aging in Arab Countries', *International Handbook of Population Aging*, New York: Springer, pp. 277–315.
Zita, Jacqueline N. (1997), 'Heresy in the Female Body: The Rhetorics of Menopause', in Marilyn Pearsall (ed.) (1997), *The Other Within Us: Feminist Explorations of Women and Aging*, Boulder: Westview Press, pp. 95–112.

Index

'An Abandoned Winter' (*Shita' Mahjour*) (al-Hayek), 74–5, 76–81, 99
Abdel-Nasser, Gamal, 10
age
  chronological, 8–9, 113
  as a cultural construct, 82
  'mirror stage' of old age, 74, 76–81, 78, 79, 99
  mystique of, 9
  of retirement, 8, 112, 118
ageing
  constructionist social model of, 3
  as a continuum, 55–63
  denial of, 125
  essentialist model of, 2–3, 79, 105
  gendered process of, 11
  and identification, 80, 143
  process of, 14–17
  studies of, 1–5
ageism, 63, 75, 78, 92
  and gender, 120
  middle ageism, 98, 169
  and sexism, 12, 85, 95, 96, 97, 100
al-Aswany, Alaa: *The Yacoubian Building* (*Imaret Ya'qubyan*), 48–9, 55–63
al-Daif, Rashid, 15, 97
  Dear Mr. Kawabata (*Azizi al-Sayyid Kawabata*), 7, 8
  'O.K. Good-bye' (*O.K. ma' al-Salama*) 14, 105, 121–8
  'Tactics of Wretchedness' (*Taqaniyyat al-Bu's*), 11
al-Hayek, René
  'An Abandoned Winter' (*Shita' Mahjour*), 74–5, 76–81, 99
  Beirut, 10
al-Isfahani, Raghib, 6
al-Salimy, al-Habib: 'The Lovers of Bayya' ('*Ushshaq Bayya*), 104, 105–12, 128

al-Takarli, Fuad: *The Long Way Back* (*Al-Raj al-Ba'id*), 11, 20, 21–7, 43, 168
'The Album of Defeat' (*Album al-Khasara*) (Baydun), 15, 134, 156–61, 162
Aleppo, 48, 49, 63, 66, 67, 68, 69, 170
The American Granddaughter (*al-Hafida al-Amirikiyya*) (Kachachi), 11, 21, 35–43, 44, 168
Anishchenkova, Valerie, 135, 138
Anta Mundhu Al-Yawm (Subul), 7–8
autobiography, 1, 13, 170
  No Knives in This City's Kitchens (Khalifa,) 49, 63–70, 170
  'O.K. Good-bye' (al-Daif), 14, 63–70, 105, 121–8
  'An Unheroic Autobiography' (Khalidy), 5, 14–15, 133–4, 143–56, 162

Barakat, Halim, 7
Baydun, Abbas: 'The Album of Defeat' (*Album al-Khasara*), 15, 134, 156–61, 162
Beirut, 11, 87, 88, 94, 156
Beirut (al-Hayek), 10
belonging: sense of, 34, 40, 139–40
Bhabha, Homi, 138
Bible: longevity in, 6
Biggs, Simon, 92
birthdays, 144, 147, 148
Bitar, Haifa: 'A Woman of Fifty' (*Imra'a fi al-Khamsin*), 12, 75, 92–9, 100
Borrowed Time (*Ayyam Za'ida*) (Daoud), 13–14, 104–5, 112–21
Butler, Judith, 3

Cairo, 48, 49–50, 55, 56, 57, 60–1, 71, 136, 139
Calasanti, Toni M., 5

183

childhood, 80, 133, 143
Chivers, Sally, 3–4
Christianity, 37, 38, 140; *see also* Bible
city life, 167; *see also* Aleppo; Beirut; Cairo
Cole, Thomas, 17
consumer culture, 13, 99, 169
cultural difference, 139, 170
cultural displacement, 138
cultural norms, 5–6

Daoud, Hassan: *Borrowed Time* (*Ayyam Za'ida*), 13–14, 104–5, 112–21
de Beauvoir, Simone, 4, 75
Dear Mr. Kawabata (*Azizi al-Sayyid Kawabata*) (al-Daif), 7, 8
death
 fear of, 75, 104–5, 105–6, 111, 122, 128
 preparedness for, 2, 26–7, 29, 32, 37, 38, 49, 52, 54, 58, 68, 69, 107, 111–12, 121, 161
 see also funeral rites
dementia, 91, 115, 122, 127, 134, 148, 149

families
 and belonging, 140
 conflict in, 82, 86–7
 control of, 38, 43, 116
 extended, 27, 90–1, 117, 140–1
 hierarchies in, 9–11, 168
 and identity, 7, 135–7
 and neglect, 113–14, 118
 role of, 106, 140, 156, 168
 role reversals in, 78, 105
 see also grandfathers; grandmothers; mothers; patriarchy; siblings
Faraman, Gha'ib To'mi: 'The Pains of Mr Ma'ruf' (*Alam al-Sayyid Ma'ruf*), 14
fathers *see* patriarchy
Featherstone, Mike, 4, 14, 127, 169
Fiedler, Leslie, 2
friendships, 13, 51, 60, 65, 88, 89, 96, 100, 111–12, 118, 136, 142, 149
funeral rites, 91
Furman, Frida Kerner, 96

gender, 2–3, 63–70, 152
 and ageism, 120
 de-genderisation, 7, 22
 and education, 138, 139
 and image, 11, 34

and sexuality, 75, 124, 149; *see also under* men; women
and tradition, 43
Giddens, Anthony, 91–2
Gilbert, Sandra M., 94
globalisation, 9, 10, 88, 91, 93, 99, 123, 128, 169, 170
grandfathers, 13–14, 34, 41, 79, 112, 117, 156
grandmothers
 and conflict, 11, 20–1
 coping strategies of, 35–43
 and nationalism, 40–1, 42, 44, 168
 and religion, 31, 32, 37, 38
 and superstition, 31
 traditional role of, 11, 23, 28–35, 36, 43–4
Gravagne, Pamela H., 4
Grosz, Elizabeth, 2
Gubar, Susan, 94
Gullette, Margaret Morganroth, 2, 124, 129, 149

hajj (pilgrimage), 108
health, 127, 156, 158; *see also* dementia
Hepworth, Mike, 4, 14, 127, 169
Holstein, Martha, 96

ibn al-Khattab, 'Umar, 6
Improvisations on a Missing String (*Taqassim 'la watarin Da'i'*) (Yared), 15, 133, 134–43, 162
In Search of Walid Massoud (Jabra), 10
The Inheritance (*al-Mirath*) (Khalifah), 12, 75, 81–7, 99
Islam 150; *see also* Qur'an

Jabra, Jabra Ibrahim: *In Search of Walid Massoud*, 10
Joseph, Souad, 1, 147
The Journey of Little Gandhi (*Rihlat Gandhi al-Saghir*) (Khoury), 10–11

Kachachi, Inaam: *The American Granddaughter* (*al-Hafida al-Amirikiyya*), 11, 21, 35–43, 44, 168
Khalidy, Randa: 'An Unheroic Autobiography' (*Sira Ghayr Butuliyya*), 5, 14–15, 133–4, 143–56, 162
Khalifa, Khalid: *No Knives in This City's Kitchens* (*La Sakakin fi Matabikh hadhihi al-Madina*), 49, 63–70, 170

INDEX | 185

Khalifah, Sahar: *The Inheritance (al-Mirath)*, 12, 75, 81–7, 99
Khan Zada (Kreidiyyeh), 75–6, 87–92, 99–100
Khoury, Elias
   The Journey of Little Gandhi (Rihlat Gandhi al-Saghir), 10–11
   White Masks (Al-Wujuh al-Bayda'), 10
King, Jeannette, 82
Kreidiyyeh, Lina: *Khan Zada*, 75–6, 87–92, 99–100
Kristeva, Julia, 63

Le Gassick, Trevor, 4
The Long Way Back (Al-Ra'al-Ba'id) (al-Takarli), 11, 20, 21–7, 43, 168
'The Lovers of Bayya' (*'Ushshaq Bayya*) (al-Salimy), 104, 105–12, 128

Mahfouz, Naguib: *Sugar Street (al-Sukariyya)*, 11, 48, 49–55
Mamdouh, Alia: *Mothballs (Habbat al-Naphtalin)*, 5, 11, 20–1, 28–35, 43–4, 168
masculinity, 56–7, 61, 62–3, 93–4, 104–29, 149
'matrophobia', 78
memories, 14, 26, 28, 48, 49, 88, 90, 111, 122, 127, 134, 135, 144, 147, 159–60; *see also* nostalgia
men
   ageing, 2–3, 13–14
   authority of, 50
   behaviour of, 84, 105, 109–10, 115, 118, 119, 125–6, 152–3
   effeminisation of, 36, 79, 105, 114, 115, 120
   and exclusion, 110–11
   and friendships, 51–2
   and identity loss, 53, 54
   infantilisation of, 78, 107, 118, 119
   and 'male menopause', 14, 127, 128
   marginalised, 117, 118
   middle-aged, 79, 169
   otherness of, 58, 112–21, 114
   and physical appearance, 55–6, 57–8, 85, 92, 95, 99, 107–8, 114, 122, 123, 125, 151
   and prestige, 26
   and religion, 26–7, 61–2, 119
   and retirement, 36, 41, 70, 112–13
   and sexuality, 14, 48, 51, 53, 56–7, 59, 61–3, 69, 109, 117, 120, 124–5, 126, 129, 149, 158
   see also masculinity; patriarchy
Millet, Kate, 43
misogyny, 71, 124, 128
modernity, 48, 50, 54, 55, 88, 123, 168–9, 170
Morris, Pam, 29
Mothballs (Habbat al-Naphtalin) (Mamdouh), 5, 11, 20–1, 28–35, 43–4, 168
mothers, 9, 89–90, 95; *see also* 'matrophobia'

narcissism, 62, 74, 87, 92
Nasser, Gamal Abdel *see* Abdel-Nasser, Gamal
No Knives in This City's Kitchens (La Sakakin fi Matabikh hadhihi al-Madina) (Khalifa), 49, 63–70, 170
nostalgia, 28, 54, 60–1, 63, 64, 79, 80, 84, 88, 147; *see also* memories; reminiscence

'O.K. Good-bye' (*O.K. ma' al-Salama*) (al-Daif), 14, 105, 121–8

'The Pains of Mr Ma'ruf' (*Alam al-Sayyid Ma'ruf*) (Faraman), 14
Palestine, 136, 137–8
Palestine Liberation Organization (PLO), 10, 146
past: and present, 133, 134–5
patriarchy, 6–9, 21, 43
performativity theory, 3
photographs, 34, 69, 70, 89, 144, 145, 149, 159

Qur'an 6, 29, 31, 32, 106–7, 119

Ray, Ruth E., 90
religion, 5–6, 140, 150; *see also* Christianity; Islam
reminiscence, 134–5; *see also* memories; nostalgia
retirement *see* age: of retirement
Rich, Adrienne, 78
Robertson, Ann, 115

Said, Edward, 128
Saleh, Tayyib: *Season of Migration to the North*, 11–12

Season of Migration to the North (Saleh), 11–12
secularism, 8, 10
Segal, Lynne, 81
self
 changeability of, 91, 92–3, 135, 139
 and identity, 4, 5, 11, 13, 16, 29, 34, 35, 37, 39, 42, 52, 59, 66, 74–5, 77, 79–80, 81–2, 83, 96, 97, 113, 134, 138, 142, 144, 145, 146, 148, 151, 153, 155, 156, 162, 169–70
sexism, 12, 95, 97; *see also* misogyny
sexuality, 2, 75, 124, 149; *see also under* men; women
Shami, Steney, 5–6
Shuraydi, Hasan, 6
Sibai, Abla M., 7
siblings, 58, 70, 92, 138–9, 140
Silver, Catherine B., 74
social class, 21, 27, 30, 39, 53, 55, 56, 59, 65, 68, 70, 84, 136, 145, 153, 170
stereotypes, 77, 117, 128, 129, 145–6, 150, 162, 169
Stoltenberg, John, 125
Subul, Taysir: *Anta Mundhu Al-Yawm*, 7–8
Sugar Street (*al-Sukariyya*) (Mahfouz), 11, 48, 49–55

'Tactics of Wretchedness' (*Taqaniyyat al-Bu's*) (al-Daif), 11
Thompson, Edward H., 125
time
 and anxiety, 106
 calculation of, 112, 144
 and change, 78
 and identity, 145
 and memories, 135
 passing of, 8–9, 48, 64, 70, 75, 81, 96–7, 107, 141
 past and present, 15

'An Unheroic Autobiography' (*Sira Ghayr Butuliyya*) (Khalidy), 5, 14–15, 133–4, 143–56, 162

Violence, 8, 33, 61, 71, 110, 140, 153, 160

White Masks (*Al-Wujuh al-Bayda'*) (Khoury), 10
'A Woman of Fifty' (*Imra'a fi al-Khamsin*) (Bitar), 12, 75, 92–9, 100
women
 ageing, 2–3
 and education, 50, 138, 139, 142, 152, 153
 and independence, 145, 147–8, 151, 168
 infantilisation of, 22–3, 37
 marginalised, 16, 21–7, 52–3, 80, 81–3, 85, 91, 94, 95, 99, 116, 150–1, 153
 and marriage, 144, 150, 151–2, 154, 155–6
 menopausal, 12–13, 74–100, 169
 modern, 96–7, 100
 otherness of, 68, 71, 75, 138
 and physical appearance, 6, 11, 12, 24–5, 30, 33, 37–8, 39, 53, 58, 65, 74, 77, 78, 79–80, 83, 84, 91, 92, 93, 97–8, 116, 136–7, 138, 139, 140, 147, 169
 and religion, 52, 140
 and sexuality, 11–12, 13, 20, 33, 34, 39, 53, 67, 75, 83, 84, 85, 86, 93–4, 97, 100, 124, 145–6, 158
 and tradition, 20–1, 22
 unmarried, 11, 25, 53, 81–7, 83, 85, 87, 90, 97–8, 99, 137
 see also grandmothers; mothers
Woodward, Kathleen M., 4, 5, 14, 74, 80
Wyatt-Brown, Anne, 13

The Yacoubian Building (*Imaret Ya'qubyan*) (al-Aswany), 48–9, 55–63
Yared, Nazik: *Improvisations on a Missing String* (*Taqassim 'la watarin Da'i'*), 15, 133, 134–43, 162
Young, William C., 5–6
Yount, Kathryn M., 7
youth
 and age, 2–3, 7, 8, 9, 13, 24, 113, 125, 160
 experiences of, 133
 migration of, 10

EU representative:
Easy Access System Europe
Mustamäe tee 50, 10621 Tallinn, Estonia
Gpsr.requests@easproject.com

www.ingramcontent.com/pod-product-compliance
Lightning Source LLC
Chambersburg PA
CBHW070357240426
43671CB00013BA/2541